SETTLER COLON
VICTORIAN LIT

MW00604508

How did the emigration of nineteenth-century Britons to colonies of settlement shape Victorian literature? Philip Steer uncovers productive networks of writers and texts spanning Britain, Australia, and New Zealand to argue that the novel and political economy found common colonial ground over questions of British identity. Each chapter highlights the conceptual challenges to the nature of "Britishness" posed by colonial events, from the gold rushes to invasion scares, and traces the literary aftershocks in familiar genres such as the bildungsroman and the utopia. Alongside lesser-known colonial writers such as Catherine Spence and Julius Vogel, British novelists from Dickens to Trollope are also put in a new light by this fresh approach that places Victorian studies in colonial perspective. Bringing together literary formalism and British world history, *Settler Colonialism in Victorian Literature* describes how what it meant to be "British" was reimagined in an increasingly globalized world.

PHILIP STEER is Senior Lecturer in English at Massey University. He is co-editor with Nathan K. Hensley of *Ecological Form: System and Aesthetics in the Age of Empire* (Fordham University Press, 2018), and his essays have appeared in *Victorian Studies* and *Victorian Literature and Culture*, as well as in *Modernism, Postcolonialism, and Globalism* (Oxford University Press, 2018) and *A History of New Zealand Literature* (Cambridge University Press, 2016). He completed his doctorate at Duke University after being awarded a Fulbright Scholarship. He is also the recipient of a Marsden Fund Fast-Start Grant from the Royal Society of New Zealand.

CAMBRIDGE STUDIES IN NINETEENTH-CENTURY LITERATURE AND CULTURE

General editor
Gillian Beer, *University of Cambridge*

Editorial board
Isobel Armstrong, *Birkbeck, University of London*
Kate Flint, *University of Southern California*
Catherine Gallagher, *University of California, Berkeley*
D. A. Miller, *University of California, Berkeley*
J. Hillis Miller, *University of California, Irvine*
Daniel Pick, *Birkbeck, University of London*
Mary Poovey, *New York University*
Sally Shuttleworth, *University of Oxford*
Herbert Tucker, *University of Virginia*

Nineteenth-century British literature and culture have been rich fields for inter-disciplinary studies. Since the turn of the twentieth century, scholars and critics have tracked the intersections and tensions between Victorian literature and the visual arts, politics, social organization, economic life, technical innovations, scientific thought – in short, culture in its broadest sense. In recent years, theoretical challenges and historiographical shifts have unsettled the assumptions of previous scholarly synthesis and called into question the terms of older debates. Whereas the tendency in much past literary critical interpretation was to use the metaphor of culture as "background," feminist, Foucauldian, and other analyses have employed more dynamic models that raise questions of power and of circulation. Such developments have reanimated the field. This series aims to accommodate and promote the most interesting work being undertaken on the frontiers of the field of nineteenth-century literary studies: work that intersects fruitfully with other fields of study such as history, or literary theory, or the history of science. Comparative as well as interdisciplinary approaches are welcomed.

A complete list of titles published will be found at the end of the book.

CAMBRIDGE
UNIVERSITY PRESS

University Printing House, Cambridge CB2 8BS, United Kingdom

One Liberty Plaza, 20th Floor, New York, NY 10006, USA

477 Williamstown Road, Port Melbourne, VIC 3207, Australia

314-321, 3rd Floor, Plot 3, Splendor Forum, Jasola District Centre, New Delhi - 110025, India

103 Penang Road, #05-06/07, Visioncrest Commercial, Singapore 238467

Cambridge University Press is part of the University of Cambridge.

It furthers the University's mission by disseminating knowledge in the pursuit of education, learning and research at the highest international levels of excellence.

www.cambridge.org
Information on this title: www.cambridge.org/9781108735858
DOI: 10.1017/9781108695824

First published 2020
First paperback edition 2022

A catalogue record for this publication is available from the British Library

Library of Congress Cataloging in Publication data
NAMES: Steer, Philip, 1979– author.
TITLE: Settler colonialism in Victorian literature : economics and political identity in the networks of empire / Philip Steer, Massey University, Auckland.
DESCRIPTION: New York : Cambridge University Press, 2020. | Series: Cambridge studies in nineteenth-century literature and culture | Includes bibliographical references and index. | Contents: Introduction: Settler Colonialism and Metropolitan Culture – 1. The Transportable Pip: Liberal Character, Territory, and the Settled Subject – 2. Gold and Greater Britain: The Australian Gold Rushes, Unsettled Desire, and the Global British Subject – 3. Speculative Utopianism: Colonial Progress, Debt, and Greater Britain – 4. Manning the Imperial Outpost: The Invasion Novel, Geopolitics, and the Borders of Britishness – Conclusion.
IDENTIFIERS: LCCN 2019038893 (print) | LCCN 2019038894 (ebook) | ISBN 9781108484428 (v. 122 ; hardback) | ISBN 9781108735858 (v. 122 ; paperback) | ISBN 9781108695824 (epub)
SUBJECTS: LCSH: English fiction–19th century–History and criticism. | Commonwealth fiction (English)–19th century–History and criticism. | Imperialism in literature. | Colonies in literature. | National characteristics in literature. | Identity (Psychology) in literature.
CLASSIFICATION: LCC PR830.I544 S74 2020 (print) | LCC PR830.I544 (ebook) | DDC 823/.809–dc23
LC record available at https://lccn.loc.gov/2019038893
LC ebook record available at https://lccn.loc.gov/2019038894

ISBN 978-1-108-48442-8 Hardback
ISBN 978-1-108-73585-8 Paperback

SETTLER COLONIALISM IN VICTORIAN LITERATURE

*Economics and Political Identity in
the Networks of Empire*

PHILIP STEER

Massey University

CAMBRIDGE
UNIVERSITY PRESS

point of view is not London or Paris, but Melbourne," *The Athenaeum* reflected: "In this forecast, in fact, Europe loses altogether the precedence it has enjoyed."[3] The Oxford-educated Pearson had been in his mid-thirties when he first traveled to Australia in 1864 for health reasons; by the 1870s, he had taken up residence in the colony of Victoria, becoming involved in politics, and eventually being appointed minister of education; he was still in Australia when he wrote *National Life and Character*. "Twenty years' residence under the Southern Cross," he argued in its opening chapter, "has forced me to consider a new side of this particular question: whether the capacity of European races to form new homes for themselves is not narrowly limited by climate."[4] Australia shaped Pearson's thoughts not only by convicting him of the truth of climatic determinism, but also by opening his eyes to the progressive nature of the colony's emerging political culture. Freedom from "the limitations of English tradition" had led to "political experiments ... [that] deserve attention as an indication of what we may expect in the future."[5] In addition to providing ammunition for his claims, Pearson's colonial experience was manifested in his propensity for formal innovation. "[H]is history has divested itself of narrative," the *Athenaeum* remarked, "he ... has, perhaps, invented a new variety of historical composition."[6] In its active transformation of metropolitan form, however, *National Life and Character* merely provided the most recent example of a long-standing tendency for Victorian conceptions of British political identity to be transformed as they were routed through the settler empire.

This book argues that the development of Victorian literature and political economy is part and parcel of the history of settler colonialism. Throughout the Victorian era, Britain and its settler empire were linked by flows of capital, population, material goods, and culture that were seen at the time to be qualitatively different from exchanges with other parts of the empire. "Transfers of things, thoughts, and people, lubricated by shared language and culture, were easier within them than from without," James Belich observes of this transnational British community: "Changes flowed

---

[3] Rev. of Pearson, *Athenaeum*, 273. For an extensive account of the colonial background to, and international reception of, Pearson's work, see Marilyn Lake, "'The Day Will Come': Charles H. Pearson's *National Life and Character: A Forecast*," in *Ten Books That Shaped the British Empire: Creating an Imperial Commons*, ed. Antoinette M. Burton and Isabel Hofmeyr (Durham: Duke University Press, 2014).

[4] Charles H. Pearson, *National Life and Character: A Forecast* (London: Macmillan, 1893), 16.

[5] Ibid., 17.   [6] Rev. of Pearson, *Athenaeum*, 273.

Introduction
Settler Colonialism and Metropolitan Culture

> But the New World would also act upon the European communities
> themselves, modifying their occupations and ways of life, altering
> their industrial and economical character. Thus the expansion of
> England involves its transformation.
>
> J. R. Seeley, *The Expansion of England*

> How one goes about identifying the social and political reverber-
> ations between colony and metropole is a difficult task.
>
> Ann Laura Stoler and Frederick Cooper, "Between Metropole
> and Colony: Rethinking a Research Agenda"

In 1893, the Victorian cultural and political firmament was agitated by
Charles H. Pearson's *National Life and Character: A Forecast*, a work of
speculative history that argued that global history was in essence a race war
that Anglo-Saxons were destined to lose. Reviewers found it to be a
"remarkable, though melancholy, book"; "hopelessly discouraging …
[and] almost unmitigatedly grim and wretched"; and infused by a "fine
tone of somber fatalism."[1] Gladstone recommended Pearson's work to
visitors to Downing Street, while across the Atlantic, Theodore Roosevelt
ranked it alongside Alfred Thayer Mahan's *The Influence of Sea Power upon
History* (1890) for its geopolitical import.[2] Nothing could seem more
quintessentially Victorian than this *fin de siècle* fever dream of racial
decline, yet its distinctive approach and insights – its virulent racism, its
fascination with population growth, and its interest in the future – were
frequently attributed to its origins on the edge of the empire, and specifically in a settler colony. "The reader can indeed discern that Mr. Pearson's

---

[1] Unsigned review of *National Life and Character: A Forecast*, by Charles H. Pearson, *The Edinburgh Review* 178, no. 366 (1893): 277; Unsigned review of *National Life and Character: A Forecast*, by Charles H. Pearson, *The Athenaeum*, no. 3410 (1893): 209; A. C. Lyall, review of *National Life and Character: A Forecast*, by Charles H. Pearson, *The Nineteenth Century* 33, no. 195 (1893): 893.
[2] Marilyn Lake, "The White Man under Siege: New Histories of Race in the Nineteenth Century and the Advent of White Australia," *History Workshop Journal* 58, no. 1 (2004): 41.

Greater Britain: Jevons, Trollope, and Settler Colonialism," *Victorian Studies* 58, no. 3 (2016): 436–63. It is reprinted with the permission of Indiana University Press. A version of Chapter 4 was published a long time ago as "Greater Britain and the Imperial Outpost: The Australasian Origins of *The Riddle of the Sands* (1903)." This article was first published in the *Victorian Review*, 35.1 (2009): 79–95. Copyright © 2009 Victorian Studies of Western Canada. Reprinted with permission by Johns Hopkins University Press.

and rewritten due to a Marsden Fund Fast-Start Grant, awarded by the Royal Society of New Zealand.

Early on, a period as a resident scholar at the Stout Centre for New Zealand Studies, Victoria University of Wellington, allowed me to realize that there was a forgotten colonial story to be told about the invasion novel. Near the end, a visiting research fellowship at the University of Sydney's School of Literature, Art and Media allowed me to finish the proposal. Throughout, I have been more than ably assisted by librarians at several remarkable institutions: the Mitchell Library, State Library of New South Wales; the Alexander Turnbull Library, National Library of New Zealand Te Puna Mātauranga o Aotearoa; Duke University Libraries; and the Massey University Library Te Putanga ki te Ao Mātauranga, who also kindly overlooked my overdue fines.

I have been incredibly fortunate to find interlocutors and encouragers around the world: Tim Alborn, Nancy Armstrong, Duncan Bell, Simon During, Ingrid Horrocks, Ian Huffer, Edmund King, Dougal McNeill, Liz Miller, John Plotz, Sarah Ross, Jason Rudy, Tess Shewry, Vanessa Smith, and Lydia Wevers. The North American Victorian Studies Association and Vcologies have proved the most stimulating and supportive of intellectual communities. At Cambridge University Press, I am so grateful to my editor, Bethany Thomas, for being willing to take a further look at the project; to the two anonymous readers who provided such valuable feedback; to Carrie Parkinson and Bethany Johnson for guiding me through the whole process; and to Yassar Arafat for overseeing the production, and Christine Dunn for astute and patient copyediting

At the heart of it all has been family, and faith. My parents, Michael and Susan, have been unfailing in their love, encouragement, and interest from the very first. My in-laws, Des and Louise, have also been a source of great kindness on the journey. All Saints' Church has provided a spiritual home, and a community, and both have sustained this work. My wife, Sarah, has been there every step of the way, in every country and every challenge, and words cannot describe how grateful I am for her love, support, and patience throughout. My working life has been immeasurably enriched by our children, Esther, Silas, Joseph, and Amos. Probably none of you will quite believe this is now actually finished. Dedicating this book to you all is really the least I could do.

The cover image is a detail from Henry Gritten's painting, *Hobart Town 1856*, reproduced courtesy of the Australian National Maritime Museum Collection, object 00018553, purchased with USA Bicentennial Gift funds. A version of Chapter 2 was previously published as "Gold and

Acknowledgments

At the end of this long, long journey, all I can recall is kindness and generosity. This book originated in a doctoral dissertation, undertaken in the generative environment of Duke University, and supported by a James B. Duke Fellowship. My presence there, which still seems little short of miraculous, was enabled by the unfailing support of my teachers in the School of English, Film, and Theatre Studies at Victoria University, and in material terms by a graduate award from Fulbright New Zealand. I was sustained and encouraged throughout my time there by the hospitality and brilliance of my grad student colleagues. Of the faculty I want to especially acknowledge Michael Valdez Moses and Charlotte Sussman. Above all, my advisor, Kathy Psomiades, taught me lessons in how to write and think that I am still learning: she remains my imagined reader, and will always exemplify for me the best things in this profession. Out of my time at Duke, I also gained the inestimable friendship of the remarkable Nathan Hensley, reader of innumerable chapter drafts and provider of wise counsel at every turn, whose conceptual rigor and narrative style have brought me further in my own work than I ever imagined possible, and who remains even at this distance perhaps the best person I could ever possibly hope to meet.

The Division of English at Nanyang Technological University offered me my first job. The School of English and Media Studies at Massey University has witnessed my slow movement from dissertation to book, and I am grateful for the support provided by successive heads of school – John Muirhead, Joe Grixti, and Jenny Lawn – as well as the administrative assistance of Carol Seelye and Janet Lowe in particular. The College of Humanities and Social Sciences has provided support through a period of long leave, as well as several grants from the Massey University Research Fund for invaluable research assistants: Bonnie Etherington, Danielle Calder, and Kirsten Ellmers. The entire project was able to be rethought

Figures

Contents

For Sarah
and Esther
and Silas
and Joseph
and Amos

more easily within the system, and were received more readily."[7] Within this imperial system, the colonies of Australia and New Zealand – collectively termed Australasia – were regarded as archetypal expressions of the Victorian effort to replicate the entirety of their society around the globe.[8] "New Zealand is essentially a product of the Victorian era," observed its former premier, Julius Vogel, in the year *National Life and Character* was published: "It was during the present reign that its sovereignty was acquired, and that it was constituted into a British colony."[9] This privileged status was intensified by the symbolism of Australasia's antipodal relationship to Britain, its geopolitical isolation from other imperial competitors, climatic similarities and suitability for agricultural production, and fervently pro-imperial sentiments. "[O]f all the colonial provinces of the British crown," reflected the geologist Ferdinand von Hochstetter at mid-century, "New Zealand bears the most resemblance to the mother-country by virtue of its insular position, its climate, its soil, and the whole form and structure of the country."[10] In the "extreme case" offered by New Zealand, moreover, its vast distance from Britain was belied by the speed at which its ecosystems were overthrown and the indigenous Māori population was dispossessed.[11] In Australia, which had been the destination of transported convicts since the 1780s, a far more massive flow of "free" settlers was also a distinctive product of the Victorian era: more than 1,132,000 emigrants traveled voluntarily to the southern continent in the second half of the century.[12] This history of settlement recurs in H. G.

---

[7] James Belich, *Replenishing the Earth: The Settler Revolution and the Rise of the Anglo-World, 1783–1939* (Oxford: Oxford University Press, 2009), 49.

[8] Although the term fell out of favor during the twentieth century, as distinct national identities coalesced in Australia and New Zealand, "Australasia" was used widely and flexibly in the nineteenth century to describe Britain's imperial possessions in the South Pacific, and the shared cultural and economic linkages between them. Thus James Belich describes "a series of trans-Tasman industries ... in which the distinction between Australia and New Zealand was artificial" during the course of the nineteenth century. James Belich, *Making Peoples: A History of the New Zealanders, from Polynesian Settlement to the End of the Nineteenth Century* (Auckland: Penguin, 1996), 132. See also Donald Denoon, "Re-Membering Australasia: A Repressed Memory," *Australian Historical Studies* 34, no. 122 (2003); Philippa Mein Smith, Peter Hempenstall, and Shaun Goldfinch, *Remaking the Tasman World* (Christchurch: Canterbury University Press, 2008).

[9] Julius Vogel, *New Zealand: Its Past, Present and Future* (London: Waterlow and Sons, 1893), 3–4.

[10] Ferdinand von Hochstetter, *New Zealand: Its Physical Geography, Geology and Natural History, with Special Reference to the Results of Government Expeditions in the Provinces of Auckland and Nelson,* trans. Edward Sauter (Stuttgart: Cotta, 1867), 44–45.

[11] John Darwin, *The Empire Project: The Rise and Fall of the British World-System, 1830–1970* (Cambridge: Cambridge University Press, 2009), 168.

[12] Robert Hughes, *The Fatal Shore* (New York: Knopf, 1987), 162; P. J. Cain, "Economics and Empire: The Metropolitan Context," in *The Nineteenth Century,* ed. Andrew Porter, The Oxford History of the British Empire (Oxford: Oxford University Press, 1999), 47.

Wells's *The War of the Worlds* (1898), when the narrator attempts to put the ruthless Martian invasion in context: "The Tasmanians, in spite of their human likeness, were entirely swept out of existence in a war of extermination by European immigrants, in the space of fifty years."[13] By the turn of the twentieth century, the indigenous population in Australia had plummeted some 70 percent – to perhaps 94,500 – and in New Zealand by 60 percent, to an estimated 42,000.[14] As Wells's passing reference indicates, the story of Victorian literature in the settler colonies is not just a tale of the colonial acclimatization of British writing. Within the common bounds of "shared language and culture," the evolving frenzy of exploitation and transformation in the settler colonies put pressure on metropolitan forms of the novel and political economy, and provided new conceptual vocabularies for understanding British society and subjectivity.

Our understanding of Victorian literature and culture – its global reach, pathways of development, and political significance – has been impoverished by a failure to find the terms and methodologies necessary to grapple with the impact of the Victorian settler empire. Yet to make such a claim is to immediately confront the fact that, barring a few brief mentions in a few exceptional texts – most famously, the scene-stealing portrayal of the convict Magwitch in Charles Dickens's *Great Expectations* (1861) – its literary traces seem at first glance barely discernible. Take, for example, a moment mid-way through Anthony Trollope's *Phineas Finn* (1869):

> General Effingham ... and Lord Brentford had been the closest and dearest of friends. They had been young men in the same regiment, and through life each had confided in the other. When the General's only son, then a youth of seventeen, was killed in one of our grand New Zealand wars, the bereaved father and the Earl had been together for a month in their sorrow.... Now the General was dead, and Violet, the daughter of a second wife, was all that was left of the Effinghams. This second wife had been a Miss Plummer, a lady from the city with much money, whose sister had married Lord Baldock. Violet in this way had fallen to the care of the Baldock people, and not into the hands of her father's friends.[15]

The typicality of this moment lies equally in its brevity – nothing more will be heard of New Zealand in the novel – and in its function as mere

---

[13] H. G. Wells, *The War of the Worlds*, ed. Andy Sawyer (London: Penguin, 2005), 9.
[14] Australian Bureau of Statistics, "Australian Historical Population Statistics, 2008," Commonwealth of Australia; Statistics New Zealand, "Historical Population Estimates Tables," Statistics New Zealand.
[15] Anthony Trollope, *Phineas Finn* (London: Oxford University Press, 1973), 100–1.

background to the financial and genealogical plotting of metropolitan realism. Yet this fictional trace belies the prominence of the subject at the time: just five years before *Phineas Finn* was published, there were 12,000 imperial soldiers in the colony, "more than were available for the defence of England at the time," mobilized to fight approximately 4,000 of the indigenous Māori population in the largest of the century's "grand New Zealand wars."[16] Britain's subsequent decision to withdraw these troops produced "an acute crisis in Imperial relations" and prompted vigorous debate in the metropole and the settler colony.[17] The point is not that *Phineas Finn* should somehow have made more of New Zealand – the novel is, after all, preeminently concerned with another imperial zone, Ireland – or that Trollope was blind to colonial questions, for empire was more central to his thought than to most metropolitan writers of the period. Instead, the brief tale of the general's ill-fated son suggests that a paucity of direct literary references cannot necessarily be treated as indicative of the scale or nature of Britain's settler-colonial entanglements.

Yet given the scale of the settler empire, can our current critical tools help us discern the extent of its literary influence? After all, as J. R. Seeley put it, at the height of interest in what the Victorians came to call Greater Britain, "the expansion of England involves its transformation."[18] This poses something of a methodological dilemma for Victorian studies, because the procedures we have developed for recognizing empire's literary traces have left settler colonialism as something of a constitutive absence within our thinking, akin to the "absence of mind" about empire that Seeley famously attributed to his contemporaries.[19] The root of our current approach can be traced in large part to Edward Said's influential reading of *Mansfield Park* (1814), which dwells on the relationship between the richly imagined social milieu of the Bertrams' English estate, and their slave-owning sugar plantation in Antigua that bankrolls the family but is only alluded to in passing. Said's approach attends to a

---

[16] James Belich, *The New Zealand Wars and the Victorian Interpretation of Racial Conflict* (Auckland: Penguin, 1998), 125.

[17] Peter Burroughs, "Defence and Imperial Disunity," in *The Nineteenth Century*, ed. Andrew Porter, The Oxford History of the British Empire (Oxford: Oxford University Press, 1999), 329. See also J. A. Froude's comments on "the withdrawal of the troops" in James Anthony Froude, "England and Her Colonies," in *Short Studies on Great Subjects* (New York: Scribner, Armstrong, 1874), 156–58; James Anthony Froude, "The Colonies Once More," in *Short Studies on Great Subjects* (New York: Scribner, Armstrong, 1874), 287–88.

[18] John Robert Seeley, *The Expansion of England: Two Courses of Lectures*, 2nd ed. (London: Macmillan, 1921), 93.

[19] Ibid., 10.

"counterpoint between overt patterns in British writing about Britain and representations of the world beyond the British Isles. The inherent mode for this counterpoint is not temporal but spatial."[20] The key terms here are "representations" and "spatial": Said's analysis focuses on "overt" mentions of empire as indexical of its limited prominence in British thought, and as a consequence maintains that the geographic separation of metropole and colony is matched by their cultural and intellectual isolation from each other. Yet as Elaine Freedgood points out in response to Said, the invisibility of empire in the "enduring cultural monuments of the nineteenth century" (in her discussion, *Great Expectations*) is belied by its visibility in the periodical press, compromising the assumption that "many historicist critics, myself included, frequently disavow but endemically rely upon: the relationship ... between the realist novel and social reality, or our critical ability to pry that reality from recalcitrant representations."[21] Put another way, the imperial content of the Victorian novel is in itself no clear indication of the degree of entanglement between the metropole and the settler colonies.

If not content, then form? The possibility that imperial insights might be gained from a new formalist criticism that "makes a continuum with new historicism," as Marjorie Levinson puts it, is exemplified by Garrett Stewart's contribution to *Modern Language Quarterly*'s iconic special issue, "Reading for Form," which argues that the influence of empire pervades the very grammar of metropolitan realism, playing out as "a structuring of consciousness rather than a conscious object."[22] Stewart zeroes in on Dickens's widespread use in *Dombey and Son* of sylleptic constructions: the grammatical linking of unlike things, literal and figurative, through a "predication [that] splays out in two different but syntactically absorbable senses."[23] These formations, he maintains, both enact and illuminate the metropolitan conceptual operations that could simultaneously avoid and mystify the realities of imperialism, "the tenuous ligatures of colonial interdependency ... refigured as immaterial, distanced, disembodied, impersonal, abstracted to all that remains unseen to be believed, believed in as British fortitude rather than exploitation."[24] For all the startling suggestiveness of this analysis, however, its conception of the relationship

[20] Edward W. Said, *Culture and Imperialism* (New York: Knopf, 1993), 81.
[21] Elaine Freedgood, "Realism, Fetishism, and Genocide: 'Negro Head' Tobacco in and around *Great Expectations*," *Novel* 36, no. 1 (2002): 28, 31.
[22] Marjorie Levinson, "What Is New Formalism?," *PMLA* 122, no. 2 (2007): 559; Garrett Stewart, "The Foreign Offices of British Fiction," *Modern Language Quarterly* 61, no. 1 (2000): 193.
[23] Stewart, "Foreign Offices of British Fiction," 186.   [24] Ibid., 204.

between culture and imperialism remains firmly circumscribed within metropolitan horizons. Most immediately, the forensic attention to "minuscule syntactic wrinkles" that grounds Stewart's analysis contrasts with its rough-hewn sense of empire, which is figured in the most generalized of terms: "colonial armatures," the "myth of empire," "global transformation."[25] This comparative unevenness in turn highlights an underlying assumption that the primary impact of imperialism upon the metropolitan novel occurred at second hand, through its registering of the "cultural tensions" generated at home by those unsavory and invisible offshore activities.[26] I shall suggest instead that the formal traces of the Victorian settler empire can be brought to light more effectively through renovating a materialist tradition of formal analysis. "Every element of form has an active material basis," insists Raymond Williams; at the same time, he avers, "form is inevitably a relationship."[27] Britain's entangled histories with Australia and New Zealand in the nineteenth century had significant implications, as much relational as material, for literary form. Both the unfolding local histories of Britain's settler projects and the shifting geopolitical status of the settler empire as a whole, I shall argue, left formal traces upon metropolitan literature by way of specific networks of literary influence and exchange that emerged out of that distinct imperial framework.

British Identity, Literature, and the Victorian Settler Empire

When Karl Marx turned his excoriating gaze on Edward Gibbon Wakefield's influential theories of settler colonization, at the conclusion of his analysis of primitive accumulation in *Capital* (1867), he found their "great merit" lay in having "discovered, not something new *about* the colonies, but, *in* the colonies, the truth about capitalist relations in the mother country."[28] This book's central wager follows Marx in arguing that settler colonialism's most significant influence on Victorian literature was brought to bear through one of its most obvious yet least remarked structural features: the centrality of British identity to the attempt to replicate Victorian society on a global scale. The potential of Britishness as a collective political identity to underpin nation and empire building

---

[25] Ibid., 187, 192, 194.   [26] Ibid., 200.
[27] Raymond Williams, *Marxism and Literature* (Oxford: Oxford University Press, 1977), 187, 190.
[28] Karl Marx, *Capital: A Critique of Political Economy: Volume One*, ed. Ernest Mandel, trans. Ben Fowkes (London: Penguin, 1976), 830, 932. See also Gabriel Piterberg and Lorenzo Veracini, "Wakefield, Marx, and the World Turned Inside Out," *Journal of Global History* 10, no. 3 (2015).

was crystallized in the eighteenth century, as Linda Colley has argued, when its capaciousness and flexibility as a concept provided a means of unifying England, Scotland, and Wales in response to the threat of European war.[29] Defined in opposition to other nationalities and ethnicities, the conviction of a shared British identity helped bolster a particularly potent form of the "deep, horizontal comradeship" that Benedict Anderson locates in all national identities, a shared identification that binds a dispersed and numerous population together despite a lack of personal connection or knowledge between its members, so that "in the minds of each lives the image of their communion."[30] By the last quarter of the nineteenth century, a rhetoric of Britishness that conflated racial and national identity was being mobilized to imagine a common political purpose across the settler empire, providing "a form of social cement connecting the scattered elements of the empire, and allowing it to be represented both as a natural outgrowth of England and as a cohesive whole."[31] Yet, to borrow the terms of Anderson's most influential formulation of national identity, Britishness proved at a global scale to be neither a "homogeneous" nor an "empty" concept. In the process of being transported from Britain and imposed violently and unevenly in Australia and New Zealand, key concepts underpinning British political identity were repeatedly challenged and reconfigured in the colonies as settlement took unexpected turns. It is through the torqueing of Victorian narrative forms in the colonial environment, I shall suggest, that we can best grasp the new claims made for British identity by settler populations independent of its ostensible metropolitan arbiters.

The persistence of Britishness as a unifying political identity within the Victorian settler empire throughout the century is a divergence from the path toward colonial nationalism that Benedict Anderson has taught us to expect. *Imagined Communities* points out that nationalist sentiment emerged in the Americas amongst creoles (European-descended but

---

[29] Linda Colley, *Britons: Forging the Nation, 1707–1837* (New Haven: Yale University Press, 1992). For the political import of the relationship between conceptions of "Englishness" and "Britishness," see Ian Baucom, *Out of Place: Englishness, Empire, and the Locations of Identity* (Princeton: Princeton University Press, 1999), 3–40.

[30] Benedict R. O'Gorman Anderson, *Imagined Communities: Reflections on the Origin and Spread of Nationalism*, rev. ed. (London: Verso, 2006), 6, 7.

[31] Duncan Bell, *The Idea of Greater Britain: Empire and the Future of World Order, 1860–1900* (Princeton: Princeton University Press, 2007), 119. On the historiographical questions for "British history" raised by the attempted "duplication of British nationality, politics and social structure under conditions of settlement," see J. G. A. Pocock, "The Neo-Britains and the Three Empires," in *The Discovery of Islands: Essays in British History* (Cambridge: Cambridge University Press, 2005), 187.

colonial-born) despite the existence of "a common language and a common descent" that ought to continue to bind it to the metropole.[32] The drivers of colonial separatism are located in their political and cultural marginalization by the metropole, whereby "the accident of birth in the Americas consigned him [i.e., the colonial functionary] to subordination – even though in terms of language, religion, ancestry, or manners he was largely indistinguishable from the Spain-born Spaniard."[33] In contrast to the revolutionary path taken by British settlers in North America in the eighteenth century, however, Britain's nineteenth-century settler colonies attained a significant degree of political independence (creole nationalism) yet chose to retain their imperial allegiance (imagined community). Imperial historian John Darwin describes this seemingly paradoxical state of affairs as "Britannic nationalism," whereby "national identity was asserted by rejecting subservience to the British *government*, but by affirming equality with Britain as 'British peoples' or 'nations.'"[34] James Belich goes further in proposing a process of "recolonization," or "metropolitan reintegration," whereby antiparallel economic and cultural flows surprisingly strengthened aging imperial bonds:

> Economic staples flowed one way, from newlands to old; cultural staples and manufactures flowed the other way. The relationship between oldland and new tightened, against the grain of expectations about the steady emergence of independence or parity. Collective identities shared by old-land and new strengthened along with economic re-integration, though the one did not necessarily determine the other.[35]

These broad-brush invocations of Britishness nevertheless remain unable to say anything very specific about the conceptions of identity that did gain purchase across the empire, how they might have altered in the process of their global transit, or the means by which a given narrative model might have become influential in colonial or metropolitan environments. Moreover, I wish to suggest that in this complex environment of shared and divergent political affiliations – racial, national, imperial – British identity comes into focus as something to be claimed, contested, and mobilized. At least, that is, by those who have a stake in it.

---

[32] Anderson, *Imagined Communities*, 7, 47.   [33] Ibid., 58.
[34] Darwin, *Empire Project*, 147, original emphasis.
[35] Belich, *Replenishing the Earth*, 179. The phrase "metropolitan reintegration" is suggested by P. J. Cain, "The Economics and Ideologies of Anglo-American Settlerism, 1780–1939," *Victorian Studies* 53, no. 1 (2010): 106.

My thinking in the following pages about the formal work that literature performed within the Victorian settler empire both draws on and diverges from imperial historians' use of world-systems approaches to foreground the powerful economic and ethnic linkages between Britain and its settler populations. A focus on networks is far from unique to this body of work, for there is now a "consensus amongst many, if not all, historians of empire," as Tony Ballantyne points out, "that reconstructing the movement of plants and animals, people, capital, commodities, information, and ideas is fundamental to understanding how the empire developed and how it operated on a day to day basis."[36] World-systems histories have largely focused on "people, capital, [and] commodities," seeking to highlight the settler empire's sheer scale by outlining the globe-changing consequences of trade and migratory flows that derived their effectiveness from the substrate of shared British culture.[37] The potential that such frameworks offer for reconsidering the literary dimensions of the settler empire lies equally in their transnational scope, the importance they ascribe to identity, and their emphasis on the material drivers of imperial culture. From another angle, however, "British World" scholarship appears to offer a severely diminished horizon for criticism. A general lack of interest in the nuances of cultural production is often underpinned by a thoroughgoing suspicion of postcolonialism, both for its privileging of textual representations and its apparent neglect of white populations. These possibilities and pitfalls are equally on display in Darwin's *The Empire Project* (2009), where a rejection of postcolonialism's cultural turn is part and parcel of the historiographic claim to redress "the place of the white dominions [that] has been all but ignored by two generations of imperial historiography":

> Least of all will it help to fall back upon a crude stereotyping of conflicting "imaginaries," in which "British" conceptions of mastery are contrasted with the values of their indigenous subjects.... Most important of all, discerning the impact of "imaginings," "representations," or "colonial

---

[36] Tony Ballantyne, "The Changing Shape of the Modern British Empire and Its Historiography," *The Historical Journal* 53, no. 2 (2010): 442.

[37] For useful surveys of the changing fortunes of British imperial historiography, see ibid.; Durba Ghosh, "Another Set of Imperial Turns?," *American Historical Review* 117, no. 3 (2012). Overviews of "British World" scholarship are offered by Rachel K. Bright and Andrew R. Dilley, "After the British World," *The Historical Journal* 60, no. 2 (2017); Stephen Howe, "British Worlds, Settler Worlds, World Systems, and Killing Fields," *Journal of Imperial and Commonwealth History* 40, no. 4 (2012); Dane Kennedy, *The Imperial History Wars: Debating the British Empire* (London: Bloomsbury Academic, 2018), 73–147.

knowledge" requires something more than a sampling of texts: the careful reconstruction of economic and political contexts must be the starting point of enquiry.[38]

Such suspicions play out as a refusal to acknowledge or interrogate the political work performed by British identity and culture. Indeed, British World scholarship at times shades imperceptibly into formulations that the Victorians might have used – Dane Kennedy sees it as "tinged with nostalgia" – as in Bridge and Federowich's desire to reconnect with "the heart of the imperial enterprise, the expansion of Britain and the peopling and holding of the trans-oceanic British world."[39] These methodological dispositions mean that, for all its generative potential, British World scholarship cannot simply be imported wholesale into literary studies.

Although British World historiography and Victorian studies diverge sharply over questions of culture and identity, literature can reshape our understanding of the settler empire at global scale through its foregrounding of the construction and contestation of Britishness as a collective political identity. Dror Wahrman argues that the British World offers a challenge and an invitation to Victorianists, "especially the cultural historians and the literary critics," because the claims made for its significance demand a more thorough understanding of the culture of imperialism: "If they cannot produce the remains of the veins and sinews of this global nineteenth-century multi-headed English-speaking hydra, then it probably never lived."[40] Taking up this challenge requires overcoming further methodological differences centered on questions of scale and its implications for textual interpretation. On the historiographic side of the ledger, individual texts or authors tend to pale into insignificance in comparison with the scale and volume of material and information flows within the settler empire. Belich, for example, has little need of plot or theme when he can literally weigh the extent of imperial sentiment: "Canada's link with Britain was fifty-eight times as strong as India's" by the turn of the twentieth century, he concludes, based on the volume of mail sent and

[38] Darwin, *Empire Project*, 7. In an important critique, Bill Schwarz sums up Darwin's historiography as "steadfast in his indictment of all that convenes under the banners of postcolonial history, or of the so-called new imperial history, or of cultural history or of what he chooses at one point to designate by the catch-all notion of 'subaltern history'" – and concludes that "his indictment represents – in every respect – a serious misreading." Bill Schwarz, "An Unsentimental Education: John Darwin's Empire," *Journal of Imperial and Commonwealth History* 43, no. 1 (2015): 126, 135.
[39] Carl Bridge and Kent Fedorowich, "Mapping the British World," in *The British World: Diaspora, Culture and Identity*, ed. Carl Bridge and Kent Fedorowich (London: Frank Cass, 2003), 11.
[40] Dror Wahrman, "The Meaning of the Nineteenth Century: Reflections on James Belich's *Replenishing the Earth*," *Victorian Studies* 53, no. 1 (2010): 99.

received on a pounds per capita basis.[41] Further, conceiving of the settler empire in such aggregate terms inevitably comprehends British political identity as firmly centered on London, "the cultural and economic capital of Greater Britain."[42] Within literary studies, by contrast, the continuing dominance of the nation as a basis of comparison and analysis militates against reading and arguing in transnational terms. Reflecting on the "relative dearth of literary and cultural studies work on global Britishness," Steven Howe argues that traditions of national literary study have fostered "almost entirely 'internalist'" accounts of colonial writing, a bounded approach that eschews "wider arguments about identity."[43] Historiography comes within touching distance of criticism, however, when British identity is viewed as more than a mere vector of transnational information transfer. Belich even gestures toward the possibility that settler populations performed a more active, agentive role in defining what it meant to be British when he suggests that they "considered themselves co-owners of London, the Empire, and British-ness in general."[44] British political identity comes into view as neither fully prefabricated in Britain, nor harmoniously co-constructed between the metropole and settler colonies, but as contested and reshaped in the course of its imperial transit and deployment.

Perhaps the most powerful lesson of the British World historians is the reminder that the reimagining of British identity in the settler colonies did not occur in isolation from the wider forces of empire, but took place in the context of the cultural and economic exchanges that linked the settler empire. At a fundamental level, the cultural texts of settler colonialism were inseparable from its financial considerations throughout the Victorian period because the ability to imagine settled outposts defined by the virtues of British character played an integral role in the global expansion of British finance capital. "Being seen to be British paid dividends," point out the economic historians Gary B. Magee and Andrew S. Thompson, because the idea of a common British identity functioned as a shorthand for the full panoply of institutions and character traits thought to guarantee a safe investment.[45] The implications of this insight for literary form are profound because it suggests that there is no clearly demarcated relationship between economic base and cultural superstructure within the genres that flourished

---

[41] Belich, *Replenishing the Earth*, 461.   [42] Ibid., 460.   [43] Howe, "British Worlds," 700–1.
[44] Belich, *Replenishing the Earth*, 209.
[45] Gary B. Magee and Andrew S. Thompson, *Empire and Globalisation: Networks of People, Goods and Capital in the British World, c. 1850–1914* (Cambridge: Cambridge University Press, 2010), 212.

and circulated within the settler empire. Thus, while my concern with form is largely informed by Marxist modes of analysis, it diverges from them over the interrelationship between cultural and financial considerations: concurring with Fredric Jameson's insistence on "the priority of the political interpretation of literary texts," for example, but not following him to the point of finding "an ultimate determination by the mode of production."[46] The approach taken here is more of a piece with Raymond Williams's recognition of "the indissoluble connections between material production, political and cultural institutions and activity, and consciousness," and a concomitant understanding of form as "a relationship" with a broadly construed set of social systems.[47] If "new formal possibilities ... are inherently possibilities of a newly shared perception, recognition and consciousness," then attending to the adaptation and circulation of genres in the Victorian settler empire reveals the social function of literary form as a complex interface operating on two levels: enabling the "overlapping" or intersection between metropolitan and colonial spatial and social orders; and providing a means of mediating between material flows (of migrants, capital, and commodities) and ideological systems (of political economy, aesthetics, and novelistic plotting employed to make sense of them).[48] That is, I am arguing for the need to see the imagined community of global Britishness neither as a homogeneous nor as a purely cultural formation, but as fractured by the different ways that British identity was imagined and asserted in response to economic and political pressures in its disparate metropolitan and colonial locations.

Stadial Theory, Settlement, and Literary Form

Admittedly, though, one key reason settler literature has not generally been held in high regard is precisely because of its perceived formal failings. "I never yet could get the proper knack of telling a story," reflects F. E. Maning, one of the few New Zealand writers to have escaped that general opprobrium, six chapters into *Old New Zealand: A Tale of the Good Old Times* (1863), his circuitous fictionalized memoir of settling in the north of the colony in the early 1830s.[49] "I begin to fancy I have not been born under a storytelling planet," he adds in a later chapter, "for by no effort

---

[46] Fredric Jameson, *The Political Unconscious: Narrative as a Socially Symbolic Act* (Ithaca: Cornell University Press, 1981), 17, 45.
[47] Williams, *Marxism and Literature*, 80, 187.   [48] Ibid., 189.
[49] F. E. Maning, *Old New Zealand: A Tale of the Good Old Times* (Auckland: Creighton and Scales, 1863), 85.

that I can make can I hold on to the thread of my story, and I am conscious the whole affair is fast becoming one great parenthesis."[50] At least since the first known review of Australian literature, when Frederick Sinnett described them in 1856 as "books of travels in disguise," and their authors as "voyagers sailing under the false colors of novelists," settler novels have generally been dismissed for their structural and narrative quirks.[51] Indeed, the consolidation of distinct literary traditions in both Australia and New Zealand during the first half of the twentieth century was in each case founded in large part on the dismissal of settler writing's bent and broken forms. For E. H. McCormick, writing in the 1940s of New Zealand's colonial novelists, "Their minds were immature, their work provincial in its form and outlook. The fact was they lived in a society still inchoate."[52] Three decades later, Geoffrey Serle similarly described the afterlife of English literary tradition in Australia as "a kind of negative asset, tied-up capital which could not be productively used": "Culture is a highly perishable growth which, transplanted, cannot bloom as before. Once the geographical break was made, in creative terms the tradition was broken or became very tenuous."[53] Yet far from marking a failure of perception, only capable of remedy once aesthetic vision could again be adequately bounded by the emergence of a nation-state, these narrative tendencies might be seen more productively as direct engagements with the principles and processes of settler colonization. Maning, for example, is highly aware that settlement can be grasped as a formal problem:

> Here I am now, a good forty years ahead of where I ought to be, talking of "title deeds" and "land commissioners," things belonging to the new and deplorable state of affairs which began when this country became "a British colony and possession," and also "one of the brightest jewels in the British crown." I must go back.[54]

---

[50] Ibid., 165. Upon its reprinting, the *Athenaeum* enthusiastically described it as "the best book ever written about a savage race," as well as "one of the most mirth-making that we know." Unsigned review of *Old New Zealand, a Tale of the Good Old Times*, by F. E. Maning, *The Athenaeum*, no. 2560 (1876): 653. For Maning's life, and the publication history of *Old New Zealand*, see Alex Calder, "Introduction," in *Old New Zealand and Other Writings* (London: Leicester University Press, 2001).

[51] Frederick Sinnett, "The Fiction Fields of Australia," in *The Writer in Australia: A Collection of Literary Documents, 1856 to 1964*, ed. John Barnes (Melbourne and New York: Oxford University Press, 1969), 17.

[52] E. H. McCormick, *Letters and Art in New Zealand* (Wellington: Department of Internal Affairs, 1940), 125.

[53] Geoffrey Serle, *From Deserts the Prophets Come: The Creative Spirit in Australia 1788–1972*, new ed. (Clayton: Monash University Publishing, 2014), 52.

[54] Maning, *Old New Zealand*, 165.

These self-conscious formal contortions register the collision between different cultural and political regimes in the settler colony. Not only are British economic principles ("title deeds") and their intersection with identity claims ("brightest jewels in the British crown") held up for ironic scrutiny, but both are shown to be actively confronted by indigenous protocols of social and spiritual order. In addition to those imported formations, the "all-pervading" system of *tapu* also structures, or rather deforms, his ability to narrate the settler colony: "If I could only get clear of this *tapu* I would try back. I believe I ought to be just now completing the purchase of my estate."[55] Narrative form – "story," as Maning puts it – thus provides a central means of identifying and exploring the limits and contradictions of settler colonialism's cultural and economic principles.

A more awkward – and thus more typical – settler novel casts further light on the formal stakes of such works. Charles Rowcroft's *Tales of the Colonies, or, The Adventures of an Emigrant* (1843), based on his experiences as one of the earliest "free" settlers in Van Diemen's Land in the 1820s, tells the story of William Thornley, who arrives in the colony determined to settle on a piece of land and establish a farm and family home. The first hundred pages generally follows the colonial narrative template established by Daniel Defoe's *Robinson Crusoe* (1719) in presenting the transformation of new land into British space through a journal of diligent, if dull, labor:

> *Monday, March 4.* – Chopping and sawing.
> *Tuesday, March 5.* – Sawing and chopping.
> *Wednesday, March 6.* – Chop, chop, chop, saw, saw, saw.
> ...
> *Saturday.* – More chopping and sawing.
> *Sunday.* – Passed as before.[56]

This testament to Thornley's regular and persistent work helps create the impression that the new colony is a fit place for what Walter Scott called "the ordinary train of human events, and the modern state of society."[57] The effect is complicated, however, by points when the narrative is suspended in favor of another mode altogether – that of political economy:

[55] Ibid., 119, 65.
[56] Charles Rowcroft, *Tales of the Colonies, or, the Adventures of an Emigrant* (London: Saunders & Otley, 1843), 71–72.
[57] Walter Scott, "An Essay on Romance," in *Essays on Chivalry, Romance, and the Drama, The Miscellaneous Prose Works of Walter Scott* (Edinburgh: Cadell, 1834), 129.

In taking stock last month, the numbers of my sheep stood thus: –

180 ewes, bought in March, 1817   180
Their lambs, then five months old, viz., 100 ewes and 80
   wethers 180

2 wethers, left out of the 40 bought in March last   2
220 lambs, three months old, dropped in November,
   by the 180 ewes bought in March last; viz. 120 ewe
   lambs and 100 wethers   220

The 100 ewe lambs, bought in March last, produced
   me this February 120 lambs; viz., 64 ewes and 56
   wethers 120
                                            702[58]

A similar statistical intrusion occurs, on an even broader social scale, when Thornley recounts that "a careful census was taken of the statistics of the colony, which I find in my journal to stand thus: – Number of inhabitants, 7,185; acres in cultivation, 14,940; sheep, 17,000; horses, 350."[59] The enumeration of horses and sheep, and the detailing of tedious exertions, are linked not only by the equal likelihood that they will be skimmed or skipped. These blunt juxtapositions of labor and livestock also reflect the common ground shared by the novel and political economy in the settler colony, for both depend upon the evidence of a settled pastoral space to be able to imagine a civilized British society. The formal qualities of Victorian writing in and about the settler colonies, I shall argue, stem from these intersecting concerns of culture, cultivation, and capital.

The Victorian settler empire was founded upon the long-standing principle of liberal political economy theory of an underlying structuring relationship – simultaneously political, economic, and cultural – between territory and sociality. If a desire to control and exploit territory is "settler colonialism's specific, irreducible element," as Patrick Wolfe asserts, the Victorian commitment to settlement was equally predicated on "an act – or at least a fantasy – of mimetic transfer" of British institutions, social structures, and cultural norms.[60] At the heart of those twinned fantasies of control and imitation were John Locke's theories of private property, and the Scottish Enlightenment's "stadial" theory of societal development. In

---

[58] Ibid., 98.   [59] Ibid., 104.
[60] Patrick Wolfe, "Settler Colonialism and the Elimination of the Native," *Journal of Genocide Research* 8, no. 4 (2006): 388; Duncan Bell, *Reordering the World: Essays on Liberalism and Empire* (Princeton: Princeton University Press, 2016), 38.

Locke's *Second Treatise of Government* (1690), where the possession of the *"earth itself"* is proposed as the basis of all property relations, it is the individual's labor that famously transforms nature from a common possession of all humanity into the simplest form of individual title: *"As much land* as a man tills, plants, improves, cultivates, and can use the product of, so much is his *property.* He by his labour does, as it were, inclose it from the common."[61] In the hands of Scottish Enlightenment thinkers such as Adam Smith, Dugald Ferguson, and John Millar, the creation of property from nature through labor became the crux of a sweeping theory of sociocultural evolution. According to this "stadial" narrative, the path from savagery to civilization is marked by four stages: as Smith succinctly put it in his lectures on jurisprudence, "1st, the Age of Hunters; 2dly, the Age of Shepherds; 3dly, the Age of Agriculture; and 4^{thly}, the Age of Commerce."[62] Each stage represents a distinct mode of subsistence and social organization, originating in a specific economic relationship to territory, but the most radical break in the developmental narrative occurs with the act of settlement – agriculture – as the Lockean cultivation of the soil reduces a nomadic existence to stasis, and enables for the first time the accumulation of private property. Thus the arbiter of early Victorian economic orthodoxy, J. R. McCulloch, could assert, "The *third* and most decisive step in the progress of civilisation – in the great art of producing the necessaries and conveniences of life – is made when the wandering tribes of hunters and shepherds renounce their migratory habits, and become agriculturalists and manufacturers."[63] During the Victorian renewal of British settler colonialism, stadialism proved "undoubtedly influential in informing policies and practices on native title."[64] At the same time, because settlement was most typically envisaged as a pastoral economy in the midst of limitless colonial "waste," the British settler population occupied an unstable conceptual niche between the sociospatial orders of savagery and wandering, and stasis and civilization. Political

---

[61] John Locke, *Second Treatise of Government*, ed. C. B. Macpherson (Indianapolis: Hackett, 1980), 21, original emphasis. On the relationship between Locke's political theory and the emergence of political economy, see Andrew Sartori, *Liberalism in Empire: An Alternative History* (Oakland: University of California Press, 2014), 8–20.

[62] Adam Smith, *Lectures on Jurisprudence*, ed. Ronald L. Meek, D. D. Raphael, and Peter Stein, The Glasgow Edition of the Works and Correspondence of Adam Smith (Oxford: Clarendon Press, 1978), 14. Ronald L. Meek outlines the development of stadial theory in Scotland in the 1750s in *Social Science and the Ignoble Savage* (Cambridge: Cambridge University Press, 1976), 99–130.

[63] J. R. McCulloch, *The Principles of Political Economy; With a Sketch of the Rise and Progress of the Science*, 2nd ed. (London: Tait, 1830), 68.

[64] Mark Hickford, *Lords of the Land: Indigenous Property Rights and the Jurisprudence of Empire* (Oxford: Oxford University Press, 2011), 29.

economist Herman Merivale succinctly captured this tension in his influential *Lectures on Colonization and Colonies* (1841), in discussing the effects of the "wide extent of fertile soil" on the settler population in Australia: there, worryingly for him, "the inclination of men for the ease and independence of pastoral, semi-savage life" seemed a more powerful instinct than that for the accumulation of private property, and therefore "placed great obstacles in the way of civilization."[65] From the earliest days of Victorian settler colonialism, that is, what it meant to be British appeared to be defined as much by its spatial parameters as by racial or cultural inheritance.

The novel stands out as the Victorian literary form most thoroughly infused with the logic of stadialist thought, and thus most keenly attuned to the task of conceptualizing British identity in the settler colonies.[66] From Cathy Linton's planting a garden at Wuthering Heights to dispel Heathcliff's vagrant energies, through to the Wessex novels' concern for the "destruction of a local sense and the substitution of nothing in its place," the novel's investment in states of spatiotemporal settlement can be glimpsed at the level of characterization – as disposition; as propensity for geographic mobility – and in the sharpening distinction between realism and romance forms.[67] This formal logic enters into early Victorian literary culture by way of the "massively influential new form of historiographic practice" enacted in Walter Scott's Waverley novels.[68] Furthermore, as Katie Trumpener points out, not only were Scott's works, along with Shakespeare and Dickens, the "most widely circulated British literature in … the whole English-speaking world," but they were also "by mid-century … so deeply embedded in the colonial imagination that their full influence is not always understood."[69] Yet whereas Trumpener stresses the

---

[65] Herman Merivale, *Lectures on Colonization and Colonies*, 2 vols. (London: Longman, Orme, Brown, Green, and Longmans, 1841), 1.266–67.

[66] Recent works have made strong claims for focusing on altogether different forms of writing in the settler colonies. As Jason R. Rudy argues, "Poetry's portability – readily scribbled on a scrap of paper, reprinted in a letter, or fixed in an emigrant's memory – meant it could circulate with ease through Britain's colonies, spaces that at first were not equipped to publish longer works." Jude Piesse, by contrast, sees the "inherently mobile form" of the periodical as offering "unrivalled capacity to register emigration." Jason R. Rudy, *Imagined Homelands: British Poetry in the Colonies* (Baltimore: Johns Hopkins University Press, 2017), 7; Jude Piesse, *British Settler Emigration in Print, 1832–1877* (Oxford: Oxford University Press, 2016), 2.

[67] John Barrell, "Geographies of Hardy's Wessex," in *The Regional Novel in Britain and Ireland, 1800–1990*, ed. K. D. M. Snell (Cambridge: Cambridge University Press, 1998), 101.

[68] James Chandler, *England in 1819: The Politics of Literary Culture and the Case of Romantic Historicism* (Chicago: University of Chicago Press, 1998), 127.

[69] Katie Trumpener, *Bardic Nationalism: The Romantic Novel and the British Empire* (Princeton: Princeton University Press, 1997), 246, 247.

Waverley novels' ability to reconcile the United Kingdom's competing ethnic nationalisms under the banner of Britishness, by dissociating cultural distinctiveness from political autonomy, I wish to highlight the consequences of Scott's distillation of stadialist theory into genre categories. As James Chandler points out, the Waverley novels self-consciously enact a narrativized "logic of uneven development," juxtaposing Scotland with England in terms that are simultaneously developmental and temporal.[70] Scott discusses the relationship between stadial thought and genre choice more directly in his "Essay on Romance" (1824), which links the emergence of the novel out of the romance to the transition from primitive to modern society. On the one hand, Scott defines the romance as a "fictitious narrative in prose or verse; the interest of which turns upon marvellous and uncommon incidents."[71] In his hypothetical account of literature's origins, those extravagances of plot are indexed to a nomadic state of society: "The father of an isolated family, destined one day to rise into a tribe, and in farther progress of time to expand into a nation, may, indeed, narrate to his descendants the circumstances which detached him from the society of his brethren, and drove him to form a solitary settlement in the wilderness."[72] In the realist novel, on the other hand, "events are accommodated to the ordinary train of human events, and the modern state of society."[73] The novel thus constitutes a more appropriate form for civil society, reflecting its "settled" qualities at the level of plot in its concern for the quotidian and its constraint within the "bounds of probability or consistency."[74] At the advent of "free" settlement, then, the realist novel and the romance were equally available, and primed by stadial theory, to be applied and adapted by Victorian writers in the course of establishing of a British polity in colonial space.

My approach the novel and political economy has been enabled by the return to formalism that has characterized much literary criticism in recent years, and more especially the debates that have flourished in Victorian studies. The elements of form taken up in the following pages encompass "internal" narrative qualities – character, systems, plot, spatiality, temporality – alongside broader "external" categories of mode, genre, and even domains of knowledge. That is, I will treat form as synonymous with structure, while also regarding form as commensurate with genre. This

---

[70] Chandler, *England in 1819*, 131.   [71] Scott, "Essay on Romance," 129.

[72] Ibid., 134. Scott's stadialist thinking is most explicit when he quotes Robert Southey's opinion that "in similar stages of civilization, or states of society, the fictions of different people will bear a corresponding resemblance, notwithstanding the difference of time and scene" ibid., 174–75.

[73] Ibid., 129.   [74] Ibid., 130.

stance is in contrast to that taken by Caroline Levine in *Forms* (2015), where structure provides a means of sharply distinguishing form from genre. If genre is troublingly messy and contextual, an "ensemble of characteristics, including styles, themes, and marketing conventions," Levine argues, form instead embodies the pure and abstract principle of structural organization:

> Forms, defined as patternings, shapes, and arrangements, have a different relation to context: they can organize both social and literary objects, and they can remain stable over time.... More stable than genre, configurations and arrangements organize materials in distinct and iterable ways no matter what their context or audience. Forms thus migrate across contexts in a way that genres cannot.[75]

Narrative is accordingly reduced to little more than an arena where forms are "set in motion" and can then be monitored as they "cooperate, come into conflict, and overlap."[76] Yet Levine's positioning of genre in opposition to mobility, and of form in opposition to localized "meanings and values," elides precisely those questions of recognition and shared ownership that cluster around genres and allow them to be relocated.[77] These issues are particularly pressing in the case of the Victorian settler empire's globally dispersed British populations. The intrinsic relationship in this context between the portability of form and a shared notion of identity is evidenced by Jason Rudy's authoritative account in *Imagined Homelands* (2017) of "poetic genre … [as] a powerful mechanism supporting the cultural work of British colonialism": highlighting a widespread practice among settler poets of "literary derivativeness and reprinting," he argues that this performed a role of "cultural mediation" precisely because the poetic texts and genres that were imitated, parodied, or otherwise repurposed were "recognizable to nearly all nineteenth-century British subjects."[78] Accordingly, a more mobile approach to form is required to

---

[75] Caroline Levine, *Forms: Whole, Rhythm, Hierarchy, Network* (Princeton: Princeton University Press, 2015), 13.

[76] Ibid., 19. Levine's approach confirms at the largest scale W. J. T. Mitchell's observation that the place of form in literary criticism "has been completely overtaken by the concept of structure": "The replacement of form by structure, in fact, is one way of telling the whole story of twentieth-century criticism." W. J. T. Mitchell, "The Commitment to Form; or, Still Crazy after All These Years," *PMLA* 118, no. 2 (2003): 321.

[77] Levine, *Forms*, 7.

[78] Rudy, *Imagined Homelands*, 6, 21, 45. Rudy makes the case for "the centrality of genre – and genre's eminent reproducibility – to the work of colonial reproduction" (46) in his chapter, "Colonial Authenticity," ibid., 43–74.

illuminate the cultural work performed in the settler empire by prose narrative genres.

My claims that the spatial and temporal coordinates of British subjectivity and society are plotted in the novel and political economy, and actively revised through processes of geographic and cultural displacement, are instead more closely founded upon the strain of formal analysis that has infused Victorian studies by way of the late-twentieth-century insights of Franco Moretti. In *The Way of the World* (1987), and especially *Atlas of the European Novel 1800–1900* (1998), Moretti implicitly takes up and extends into the domain of geography the twofold challenge that Williams laid out for a materialist theory of genre: "first, that there are clear social and historical relations between particular literary forms and the societies and periods in which they were originated or practised; second, that there are undoubted continuities of literary forms through and beyond the societies and periods to which they have such relations."[79] Moretti is concerned with what he terms "symbolic form," namely, the ability of narrative to "attach a meaning" to the effects and experiences of capitalist modernity through the ordering work performed by the temporal and spatial logic of plot.[80] (Jed Esty, who has extended furthest Moretti's analysis of the bildungsroman, characterizes the relationship between literary form and political structure in terms of "reciprocal allegory" and "mutually reinforcing ideological constructions.")[81] Genre thus comes into focus as a vital category of analysis because it embodies a sustained response to political problems, its rise and fall synchronized with shifts in historical circumstance, such that it offers explanatory power over that wider material context. Formal variations at the level of structure can offer insights into processes of historical change, and illuminate especially the differences between conterminous spatio-political orders. Nathan K. Hensley has more recently described imperialism as posing "a material and conceptual problem" that was not solely worked out through the overt concerns of "plot, subject matter, and incident," but was also taken up at a deeper structural level, "as the limit case for metropolitan thought and, as such, a trigger for innovation at the level of form."[82] Moretti also proposes

---

[79] Williams, *Marxism and Literature*, 182–83.

[80] Franco Moretti, *The Way of the World: The Bildungsroman in European Culture*, trans. Albert Sbragia, New ed. (London: Verso, 2000), 5.

[81] Jed Esty, *Unseasonable Youth: Modernism, Colonialism, and the Fiction of Development* (Oxford: Oxford University Press, 2013), 2, 44.

[82] Nathan K. Hensley, *Forms of Empire: The Poetics of Victorian Sovereignty* (Oxford: Oxford University Press, 2016), 6.

that genres are "place-bound" by definition, "each of them with its peculiar geometry, its boundaries, its spatial taboos and favorite routes."[83] In essence, form is defined here not only by the kind of place it imagines but also by the kind of human movements that are permitted within it, such that plot performs a profoundly spatialized ideological work. Thus the realist novel, emerging in conjunction with the nation-state, is able in Austen's hands to replot "the painful reality of territorial uprooting," the product of capitalist modernity, presenting it as a "seductive journey: prompted by desire, and crowned by happiness." By contrast, in the imperial romance, the linear plotting that mimics the exploratory colonial journey not only diminishes indigenous populations to the status of "obstacles – and therefore, antagonists," but also lends symbolic shape to imperialism's "redirecting [of] the local economy *outwards*: towards the sea, the metropolis, the world market."[84] The corollary of such a "place-bound" view is that genres might function differently in new contexts. New geographies may, Moretti argues, "if not exactly determine, at least *encourage morphological change*," most notably through the emergence of "fragile, unstable formations" at a distance from the metropole.[85] Transported to the settler periphery and deployed there in service of replicating British society, the formal instability that becomes manifest in the Victorian novel emerges especially from the suddenly urgent need to rethink its developmental logic. At the same time, I will argue, the question of which genres come under colonial pressure at particular times is far from accidental, but making sense of this also requires attention to the physical and informational networks – of movement and interaction, influence and exchange – that linked Britain and its settler periphery.

Metropolitan Culture and the Networks of Empire

This book thus seeks to do more than simply offer yet one more account of literature's myriad one-way journeys from the metropolis to the colony. Not only charting how Victorian narrative forms were altered in and by the settler environment, it also proposes that those changes reverberated within literary culture in Britain. This aim may seem quixotic, given the settler empire's current remoteness from the concerns of mainstream Victorian literary studies, which in turn undoubtedly attests to the thousands of miles that separated Australia and New Zealand from the

---

[83] Franco Moretti, *Atlas of the European Novel, 1800–1900* (London: Verso, 1998), 5.
[84] Ibid., 18, 58, 60, original emphasis.   [85] Ibid., 32, 194, original emphasis.

imagined community of most metropolitan Britons during the Victorian era. Yet, occasionally, that distance did collapse – even to the extent that British space was reconceived in colonial terms. Take the events that unfolded in the hills of Fife and Kinross, Scotland, over three weeks in 1852, when "thousands of persons" took to "plying every kind of instrument upon them ... in search of gold, which they believed to be hidden in their recesses."[86] The upheaval was triggered by a former resident of the region, ignominiously transported to Australia some years previously, who had recently seen some of the ore from the gold rushes that were now transforming the settler colony:

> It at once struck him that he had seen abundance of the same material in his native hills, when visiting the quarries in which several of his friends and acquaintances had earned their livelihood. This impression he conveyed in a letter to his mother [in Scotland], who, as a matter of course, afforded the information to all to whom she had an opportunity of communicating it.[87]

As the dramatic completion of an imperial circuit of migration and information exchange that originated in Britain years earlier, the Fifeshire gold rush illustrates the permeability of Victorian culture to ideas and influences originating at the edges of its settler empire.[88] Crucially, for my argument what was at issue was not an explicit representation of the colonies, or colonial life, but the reconceptualizing of British territory in colonial terms. At the same time, the episode also illuminates that such influential imperial connections are far from a general condition, but come about through a series of linked circumstances, both material and textual, that are highly particularized: at a specific moment in colonial history, as a result of a specific network of personal exchange, a specific colonial representation is able to gain unexpected purchase with a metropolitan audience. Accordingly, each of the subsequent chapters will not – indeed cannot – simply address a colonial "theme" or focus on a single author, but

---

[86] "Gold-Seeking at Home," *Chambers's Edinburgh Journal,* July 24, 1852, 60. I am grateful to Tim Alborn for alerting me to this source.

[87] Ibid.

[88] The mineralogist John Calvert offered a similar reinterpretation of British territory based on his experience in Australia, arguing in *The Gold Rocks of Great Britain and Ireland* (1853) that gold was likely to be found in England on the basis of "the similarity of structure and position of the rocks to those of our Australian regions and elsewhere." John Calvert, *The Gold Rocks of Great Britain and Ireland: And a General Outline of the Gold Regions of the World, with a Treatise on the Geology of Gold* (London: Chapman and Hall, 1853), xii. To aid in this project of colonial recognition, Calvert exhibited specimens of rock and gold from Australia at Wyld's Great Globe in London, before opening his own exhibition.

will instead attempt to recover and make sense of a similarly complex series of conjunctions and exchanges.

"What enabled the reproduction of metropoles across this Anglo world, what tied its many parts together, and what unified it … ?" asks Dror Wahrman: "Much of the answer must lay, it seems to me, in the realms of language and culture."[89] In this global context, where British authors and texts moved relatively readily across the settler empire, questions of form are always also questions of mobility and exchange. Several recent attempts to rethink the place of the novel within the empire have for this reason drawn on a language of "portability." In John Plotz's influential account, novelists rendered abstract concepts of English identity portable through representing them in the guise of material objects. This procedure helped delocalize the idea of national belonging, allowing it to be reconstituted as an "isomorphic totality" across the varied spaces of empire.[90] Underpinning this operation was an overwhelming privilege enjoyed by metropolitan representation:

> It is the existence of Greater Britain that requires not just a notion of portable cultural objects, but also of *asymmetry* in portability, so that the flow of culture-bearing objects from core to periphery is not counterbalanced or interrupted by a flow in the opposite direction. The capacity of an imperium to sustain that kind of asymmetry is a crucial component of its power.[91]

In this elegant summation of the global stakes of the Victorian novel as culture-bearing commodity, novelists demarcate the borders of English identity by representing English objects in ways that confer an "immunization" against cultural difference.[92] Anglo-Indian fiction and travel literature, for example, establishes a "cordon of inattention" that distracts its English readers from the colonized populations surrounding them, "allowing English readers the option of imagining India principally via the sufferings of Anglo-Indians."[93] This model of novelistic and cultural portability across national borders, deeply imbued with an overarching

---

[89] Wahrman, "Meaning of the Nineteenth Century," 99.

[90] John Plotz, *Portable Property: Victorian Culture on the Move* (Princeton: Princeton University Press, 2008), 118.

[91] Ibid., 2, original emphasis.

[92] Ibid., 63. Such an analysis extends Moretti's earlier observation, in *Atlas of the European Novel*, that the novel is *"the most centralized of all* genres": "While the consumption of fiction was becoming more and more widespread, then, its production was becoming more and more *centralized*, both within each individual nation-state, and within the larger system of European states." Moretti, *Atlas of the European Novel*, 165, 170, original emphasis.

[93] Plotz, *Portable Property*, 46.

sense of metropolitan cultural and political dominance, proves apt for the vast majority of cultural flows within the settler empire. As Belich observes, "London, centre of the system, was not only the political capital of Britain and the British Empire, but also the cultural and economic capital of Greater Britain."[94] Nevertheless, given the relative lack of linguistic and cultural barriers between metropolitan and settler populations, a different critical framework is required to account for those occasions when – as in the case of the convict's letter – this system went into reverse, and forms of narrative did indeed flow from the periphery to the empire's core.

I propose that taking a more integrated view of Britain and its colonies in Australia and New Zealand – one that allows for the possibility that genre might be able to change in multiple locations and circulate in multiple directions – will better reveal the complex means by which ideas about British political identity were disseminated and reformulated within and across the Victorian settler empire. One useful parallel is offered by Charles W. J. Withers's spatial history of the Enlightenment, which conceives of its subject at multiple and overlapping scales of analysis – "national *and* local *and* international" – and argues Enlightenment thinking was as often as not instantiated at subnational levels, in specific localities and social spaces.[95] The broader intellectual project of Enlightenment is thus reconceived as the product of "'traffic' – the mobility of its personnel, ideas, and artifacts" across national and cosmopolitan networks.[96] More directly, my analysis is shaped by Isabel Hofmeyr's transnational history of African receptions and translations of John Bunyan's *Pilgrim's Progress* (1678), which proposes that empire be understood as "an intellectually integrated zone, instead of a divided terrain of 'center' and 'periphery'": "The imperial arena is a complex force field in which circuits of influence travel in more than one direction."[97] Those cross-border patterns of appropriation and adaptation are best revealed by focusing on the material details of the "local intellectual formations" in operation at

---

[94] Belich, *Replenishing the Earth*, 460. For analyses of how this imperial "nervous system" manifested itself through libraries in specific settler-colonial locations, see Tim Dolin, "First Steps toward a History of the Mid-Victorian Novel in Colonial Australia," *Australian Literary Studies* 22, no. 3 (2006); Lydia Wevers, *Reading on the Farm: Victorian Fiction and the Colonial World* (Wellington: Victoria University Press, 2010).

[95] Charles W. J. Withers, *Placing the Enlightenment: Thinking Geographically about the Age of Reason* (Chicago: University of Chicago Press, 2007), 7, original emphasis.

[96] Ibid., 43.

[97] Elizabeth Hofmeyr, *The Portable Bunyan: A Transnational History of* The Pilgrim's Progress (Princeton: Princeton University Press, 2004), 24.

each point in the imperial network where the text was modified.[98] Attending to "the text as a material object," Hofmeyr argues, is necessary to "bring to light the intricate circuits along which texts are funneled rather than the routes we imagine or anticipate they might traverse."[99] Rather than retracing the circulation and modification of a single text, however, I will be more concerned with the transformations of discrete genres – those "almost empty sets that shape literary history by their negation, deviation, variation, and mutation" – that occurred at different nodes in the imperial network.[100] The formal modifications that I seek to trace in this book not only reveal the settler colonies to be significant waypoints within an ostensibly metropolitan literary history but also position that literature as central to a revised understanding of the broad contours of Victorian imperial history.

This book will ultimately insist that Victorian culture be understood as produced in part by the transnational settler world that it so forcefully created. At one level, this is to argue that recognizing the multiscalar, located histories of writing in the Victorian settler empire is necessary for a full accounting of the emergence and development of Victorian culture – and thus is part of the resistance to the "implicit nationalizing of the idea of culture itself" that produces, in Irene Tucker's words, "the mistaken concept of Victorian self-evidence."[101] More than this, however, I wish to insist that there is an ethical burden upon Victorian studies to better acknowledge the material and cultural fact of nineteenth-century settler colonialism. This is not an argument for deemphasizing other parts of the empire, or other forms of imperial domination and exploitation, for, as Saree Makdisi points out,

> [S]ettler colonialism can't be hermetically sealed off from other modes of imperialism (the ones that tend toward exploiting indigenous populations rather than simply exterminating or transferring them).... The Anglo settler-colonial experience would not have been the same, or even possible, without the larger structure of British imperialism out of which it emerged, and to which it continued to be tied into the twentieth century.[102]

Yet to continue to look past Britain's settler empire is to perpetuate an act of denial that is itself characteristically Victorian. As Seeley argued at the time, the "indifference which we show towards the mighty phenomenon

---

[98] Ibid.   [99] Ibid., 25.   [100] Esty, *Unseasonable Youth*, 18.
[101] Irene Tucker, "International Whiggery," *Victorian Studies* 45, no. 4 (2003): 688.
[102] Saree Makdisi, "Riding the Whirlwind of Settler Colonialism," *Victorian Studies* 53, no. 1 (2010): 113.

of the diffusion of our race and the expansion of our state" was paralleled by a refusal to "allow it to affect our imagination or in any degree to change our ways of thinking."[103] I wish to disavow any sense of the bombast that informs these comments, and continues to underpin elements of British World historiography. Nor do I wish to present settler colonialism as if it were a hitherto unappreciated key to all Victorian mythologies. Nevertheless, I am arguing that literary scholars can no longer avoid recognizing and engaging with the enormous scale and impact of the Victorian settler empire, as one of the most egregious yet least remarked manifestations of nineteenth-century thought and culture.

Victorian Literature and the Victorian Settler Empire

In the first instance, this book seeks to demonstrate the influence of settler colonialism on Victorian literature by reframing our sense of the period in relation to settlement's history. It thus begins in 1829 with Edward Gibbon Wakefield's first public statement of a new theory of "systematic" colonization by British settlers, *A Letter from Sydney: The Principal Town of Australasia*, and concludes in 1915 with the settler invasion of Europe, when the Australian and New Zealand Army Corps stormed the Gallipoli peninsula. The chapters are arranged in a roughly chronological sequence to convey the dynamism of a global-scale cultural field shaped by an imperial context that changed radically in its economic and geopolitical significance over the course of the nineteenth century. Such historical attentiveness necessarily puts this project at odds with one of the key claims of the field of settler colonial studies, namely Patrick Wolfe's influential dictum that "invasion is a structure not an event."[104] This is not in any way to deny the desire for territory and resources that motivated colonial expansion, or to disavow the grievous structural changes wrought by settlement upon indigenous populations, or to ignore inequalities and injustices that continue to the present day. A wholesale rejection of the language of "event," however, encourages a dehistoricized criticism that potentially obscures the differences between disparate colonial spaces, while risking blindness to the changing local and geopolitical imperatives that continuously shaped each settler project.[105] The key historical

---

[103] Seeley, *Expansion of England*, 12–13.

[104] Patrick Wolfe, *Settler Colonialism and the Transformation of Anthropology: The Politics and Poetics of an Ethnographic Event* (London: Cassell, 1999), 2.

[105] This ahistoricism has played out both in psychoanalytic approaches that rest on the idea of a singular settler mindset (e.g., Stephen Turner: "Settlement may well require forgetting, a

moments discussed in the following pages are, however, offered in an avowedly nonteleological spirit, contrary both to a transhistorical, platonic notion of a settler state (as if any settler project ever achieved a stable political or cultural configuration) and to any sense of an inevitable tendency toward colonial nationalism (as if the Victorian era were simply and straightforwardly a precursor to modern nation-states). For similar reasons, I have eschewed wherever possible terms such as "Greater Britain," "Anglo-World," or "British World," despite their common currency amongst imperial historians, because they carry enduring traces of the Victorians' self-aggrandizement and their myths of peaceful colonial expansion. By preference, I instead use the phrase "Victorian settler empire": if it better conveys a sense of historical specificity, it also marks a small refusal to overlook the sustained force required to establish and maintain this imperial project. At the same time, one especially pressing consequence of adopting a transnational focus on British identity, and of concentrating on novelistic representations and economic texts that speak to this concern, is the risk of occluding the history of encounter and conflict between indigenous and settler populations. I confess at the outset I have largely failed to avoid this risk. My argument stresses where colonial writers' attempts to rethink aspects of British identity drew explicitly on examples (or counterexamples) of indigenous populations, derived at times from direct knowledge but more often from persistent stereotypes, and tries to situate their work in relation to the local progress of conquest and domination. Nevertheless, one of the deepest critical challenges of returning to the literature of the settler empire, from Wakefield's writing onward, has been finding means to avoid simply reinforcing the silences, obfuscations, and sheer ethnocentrism that structured and enabled those colonial visions.

Each chapter is structured to meet the methodological challenge of articulating Britain's literary traffic with its settler empire. First, in place of the broad-brush accounts of Australia and New Zealand that have predominated within Victorian studies – the Antipodes as archetypal "site

---

constitutive occlusion of the trauma of dislocation and unsettlement") and in formulations of genre that verge on archetypal criticism (e.g., Hamish Dalley: "In other words, because the settler-colonial relation does not resolve through synthesis, its foundational logic as a structural binary persists as long as settlement is incomplete.... For this reason we can say that settler colonies are places where 'time does not pass'"). Hamish Dalley, "The Meaning of Settler Realism: (De)Mystifying Frontiers in the Postcolonial Historical Novel," *Novel* 51, no. 3 (2018): 467; Stephen Turner, "Settlement as Forgetting," in *Quicksands: Foundational Histories in Australia and Aotearoa New Zealand*, ed. Klaus Neumann, Nicholas Thomas, and Hilary Ericksen (Sydney: University of New South Wales Press, 1999), 20.

of romance and 'space of the beyond'"; Australia as staging ground of "myths of … Arcadian redemption versus social damnation" – each chapter considers a distinct phase of colonial development or crisis that in some way challenged normative Victorian concepts of British subjectivity and sociality.[106] From William Howitt's anxiety in the 1850s that the residents of Melbourne were the "maddest speculators in the world," to J. A. Froude's dissatisfaction with Auckland in the 1880s – "The English race should not come to New Zealand to renew the town life which they leave behind them" – the progress of settlement bewildered observers as often as it seemed to satisfy their expectations.[107] In each chapter, I zoom in on a constellation of novelists and political economists who collectively experienced or engaged with the conceptual implications for British political identity of that pivotal moment in settlement history, first on the ground in Australia or New Zealand, and later in Britain. The common ties of British heritage and the dominance of Britain's literary marketplace ensured that, despite their extreme distance, those settler colonies received a surprising number of sojourners and settlers who sought to remain active in the metropolitan literary world. The most well known of these is Anthony Trollope, who visited Australia and New Zealand twice in the 1870s, but many more figures occupying somewhat less exalted positions in the Victorian cultural firmament also accrued antipodean experience.[108] These networks of influence and exchange provide the material basis for comprehending the processes of formal change that I argue took place in the novel and political economy in the course of their circulation between the settler colonies and Britain. Those formal changes were driven by the need to articulate newly pressing ideas about British identity and society.

---

[106] Helen Lucy Blythe, "*The Fixed Period* (1882): Euthanasia, Cannibalism, and Colonial Extinction in Trollope's Antipodes," *Nineteenth-Century Contexts* 25, no. 2 (2003): 1; Patrick Brantlinger, *Rule of Darkness: British Literature and Imperialism, 1830–1914* (Ithaca: Cornell University Press, 1988), 132.

[107] James Anthony Froude, *Oceana, or, England and Her Colonies* (London: Longmans Green, 1898), 212; William Howitt, *Land, Labour, and Gold; or, Two Years in Victoria: With Visits to Sydney and Van Diemen's Land*, 2 vols. (London: Longman, Brown, Green, and Longmans, 1855), 1.295.

[108] A number of canonical writers also had personal antipodean connections. Charlotte Brontë's friend Mary Taylor immigrated to New Zealand in 1845, and corresponded with Brontë while she earned a living as a shopkeeper there, until returning to England in 1860. Similarly, Robert Browning's friend Alfred Domett lived in New Zealand from 1842 to 1871, where his political career included a brief term as premier. Browning depicted Domett in his poem "Waring" (1842), and in return Domett offered the more dubious tribute of dedicating to Browning his infamous epic poem, *Ranolf and Amohia: A South-Sea Daydream* (1872). Jane Stafford, "'Remote must be the shores': Mary Taylor, Charlotte Brontë, and the Colonial Experience," *Journal of New Zealand Literature* 10 (1992); Jane Stafford, "Alfred Domett, Robert Browning and a Dream of Two Lives," *Journal of New Zealand Literature* 21 (2003).

As Australia-based economist W. E. Hearn put it in 1864, reflecting on inadequacies in the thinking evident in one of his discipline's most prominent texts, "its author had not that familiarity with a different state of facts which only residence in a new country still in course of settlement can give."[109] By following the repeated circulation of Victorian forms of thinking and writing out to Australia or New Zealand and back again, I seek to demonstrate the inescapably colonial quality of British literary culture in the nineteenth century.

What follows, then, falls roughly into two parts. The first two chapters are focused on the massive intellectual and political legacy of stadialist developmental thought, and especially its crucial spatial binary opposition between primitive wandering and civilized settlement. These early chapters reveal much of the conceptual challenge arising from settlement to be spurred by the glimpse that it apparently provided into the origins of British society, at a point when the imperial relationship was marked by a sharply stadialist distinction between a modern metropole and a semifeudal periphery. Here the focus is largely on Australia, in part because Victorian observers readily accommodated the supposedly "empty" continent and its nomadic indigenous populations to the lowest tiers of stadialist thought, and also because Britain's extensive colonizing activities since the arrival of the "First Fleet" of convict transports in 1788 meant there was a significant settler population and publishing infrastructure in place by the beginning of the Victorian era.[110] The final two chapters address the increasingly geopolitical terms in which the settler empire was thought of in the second half of the century. As colonial self-governance reshaped Britain's political and cultural relationships with its Australasian colonies, so rising threats to Britain's worldwide military dominance prompted imperial thinkers to view the settler colonies in newly strategic terms. The focus here falls more on New Zealand, which was unusually visible despite its small size: claims that it

---

[109] William Edward Hearn, *Plutology: Or, the Theory of the Efforts to Satisfy Human Wants* (London: Macmillan, 1864), 113.

[110] The first book of poetry published in Australia was by Barron Field, New South Wales judge and friend of Charles Lamb, *First Fruits of Australian Poetry* (1819); the first journal, *Australian Magazine; or, Compendium of Religious, Literary, and Miscellaneous Intelligence* (1821–22); the first novel was transported forger Henry Savery's *Quintus Servinton: A Tale Founded upon Incidents of Real Occurrence* (1831). Delys Bird, "The 'Settling' of English," in *The Oxford Literary History of Australia*, ed. Bruce Bennett and Jennifer Strauss (Melbourne: Oxford University Press, 1998); Ken Gelder and Rachael Weaver, "Beginnings and Endings: The Precarious Life of a Colonial Journal," in *The Colonial Journals: And the Emergence of Australian Literary Culture*, ed. Ken Gelder and Rachael Weaver (Crawley: UWA Publishing, 2014); David Higgins, "Writing to Colonial Australia: Barron Field and Charles Lamb," *Nineteenth-Century Contexts* 32, no. 3 (2010).

was the most British of settlements underpinned its rapid acquisition of unprecedented levels of debt in the 1870s, while its prolonged history of conflict between settlers and Māori proved a unique basis for articulating a militaristic understanding of British masculinity. In concluding at the moment of the wholehearted yet immensely costly participation of Australasia's settler populations in World War I, I ultimately suggest this can be seen not as the collapse or betrayal of the concepts of British political identity and society that sustained the settler empire, but as their apotheosis.

The first chapter offers a new genealogy of early Victorian conceptions of character by tracing two divergent theories of subject formation that emerged as the idea of character was routed through distinct forms of settler imperialism: convict transportation and "free" settlement. Edward Gibbon Wakefield's metropolitan theory of "systematic colonization" posited a stadialist model of spatial organization as the basis of replicating British character through social structure, while Alexander Maconochie's "Mark System" for the reformation of convicts derived its vision for individual character formation from the temporal understanding of self-interest familiar from bourgeois financial discipline. By charting the contrasting fates of these settler models of British character in the course of their movements between metropole and colony, I demonstrate the uneven yet influential manner in which particular networks of global exchanges could shape Victorian culture. Wakefield's metropolitan theories achieved by far the greatest public visibility, through several large-scale colonization schemes, and I suggest that their greatest impact on the metropolitan cultural sphere was to spur an imaginative expansion of the borders of Britain to encompass the settler colonies. By contrast, Maconochie's colonial ideas had a more circuitous but ultimately more powerful impact upon the metropolitan Victorian novel. Adopted by Charles Dickens for his ambitious and long-running philanthropic experiment, Urania Cottage (the "Home for Homeless Women"), I argue that these principles ultimately shaped his conception of character formation in *Great Expectations* (1861), especially through the portrayal of Pip, its metropolitan protagonist.

Chapter 2 turns to the epochal discovery of gold in Australia in the 1850s, and argues that attempts to narrate and comprehend its developmental implications necessitated the abandonment of the stadialist underpinnings of political economy and novelistic realism. I begin with Catherine Helen Spence's early work of Australian realism, *Clara Morison: A Tale of South Australia during the Gold Fever* (1854), which offers a baseline against which subsequent responses to the gold rushes can be measured: Spence couches gold digging in the language of romance, which she associates with financial speculation and the overthrow of social structures, and her novel imagines the restoration of the stadialist conjunction of culture, capital, and steady Lockean labor. The first clear formulation of a new theory of character inflected by the gold rushes can be seen in Australian-based political economist W. E. Hearn's *Plutology: or, The Theory of the Efforts to Satisfy Human Wants* (1864), which abandoned the disciplinary struts of stadialism and labor in favor of a model of consumption based upon individual desire. From here, I trace the impact of this realization back to Britain as a formal imprint on works by metropolitan writers who had previously encountered the gold rushes and now imagine the metropole and the colonies in conjunction. W. S. Jevons's pathbreaking "marginalist" *Theory of Political Economy* (1871) and Anthony Trollope's sensation novel *John Caldigate* (1878–79) both center upon and normativize a British subject defined by desire, and through this contribute to a newly deterritorialized understanding of British subjectivity.

The focus of the third chapter shifts from Australia to New Zealand, juxtaposing the utopian portrayal of colonial British identity with debates from the 1870s onward over the financial and political implications of the colony's vast debt. I argue that a formal logic of "speculative utopianism" enabled New Zealand writers to yoke the idea of the settler colony as the realm of British political identity's exemplary future with the promise that it was also an ideal destination for metropolitan financial investment. This logic can be seen taking shape in Samuel Butler's New Zealand–focused works, the nonfictional *First Year in Canterbury Settlement* (1863) and the utopian novel *Erewhon* (1872), before it was amplified dramatically as an enormous volume of borrowing was unleashed in London by new colonial policies aimed at accelerating development. As the architect of that scheme, Julius Vogel, would argue without apparent irony in the British press, "no greater benefit was ever bestowed upon the money-market of Great Britain than a colony coming forward and asking for money for the purpose of honestly and bravely developing English territory by the countrymen of those who lent the money." In the wake of a colonial credit crisis triggered in 1878–79, however, metropolitan writers increasingly attacked the assumptions of speculative utopianism, most notably Trollope's *The Fixed Period* (1882), which casts settler progress in a dystopian light. Despite this, two late settler works of speculative utopianism – Vogel's *Anno Domini 2000* (1889) and H. C. Marriott Watson's

Decline and Fall of the British Empire (1890) – point to a reformulation of the settler empire as an investment, as greater emphasis is given to the geopolitical value of the colonial British population.

Finally, Chapter 4 further expands the book's geographic scale by arguing that the adaptation of the invasion novel in Australia and New Zealand crystallized a militaristic notion of indigenized settler masculinity that soon proved adaptable to the empire's broader geopolitical needs. In response to paranoia about British decline and the perceived risk of economic and military threats from Asia, the narrative model of imperial invasion was appropriated in works such as George Ranken's *The Invasion* (1877) and Kenneth Mackay's *The Yellow Wave* (1895), which actively distinguished settler masculinity from metropolitan identity by way of its autochthonous territorial knowledge and unorthodox thinking. That defensive formulation, I argue, was soon refigured in the context of expanding arenas for settler aggression, first in the Second Anglo-Boer War (1899–1902) and ultimately in World War I. Here, the work of Erskine Childers was central to translating this colonial logic into a metropolitan idiom: alongside editing the volume on guerrilla warfare for the *Times History of the War in South Africa, 1899–1902* (1907), he reworked the invasion novel in *The Riddle of the Sands* (1903) to imagine a threat of metropolitan conflict that could only be countered by a colonial mindset. Little more than a decade later, at the height of World War I, the doomed Australian and New Zealand role in the Dardanelles Campaign would be described by British war correspondent Ellis Ashmead-Bartlett as a "southern colony, so strangely and suddenly planted on the bleak inhospitable Gallipoli coast." The figuration of this settler invasion as a heroic act of imperial sacrifice and colonial fulfillment clarifies a militarized settler form of British political identity as simultaneously the most valuable commodity produced by the Victorian settler empire, and its most disposable property, and thus brings into focus one last, terrible intersection of political economy and literary form.

Ultimately, it might still seem the case that Victorian society was transformed more visibly by an antipodean commercial invention such as refrigerated shipping (or even, as Trollope imagines in *John Caldigate*, a new method of tying mailbags) than that its literature was impacted by any single settler writer. This representational invisibility would appear to bear out Pascale Casanova's description of the workings of a "world republic of letters" that mimics the political economy of empire: "Its geography is based on the opposition between a capital, on the one hand, and peripheral dependencies whose relationship to this center is defined by their aesthetic distance from it."[111] While such metropolitan arbitration of literary value undoubtedly occurred, the history I chart counters Casanova's insistent separation of literature from the materiality of empire, whereby "literary space ... becomes progressively more autonomous, ... so that it is partially independent of the political world," and looks beyond her emphasis on a high-culture concept of literariness.[112] Instead, the literature of the settler empire was constituted by a much wider range of modes, it was more closely integrated with imperial politics and economics, and it percolated through metropolitan culture using a number of mechanisms that all hinged on personalized networks of exchange. There were undoubtedly additional pathways of imperial influence that are not mapped here, especially involving Canada and South Africa. Yet acknowledging the inevitably partial nature of the analysis that follows need not diminish the claim that literary exchanges between Britain, Australia, and New Zealand played a catalytic role within Victorian culture, exerting an inconsistent yet disproportionately significant effect on how British political identity and society was defined and demarcated across the course of the century. At its broadest level, this book is an argument for recognizing and rethinking the place of the settler colony within Victorian studies: rather than simply offering a destination for metropolitan representations, it comes into focus as playing a vital and active role in the ongoing reconfiguration of metropolitan narrative forms and the reimagination of what it meant to be British as a newly globalized world began to take shape.

[111] Pascale Casanova, *The World Republic of Letters*, trans. M. B. DeBevoise (Cambridge: Harvard University Press, 2007), 12.
[112] Ibid., 322.

CHAPTER I

The Transportable Pip
Liberal Character, Territory, and the Settled Subject

We are in a barbarous condition, like that of every people scattered
over a territory immense in proportion to their numbers.
Edward Gibbon Wakefield, A Letter from Sydney:
The Principal Town of Australasia

[T]he essential ingredient in moral Training ... is a limited amount
of *free agency*, controuled [*sic*] and guided by *moral impulse* (prospective motive).... It forms, consequently, a habit of resisting present
impulses for the sake of consequent advantages, which, when confirmed, is just the result wanted, the precise form of social virtue
which we wish to impress on our released criminals.
Alexander Maconochie, Australiana: Thoughts on Convict Management

I shall begin with the mystery of Abel Magwitch. The convict so near the
center of Dickens's *Great Expectations* (1861), transported to Australia for
life at the start of the novel only to reappear in London as the author of
Pip's social ascent, Magwitch stands for many scholars as the embodiment
of Victorian imperialism in Australia, or even of empire writ large. In
Edward Said's influential reading of the novel, in *Culture and Imperialism*
(1994), he embodies the Victorians' unwillingness to acknowledge their
empire: "subjects can be taken to places like Australia, but they cannot be
allowed a 'return' to metropolitan space, which ... is meticulously
charted, spoken for, inhabited by a hierarchy of metropolitan personages."[1] Caroline Lesjak finds a "historically specific moment of capitalist
cultural development" figured in his convict experience, while Jed Esty
argues that Magwitch's bankrolling of Pip "underscores the structural
dependence of the Victorian middle class ... on colonial wealth."[2] Yet
none of these accounts touch on the mystery of culture and imperialism

---

[1] Said, *Culture and Imperialism*, xvi.
[2] Caroline Lesjak, *Working Fictions: A Genealogy of the Victorian Novel* (Durham: Duke University
Press, 2006), 98; Esty, *Unseasonable Youth*, 52.

lying in plain sight: why Dickens, despite his close and sustained interest in Australian colonization throughout the 1850s, would make such a significant narrative investment in convict transportation, when it was by that point largely an anachronism.[3] The convict system was indeed an enormous undertaking, sending into exile some 162,000 men, women, and children, from the landing of the "first fleet" at Botany Bay in early 1788, until the arrival of the last convict ship in Western Australia in early 1868. However, by the time that *Great Expectations* was published, the total settler population in Australia numbered well over one million, and transportation had peaked decades earlier. The system's single largest year was 1833, when 6,779 convicts were exiled, and by 1840 some 93 percent of the eventual total – around 150,000 convicts – had been transported. Transportation to New South Wales, the location of Botany Bay and destination of Dickens's convict, was suspended within a few years of Victoria's accession, in 1840, and abolished in 1850; transportation to Van Diemen's Land was abolished in 1853, and the colony renamed Tasmania three years later in an attempt to leave behind its convict past. Meanwhile, it was as early as 1822 that colonial commissioner John Bigge recommended to the British government that the New South Wales economy ought to be reorganized around wool production and "free" settlement. In other words, two distinct forms of settler colonialism overlapped in Australia at the beginning of the Victorian period, as convict transportation peaked and was increasingly displaced by the rise of voluntary settler migration, yet despite this generations of scholars have turned to *Great Expectations* and found in the convict a timeless embodiment of Britain's relationship to its settler empire.

Viewed from another angle, the mystery of Magwitch centers on what an Australian convict might be doing so near the heart of one of the most prominent and enduring narrative models of Victorian character formation. Franco Moretti casts the bildungsroman as the "'symbolic form' of modernity," and in Pip he finds an archetypal "common hero," perfectly embodying the middle-class virtues of a nascent "unheroic" democratic culture.[4] Esty builds on Moretti's analysis to argue that, across the first half of the nineteenth century, the bildungsroman's model of individual

---

[3] The few who have noted the anachronism have struggled to account for it. Grace Moore, for example, maintains that it "must ... be regarded as a concerted attempt to provide his readers with the viewpoint of one who has been both socially and geographically alienated." Moore, *Dickens and Empire: Discourses of Class, Race and Colonialism in the Works of Charles Dickens* (Aldershot: Ashgate, 2004), 16.

[4] Moretti, *Way of the World*, 191, 192.

maturation and social stabilization existed in a reciprocal relationship with the idea of the nation as a bounded cultural space. From this perspective, Pip's relationship to Magwitch both reinforces this bond between individual and nation, and marks its limit. "The Magwitch plot ... seems to distend and retard Pip's growth," and as a result that prominent colonial dimension of Pip's character must ultimately be foreclosed to achieve "final resolution through an alignment between Pip and an English destiny": "The elements of danger, of wealth, of unpredictability that Magwitch represents – these have to be introduced into and then jettisoned from the national container."[5] Esty's positioning of metropolitan Pip in opposition to the external pressures of the colonial Magwitch exemplifies the spatial logic underpinning much current thinking about early Victorian ideas of subject formation, which posits that conceptions of character and its limits first took shape within a narrowly national context and were only subsequently exposed to the external forces of empire. Yet placing *Great Expectations* in the broader context of early Victorian imperial activity in Australia – widening the view to encompass "free" settlement as well as convict transportation – reveals that metropolitan conceptions of character were from the outset embedded in debates about settlement and influenced by colonial thinking.

The Victorian logic of character is, after all, infused with the language of settlement. Stefan Collini points out that a descriptive conception of character, framed in Aristotelian terms as "an individual's settled dispositions," was freighted with a more evaluative sense of character as fundamental to categories of national identity and citizenship. The "blurring" between these descriptive and evaluative senses of character, Collini maintains,

> was facilitated by the assumption that the possession of settled dispositions indicated a certain habit of restraining one's impulses. The contrast was with behaviour which was random, impulsive, feckless; and where the impulses were identified, as they often were, with the "lower self" (conceived as purely appetitive and hence selfish), then a positive connotation was conferred on the habit of restraint itself.[6]

The grounding of a nascent liberal individualism in such "settled dispositions" – asserted over and against more volatile, "impulsive" forms

---

[5] Esty, *Unseasonable Youth*, 52.
[6] Stefan Collini, *Public Moralists: Political Thought and Intellectual Life in Britain, 1850–1930* (Oxford: Clarendon Press, 1991), 96, 97. See also Kevin Timpe, "Moral Character," in *The Internet Encyclopedia of Philosophy*, ed. Bradley Dowden and James Fieser.

of behavior – was enabled by, and inseparable from, the broader developmental logic of stadial theory that also hinged on the idea of settlement. The linear narrative of societal development articulated over preceding decades by Scottish Enlightenment thinkers – across domains as varied as comparative history, anthropology, political economy, and legal scholarship – found humanity's origins in a nomadic state, and pegged the gradual emergence of capitalist modernity to the decision to settle in one place and begin cultivating the soil. In this view, "the stationary life ... made civilization feasible," J. G. A. Pocock notes, "because arable exploitation stabilizes and creates the social space across which relation, transaction and exchange become possible."[7] These individual and societal definitions of civilization as a settled state find a point of common origin in John Locke's claim in the *Second Treatise of Government* that civil society emerged out of the individual's decision to cultivate the soil. Mixing individual labor with the soil both created an economy by transforming it into private property, and also created a polity by instantiating the need for individuals to depend on others to make calculations of their long-term interest.

George Stocking has observed that, by the 1830s, "cultural ideology in Great Britain had begun to reflect a conception of civilization integrated around ideas about human labor, or in a broader sense, human productivity."[8] Yet focusing on the language of "settlement," rather than the more familiar Lockean categories of labor and production, brings to light the spatialized logic underpinning much early Victorian political debate. (Irene Tucker describes Locke's *Second Treatise* as "the birth of spatialized culture.")[9] Patrick Brantlinger and Donald Ulin have pointed out the prominence accorded to vagrancy in crime statistics and commentary in the 1830s, arguing that the vagrant embodied "a lack of certain civilizing traits that made up stationary, respectable society," while also signaling the existence of a wider range of behaviors and lifeways "beyond the pale of Victorian property relations."[10] When Carlyle attacked the deleterious social effects of widespread contract labor in *Past and Present* (1843), he drew even more explicitly on the spatial metaphors of stadialist thought. Differentiating "the civilised burgher from the nomadic savage," he

---

[7] Pocock, "*Tangata Whenua* and Enlightenment Anthropology," in *The Discovery of Islands: Essays in British History* (Cambridge: Cambridge University Press, 2005), 211.

[8] George W. Stocking, *Victorian Anthropology* (New York: Free Press, 1987), 36.

[9] Tucker, "International Whiggery," 693.

[10] Patrick Brantlinger and Donald Ulin, "Policing Nomads: Discourse and Social Control in Early Victorian England," *Cultural Critique* 25 (1993): 40, 41.

counterposes the nomad's "very house set on wheels" – a physical mobility coterminous with demands for political "liberty" – over and against an aristocratic mode of continuity and culture: "The civilised man lives not in wheeled houses. He builds stone castles, plants lands, makes lifelong marriage-contracts; ... has pedigrees, libraries, law-codes."[11] At the same time, prominent liberal theories of individual character formation also employed terminology originating in the stadialist marriage contract of civilization and territory, notably principles of "self-cultivation" and "self-culture."[12] In John Stuart Mill's espousal of a model of character formation grounded in individual liberty, these powerful and potentially threatening forces of desire and impulse are redeemed by their "cultivation," a civilizing process that transmutes them into a kind of private property, such that the subject "whose desires and impulses are his own – are the expression of his own nature, as it has been developed and modified by his own culture – is said to have a character." By contrast, that capacity of self-cultivation is notoriously denied by Mill to "those backward states of society in which the race itself may be considered as in its nonage."[13] While the stadialist opposition between mobility and settlement continued to inform a range of cultural and political debates, however, it was through the renewal of settler colonization that spatiality was introduced most forcefully into Victorian theorizing of subjectivity and society.

The social and economic consequences of settler colonization had been actively and extensively debated by political economists at least since Adam Smith canvassed the subject in Book IV ("Of Systems of Political Economy") of *The Wealth of Nations* (1776), but any claims for its merits were generally undercut by the colony's troubling of metropolitan Britain's spatial and temporal borders. A long-standing tradition of skepticism toward colonization centered on the perceived inutility of the powers of distance – that is, a perceived lack of benefit in extending either capital or

[11] Thomas Carlyle, *Past and Present* (London: Ward, Lock and Bowden, 1897), 340, 376–77.
[12] As David Wayne Thomas points out, "For in mid-Victorian liberal discourse, liberals routinely and necessarily fused sociopolitical concerns and individualism in their rhetoric of cultivation." Amanda Anderson's influential study of Victorian liberal character yokes together terms from both sides of the stadialist model of development in its key formulation – the "cultivation of distance as a distinctive topos within Victorian culture" – but the significance of these spatialized terms remain unexamined. David Wayne Thomas, *Cultivating Victorians: Liberal Culture and the Aesthetic* (Philadelphia: University of Pennsylvania Press, 2004), 3; Amanda Anderson, *The Powers of Distance: Cosmopolitanism and the Cultivation of Detachment* (Princeton: Princeton University Press, 2001), 5.
[13] John Stuart Mill, *On Liberty*, in *On Liberty and Other Writings*, ed. Stefan Collini (Cambridge: Cambridge University Press, 1989), 60, 13.

population beyond the nation's borders. Nevertheless, economists became increasingly fascinated with the insights that colonies might offer into the economic and social structures of modern British society. The utilitarian critique of convict transportation, notably laid out by Jeremy Bentham in his open letter to the Home Secretary, Lord Pelham, "Panopticon *versus* New South Wales" (1802), stemmed from a sense that sheer distance rendered the colony incapable of reforming British subjects, such that the exiled colonial population therefore amounted to little more than a form of waste, "a set of *animæ viles* – a sort of excrementitious mass, that could be projected, and accordingly was projected ... as far out of sight as possible."[14] Such views were codified in economic orthodoxy through Say's Law, adopted and promulgated in the early part of the century by James Mill and David Ricardo, which held that capital ought to exist in a steady state within the nation, such that, "so far as Britain was concerned, further accumulation [of capital] was desirable, and any loss, waste or export of capital was to be deplored."[15] Yet if such arguments made it hard to imagine the establishment of British subjectivity and society in colonial space, a prominent public debate in the 1820s about Britain's "surplus" population – "most of the leading economists of the day were drawn into the controversy"[16] – alongside the expansion of Australia's "free" settler population due to pastoralism's success increasingly rendered the settler colony a subject of interest rather than suspicion. By early in Victoria's reign, Herman Merivale could argue that "some elementary principles in Political Economy ... are illustrated by the phenomena of colonization and the growth of colonies."[17] As Britain's economic and political relationship with Australia began to shift during the 1830s, bringing the two into closer conceptual alignment within the domain of political economy, the spatial conception of character also faced similar expansionary pressures, and the need for an understanding of British political identity commensurate to a nascent settler empire became increasingly pressing.

The discussion might seem by this point to have wandered, in nomadic fashion, some distance from Dickens's convict. Yet these

---

[14] Jeremy Bentham, "Panopticon *versus* New South Wales: Or, the Panopticon Penitentiary System, and the Penal Colonization System, Compared," in *The Works of Jeremy Bentham*, ed. John Bowring (Edinburgh: Tait, 1843), 176.

[15] Donald N. Winch, "Classical Economics and the Case for Colonization," *Economica* 30, no. 120 (1963): 389–90.

[16] R. D. Collison Black, *Economic Thought and the Irish Question, 1817–1870* (Cambridge: Cambridge University Press, 1960), 209.

[17] Merivale, *Lectures on Colonization*, 1.v.

contrasting models of the colony's relationship with the metropole – as either diminishing, or as potentially generative – along with the equally contrasting settler populations – excluded convict or "free" citizen – constitute a central problem for character as it is understood in *Great Expectations*. On the one hand, the plotting of the convict's ostracism and illegal return seems to draw directly from Bentham's earlier critique of convict transportation as antithetical to subject formation. The "[c]olonizing-transportation-system" is marred by "radical incapacity of being combined with any system of inspection," Bentham maintained, and as a result neither the convict's reform nor their ongoing exile can be guaranteed, so that "many … escape from this scene of intended annihilation, to afflict their mother-country a second time with their pernicious existence."[18] On the other hand, by the time the novel was published, distance from the metropolis was no longer held to be inherently destabilizing to British character. Merivale, for example, found the settler empire newly compatible with his metropolitan perspective despite its distance:

> It is a sort of instinctive feeling to us all, that the destiny of our name and nation is not here, in this narrow island which we occupy; that the spirit of England is volatile, not fixed; that it lives in our language, our commerce, our industry, in all those channels of inter-communication by which we embrace and connect the vast multitude of states, both civilized and uncivilized, throughout the world.[19]

It is my argument in this chapter that the national horizons that continue to encompass so much Victorian literary scholarship have hidden from sight the complex transnational mechanisms of exchange and imagination linking Britain and Australia – "volatile, not fixed," as Merivale put it – by which the renewal of settler colonization helped coproduce Victorian ideas of character formation. The ultimate effect of this will be to look beyond Magwitch to Pip, and find his characterization and experience of bildung to also be structured in terms derived from the settler colonies. This argument is in turn built on a broader claim that the overlapping interests of the novel and political economy are most clearly revealed in the settler colony, where the intellectual challenges posed by the attempt to establish British society in the midst of the so-called state of nature established it as a laboratory for the testing of character and its embedding in a capitalist economy.

---

[18] Bentham, "Panopticon," 175, 191.   [19] Merivale, *Lectures on Colonization*, 1.134.

In what follows, I chart the emergence of two prominent theories of character formation during the early Victorian decades, one in Britain and one in Australia, each of which was actively and influentially proselytized by its proponents as means of harnessing political economy to the task of producing a "settled" British society. The first of these was the theory of "systematic colonization," spearheaded by Edward Gibbon Wakefield – "the most notable political economist of that period," in the eyes of Karl Marx, for his discovery "in the colonies" that "capital is not a thing, but a social relation between persons which is mediated through things."[20] Wakefield was in Newgate Prison when he published a series of anonymous articles in the *Morning Chronicle* purporting to be from a frustrated member of the gentry who had emigrated to Australia as one of the new generation of "free" settlers.[21] In what would become *A Letter from Sydney: The Principal Town of Australasia* (1829), the problem of establishing a stable form of British character in the colonies is sheeted home to the sheer surplus of "waste" colonial land, which negates the need to undertake settled cultivation because its riches encourage unconstrained movement across the land; what he proposes in response is to place a "sufficient price" on that land, thus establishing a "proportion between people and territory" that would force settlers to work. "Every new government," Wakefield's fictional settler enthuses, "possesses the power to civilize its subjects" (159). The second account of character formation I discuss had penal origins of a very different kind. Alexander Maconochie, described by historian Robert Hughes as "the one and only inspired penal reformer to work in Australia throughout the whole history of transportation," arrived in the penal colony of Van Diemen's Land as private secretary to its lieutenant governor in 1836.[22] It was there he developed and published his "Mark System" of convict discipline – soon republished in London as *Australiana: Thoughts on Convict Management* (1839) – which ultimately led to his appointment as superintendent of the Norfolk Island penal colony from 1839 to 1843. Under the Mark System, Maconochie

---

[20] Marx, *Capital*, 830, 932.
[21] Edward Gibbon Wakefield, "Australia," *The Morning Chronicle*, August 21, 1829, 2. The paper's editors, later acknowledging the English origin of the letters, claimed: "The object of the ingenious writer, in throwing his views into the form in which they appeared, was to obtain for them the attention of a class of readers too little interested in abstract speculations to have profited by them, without some such contrivance." Unsigned editorial, *The Morning Chronicle*, October 8, 1829, 2. Subsequent references will cite the version of *Letter from Sydney* published as Edward Gibbon Wakefield, *A Letter from Sydney: The Principal Town of Australasia*, in The Collected Works of Edward Gibbon Wakefield, ed. M. F. Lloyd Prichard (Glasgow: Collins, 1968).
[22] Hughes, *Fatal Shore*, 488–89.

proposed that a convict's sentence ought not be defined in terms of temporal duration but be expressed as a number of "marks" to be attained, with a given number able to be earned or lost on a daily basis depending on his behavior in certain predetermined categories. Reconceiving a space of exile as "a school for the recovery of social weakness," as Maconochie put it, the penal colony became an arena for theorizing the formation of responsible British subjects.[23] The contrasting circumstances surrounding the development and subsequent reception of Wakefield's systematic colonization and Maconochie's Mark System demonstrate the uneven and discontinuous, yet nevertheless influential, manner in which early Victorian conceptions of character took shape in the process of their circulation between Britain and Australia.

This chapter will trace two parallel flows of transnational traffic centered on Wakefield and Maconochie's divergent ideas about character, and the use of narrative forms to express them. I first consider Wakefield's theory of systematic colonization, a metropolitan adaptation of stadialist thought to the settler colony that spurred extensive colonizing projects in Australia and New Zealand. In Britain, the formal impact of systematic colonization occurred largely as a refiguring of key terms within political economy, whereas in Australia colonial writers took to the novel to conceptualize the spatial qualities that might underpin the establishment of a stable British culture. The irony that Wakefield's theories of character foundered on an inability to conceive of population mobility is most clearly on display in the formal tensions of Thomas McCombie's early colonial novel, *Arabin; or, The Adventures of a Settler in New South Wales* (1845), which invokes Walter Scott's historical romances to justify the urge to emigrate, only to then assert the value of territorial stasis as the bedrock of character formation and sociality. By contrast, despite the incipient decline of convict transportation, Maconochie's Mark System of convict discipline proved more powerfully adaptable to metropolitan contexts because its account of character focused on individual interiority rather than external spatial constraints. Maconochie's ideas proved influential in penal circles, informing prison reforms in Ireland and the United States in particular, but through his advocacy they also gained wider public prominence. In a letter dating from mid-1846, Dickens would write, "I do not know of any plan so well conceived, or so firmly grounded in a knowledge of human nature, or so judiciously addressed to it ... as what is called Captain

---

[23] Alexander Maconochie, *Australiana: Thoughts on Convict Management, and Other Subjects Connected with the Australian Penal Colonies* (London: Parker, 1839), 62.

Macconochie's [*sic*] Mark System."[24] Dickens would first apply the Mark System in his decade-long involvement with Urania Cottage, or the "Home for Homeless Women," but it is also my contention that it shaped his reconception of bildung in *Great Expectations*. In other words, what has been read as a paradigmatic account of metropolitan character formation will be shown to be in large part the product of a very particular cultural exchange across the length of the settler empire.

Stadial Theory and Systematic Colonization: *A Letter from Sydney*

There is a story we tend to tell about the Victorian idea of character and its imperial career: it first crystallized mid-century, with the simultaneous publication of Samuel Smiles's *Self-Help; With Illustrations of Character and Conduct* (1859) and John Stuart Mill's *On Liberty* (1859), and was then exported as part of the New Imperialism in the latter decades of the century, through its embodiment in the public school–educated "imperial hero."[25] Empire plays a passive, belated role in this narrative, functioning as an arena or "training ground" where prefabricated notions of character are put to the test; as a corollary, those ideas of character, and related concepts of liberal subjectivity, are firmly grounded within the borders of Britain.[26] Accordingly, different genealogies proffered by Mary Poovey and Lauren Goodlad of the individuated bourgeois subject's emergence in the 1830s and 1840s – in relation, respectively, to the reform of sanitation or the poor laws – share similarly bounded perspectives: a "British cultural formation," Poovey calls it, produced out of "the relationship between the newly emergent social sphere and the nation as an imagined community."[27] Goodlad takes up the question of character most directly, placing it at the center of her argument that a Foucauldian model of disciplinary individualism fails to adequately explain the nature of British liberalism. Character appears here as a premodern concept ("arguably traditional";

---

[24] Charles Dickens, *The Letters of Charles Dickens*, ed. Margaret Brown et al., 12 vols. (Oxford: Clarendon Press, 1965–2002), 4.553.

[25] Collini, *Public Moralists*, 116. See also P. J. Cain, "Empire and the Languages of Character in Later Victorian and Edwardian Britain," *Modern Intellectual History* 4, no. 2 (2007).

[26] Cain, "Languages of Character," 262.

[27] Mary Poovey, *Making a Social Body: British Cultural Formation, 1830–1864* (Chicago: University of Chicago Press, 1995), 21. Yet even early Victorian discussions of character in the context of poor relief invariably had an imperial dimension – indeed, the 1834 Poor Law Amendment Act contained provisions to assist the poor to immigrate to the colonies. Rita S. Kranidis, *The Victorian Spinster and Colonial Emigration: Contested Subjects* (Basingstoke: Macmillan, 1999), 22; Black, *Economic Thought and the Irish Question*, 224.

"old-fashioned"), pitted against the self-interested subject at the heart of emergent laissez-faire norms of economics and politics, and its persistence as a kind of survival in the Victorian era helps produce the distinctive "contours of Britain's idiosyncratic modernization."[28] Goodlad makes this argument to urge Victorianists to look past the Panopticon, yet to take that task seriously will also require looking beyond the borders of Britain. Doing so reveals the renewal of settler colonialism to have been the spur for some of the Victorian era's most distinctive and ambitious theoretical models of character.

Edward Gibbon Wakefield was not in Australia in 1829, but in New-gate Prison nearing the end of a three-year sentence for his sensational abduction of Ellen Turner, an underage heiress, when he began to publish a series of letters in the *Morning Chronicle* purporting to be from a frustrated member of the gentry now living in Australia as a "free" settler who owns a sizeable property of 14,000 acres.[29] Soon collected, revised, and republished – the country estate expanding in the process to 20,000 acres – what is now known as *A Letter from Sydney: The Principal Town of Australasia* (1829) told the fictional story of a newly established colony, in the midst of an uninhabited and unappropriated "waste" land, where neither the economy nor society were functioning as expected. The misrepresentation of Australia as untenanted wilderness deliberately reprises one of the most influential gestures of liberal political economy, Locke's turn to colonial territory – "Thus in the beginning all the world was *America* ... for no such thing as *money* was anywhere known" – to imagine the prior state of nature out of which private property could first emerge.[30] Yet while Wakefield's depopulated Australia resembles Locke's unappropriated America, *Letter from Sydney* inverts his most fundamental premise, so that now the surplus of "waste" land proves surprisingly unstable as a foundation for civil society. The epistolary settler's most

---

[28] Lauren M. E. Goodlad, *Victorian Literature and the Victorian State: Character and Governance in a Liberal Society* (Baltimore: Johns Hopkins University Press, 2003), 23, 24, 26.

[29] For a detailed account of the publication history of *A Letter from Sydney*, including Wakefield's likely publication in the *Morning Chronicle* of spurious letters to the editor as a strategy for "keeping his scheme and its ideas before the public," prior to its eventual anonymous publication under the "editorship" of Robert Gouger, see Tony Ballantyne, "Remaking the Empire from Newgate: Wakefield's *A Letter from Sydney*," in *Ten Books That Shaped the British Empire: Creating an Imperial Commons*, ed. Antoinette M. Burton and Isabel Hofmeyr (Durham: Duke University Press, 2014), 33–35.

[30] Locke, *Second Treatise of Government*, 29, original emphasis. Patrick Wolfe describes how eighteenth-century jurisprudence translated Locke's ideas into the Australian doctrine of *terra nullius*, and argues that its intent was "primarily a systematization of the mutual rights and obligations of rival European powers." Wolfe, *Settler Colonialism*, 26.

pressing complaint is that his estate, despite its surfeit of natural resources, has so far proved worthless:

> I imagined that a domain of that extent would be very valuable. In that I was wholly mistaken.... I could not find a purchaser, without submitting to lose great part of what I had expended in improvements.... In short, my domain has no market value. It is a noble property to look at; and "20,000 acres in a ring fence," sounds very well in England; but here, such a property possesses no exchangeable value.[31]

At the same time, his class status has been further dented by a signal failure to retain laborers, servants, or artisans in his employment. All have proved susceptible, sooner or later, to attractively high wages offered elsewhere in the colony or to the even greater temptation of acquiring land for themselves. "This is the secret both of the prosperity of the colonies and of their cancerous affliction," Marx observed of Wakefield's analysis, namely, "their resistance to the establishment of capital": given the sheer surplus of land available for appropriation, "every settler on it can therefore turn part of it into his private property and his individual means of production," so that at the most fundamental level settlers are not alienated from their own labor because "the separation of the worker from the conditions of labour and from the soil, in which they are rooted, does not exist, or only sporadically, or on too limited a scale."[32] On top of all this, in an echo of Carlyle, the colonial population is showing a worrying tendency to manifest antisocial and nomadic qualities: "in respect to wealth, knowledge, skill, taste, and whatever belongs to civilization, [they] have degenerated from their ancestors; ... ever on the move, [they] are unable to bring anything to perfection" (151). These failures of character and markets are presented as recapitulating the history of prior settlement projects, illuminating a general problem with the colonial extension of British society.

Wakefield's settler comes to the conclusion that the same cause lies at the root of all these problems. What seemed at first to be the colony's greatest asset – its seemingly limitless expanse of "waste" land – has produced a catastrophic disproportion between land and labor. "We are in a barbarous condition," he observes, "like that of every people scattered over a territory immense in proportion to their numbers" (119). This scenario of settler degeneration and wandering, which will recur throughout Wakefield's subsequent writings, is underpinned by a critical vision of

---

[31] Wakefield, *Letter from Sydney*, 102–3. Hereafter cited in text.   [32] Marx, *Capital*, 934, 935.

the progress of colonization's westward expansion in the United States. Commenting that his journey to Australia went "by way of North America," the settler recalls his experiences of "the migrating habits of the Americans": "I saw a people without monuments, without history, without local attachments founded on impressions of the past, without any love of birthplace, without patriotism – unless men constantly roaming over immense regions may be called a country" (133, 134). Indeed, Wakefield would later employ this contrast to frame an expanded account of his colonizing theory, *England and America: A Comparison of the Social and Political State of Both Nations* (1834), and Robert Grant details how his vision of ordered settlement was constructed in opposition to the idea of America as "a wild, abandoned frontier, where all that was recognizably middle class dissolved into charismatic religion, physical licence and barely veiled sexuality."[33] Although Marx takes a diametrically opposite view to "our friend E. G. Wakefield," and actively welcomes the "'barbarizing tendency of dispersion' of producers and of the wealth of the nation," their accounts of the settler colony concur in understanding individual character as overdetermined by its spatial relationship to territory.[34] That is, the degeneration of British settlers in the colony occurs not because of the proximity of a "savage" population (both Wakefield and Marx are oblivious to such a consideration) but because a capitalist form of social relations is thwarted by the nullity of colonial territory.

The spatialized understanding of British character at the heart of the theory of systematic colonization drew upon and reconfigured the familiar tropes of stadialist theory. In the stadialist model development takes a diachronic form, with one stage succeeding another in an upward historical progression from a wandering state toward agriculture and modernity. Wakefield instead offers a synchronic or "horizontal" stadialism, whereby the binary extremes of nomadism and settlement are available simultaneously to the British settler population within the horizons of the settler colony. This conceptual framework is most evident in *Letter from Sydney* in its concern with the "migratory habits" of the settler population, and its association of population mobility with a failure to establish either a functioning economy or a cultured society. Indeed, Wakefield finds this stadial logic at work across all colonial environments:

---

[33] Robert Grant, "Edward Gibbon Wakefield, England and 'ignorant, dirty, unsocial, ... restless, more than half-savage' America," *Comparative American Studies* 1, no. 4 (2003): 482.
[34] Marx, *Capital*, 936, 937. Marx's quotation is from Wakefield's *England and America*.

> It has occurred in every waste country, settled by emigrants from civilized
> countries…. [T]his colony would never be anything but a half-barbarous,
> Tartarian, ill-cultivated, poverty-stricken wilderness, until, in the course of
> nature, some hundreds of years hence, the population should become more
> dense. (112)

Civilization is not simply produced by the active renunciation of a
wandering, "Tartarian" state, but is the outcome of environmental factors
determined by what Wakefield terms "proportion."[35] A correct proportion
of population to territory will produce a settled, civilized society by
restricting its ownership to capitalists and rendering it subject to long-
term cultivation. Yet given the sheer surplus of "waste" land, Wakefield
maintains that such proportion can only be achieved by artificially limiting
its availability through imposing on it a state-controlled minimum value,
or "sufficient price." "Every new government, therefore, possesses the
power to civilize its subjects," Wakefield argues (159); Jonathan Lamb
points out that the sufficient price effectively recapitulates the history of
stadial development, "telescoped into the single transaction by which it
became settleable."[36] Marx, from a different perspective, views such a
mechanism as a "method of 'primitive accumulation,'" that is, "an accumulation which is not the result of the capitalist mode of production but
its point of departure."[37] Despite being ascribed an almost magical power
to bring about civilization, this most controversial aspect of systematic
colonization theory is nevertheless an absent center in *Letter from Sydney*.
As Wakefield's colonial correspondent openly admits, "Still, how is the
proper price to be ascertained? I frankly confess that I do not know.
I believe that it could be determined only by experience" (159). This
indeterminacy continues in the book's appendix, "Outline of a System of
Colonization," where the sufficient price is literally a blank space in the
text: "*It is suggested,* That a payment in money of – per acre be required for
all future grants of land without exception" (178, original emphasis). That
blank marks the point of intersection between Wakefield's theoretical
claims about colonization and his practical efforts to profit from the
forthcoming invasion of Australia and New Zealand.

[35] The "Tartar" was a stadialist byword for a nomadic population – McCulloch's *Principles of Political Economy* cites the "ancient Scythians and modern Tartars" as examples of precapitalist society. McCulloch, *Principles of Political Economy*, 67.

[36] Jonathan Lamb, "The Idea of Utopia in the European Settlement of New Zealand," in *Quicksands: Foundational Histories in Australia and Aotearoa New Zealand*, ed. Hilary Ericksen, Klaus Neumann, and Nicholas Thomas (Sydney: University of New South Wales Press, 1999), 89.

[37] Marx, *Capital*, 873, 939.

The cheap purchase of land from indigenous vendors (or, even more expeditiously, its appropriation at no cost whatsoever) and its subsequent high-priced sale was intended not only to place a spatial constraint on the settler population but also to bankroll the immigration process. First in the colony of South Australia, and then more extensively in New Zealand, Wakefield and his acolytes in the so-called Colonial Reform movement sought in the 1830s and 1840s to profit from settlement through the audacious mechanism they designed for the sale of land.[38] Although Wakefield withdrew at an early stage from formal involvement in the South Australian scheme, in part because he felt that it was deviating from the strict principles laid down by his theory, it is nevertheless instructive because so many of the basic mechanisms of systematic colonization – a fixed price on land, commitment to concentration of population, and assistance for emigration funded by land sales – were in place when the first fleet of nine ships of the South Australia Company landed more than 500 settlers in the colony during the second half of 1836. These first colonists had "set sail for the general region of Spencer Gulf's eastern shores with no clear idea of where they would settle" because the South Australia Company was unsure about the precise location of its colony, yet much of the land had already been sold prior to their embarkation to fund the speculative enterprise.[39] Investors in Britain had been presented with a map of the proposed settlement, divided according to a grid system, and were able to purchase "land orders" guaranteeing a certain amount of urban and rural land:

> The sole condition of purchase was to be a payment of 20/- per acre, which price was not to vary unless "any tendency to injurious dispersion" appeared among the colonists, in which event the Commissioners were to raise it to any amount not exceeding £2. In order to sell land to the value of £35,000 as required by the Act [i.e. South Australia Act (1834)], the Board offered 437 preliminary land-orders at £81, each entitling its purchaser to a country section of 80 acres and a town allotment of one acre.[40]

By March 1837, the urban settlement of Adelaide had been surveyed, and as Figure 1.1 illustrates, the Company's surveyors proceeded over the next

---

[38] For a more extensive account of the imposition of systematic colonization schemes in Australia and New Zealand, see Philip Steer, "On Systematic Colonization and the Culture of Settler Colonialism: Edward Gibbon Wakefield's *A Letter from Sydney* (1829)," *BRANCH: Britain, Representation, and Nineteenth-Century History*.

[39] Paul Carter, *The Road to Botany Bay: An Exploration of Landscape and History* (Minneapolis: University of Minnesota Press, 2010), 202.

[40] Douglas Pike, *Paradise of Dissent: South Australia 1829–1857*, 2nd ed. (Melbourne: Melbourne University Press, 1967), 120.

Figure 1.1   The South Australia Company's 1839 survey map of the Adelaide district demonstrates the spatial logic of systematic colonization. The character of individual settlers, and society in general, is guaranteed by the extensive allocation and sale of land, while the indigenous presence is rendered invisible.

two years to map 150 square miles of the surrounding land for the colony's "country sections." The success of these speculative activities, as Paul Carter points out, was therefore based on "acceptance of the proposition that land *there* could be regarded very much like land *here*," and that colonial land and society could therefore be rationalized and regulated according to metropolitan norms: "Located against the imaginary grid, the blankness of unexplored country was translatable into a blueprint for colonization: it could be divided up into blocks, the blocks numbered and the land auctioned, without the purchasers ever leaving their London offices."[41] Wakefield's equally audacious gambit was to claim that, through these spatial arrangements, British subjects could also be regarded in South Australia very much like they were in Britain.

The Romance and the Problem of Mobility: *Arabin*

Amidst the economic rhetoric, what of the novel and the question of character? If Wakefield's theories and public advocacy had a direct literary effect in Australia, it was not through spurring narratives directly concerned with systematic colonization. Indeed, Wakefield had joked in *A Letter from Sydney* that literature had no place in a settler colony: "Sir Walter Scott, Sir Humphrey Davy, and Mr. Malthus, would not earn as much in this colony as three brawny experienced ploughmen" (114). Yet Wakefield's representative literary figure, Scott, did make it to the settler colonies, at least in print form. Katie Trumpener asserts that, "by mid-century, the Waverley novels are so deeply embedded in the colonial imagination that their full influence is not always understood."[42] Trumpener claims that Scott's primary appeal lay in the narrative means he offered for absorbing the storm surge of historical change brought about by the twin forces of modernization and imperialism. I wish to argue that the Waverley novels also offered a template for settlers to imagine British society and subjectivity along the lines laid out by systematic colonization, by granting a formal logic to the ideas of settled character and settled society. That is, Scott's works gave shape to a Wakefieldian conception of settlement through their treatment of the fraught relationship between mobility and development through the possibilities of the romance form. Instead of providing neat accounts of settlement, however, early Australian adaptations of Scott display an awkwardness that reveals the difficulty of

---

[41] Carter, *Road to Botany Bay*, 203–4, original emphasis.   [42] Trumpener, *Bardic Nationalism*, 247.

reconciling the character of the emigrant with that of the settler, which is only intensified by the need to differentiate settler society from the nomadic indigenous population it was actively seeking to displace. The value and volatility of the romance for conceiving of settlement in spatial terms is most clearly on display in Thomas McCombie's *Arabin; or, The Adventures of a Settler in New South Wales* (1845), the first novel written in what would become the colony of Victoria.

It was a decade after Wakefield first began his campaign to reconceive settler colonialism when, in 1841, McCombie immigrated to the Port Phillip District of New South Wales. Although it was not established under the principles of systematic colonization, the settlement that would become its capital – Melbourne – was planned on a grid design similar to that of Adelaide, ground zero for Wakefield's project in South Australia. Having first tried and failed to make a living as a pastoralist, McCombie was by 1844 the editor and part owner of the *Port Phillip Gazette*, and a prominent member of the town's Scottish elite.[43] The plot of *Arabin* foregrounds that Scottish heritage through its young English protagonist, Godfrey Arabin, whose urge to immigrate to New South Wales is spurred by his sustained exposure to the romances of Walter Scott. Sent to board with a relative in Scotland, he encounters *Ivanhoe* and takes to wandering the mountains, "thinking on the warriors and people of the long-forgotten past, until he would inspire the dull landscape with imaginary beings."[44] As he matures, Arabin's susceptibility to the romance is shown to be in keeping with his growing dissatisfaction with the commercial orthodoxies of present-day British society. His reading interests are also in accordance with a notable lack of settled dispositions: after failing to establish himself as a surgeon, Arabin begins to "rush heedlessly into the most absurd speculations" (12). The solution to these problems appears to lie in yoking the logic of romance to the mobility of emigration: "If Edward Waverley, before him, was led by *his* youthful reading of less worthy romances to an embrace of the wrong historical cause," Trumpener comments, "Arabin finds in the Waverley novels a more appropriate guide to life and, in the development of the British settler colonies, a more worthy object for his enthusiasm."[45] Or, as Arabin more bluntly puts it, "If men were to live and die upon their cabbage-gardens, colonisation and improvement would

[43] See Alex Tyrrell, "'No Common Corrobery': The Robert Burns Festivals and Identity Politics in Melbourne, 1845–59," *Journal of the Royal Australian Historical Society* 97, no. 2 (2005).

[44] Thomas McCombie, *Arabin; or, The Adventures of a Settler in New South Wales* (London: Simmonds and Ward, 1845), 6. Hereafter cited in text.

[45] Trumpener, *Bardic Nationalism*, 258, original emphasis.

be things unknown, and might be expelled from our vernacular languages" (78–79). Here the novel first touches on the paradox of stadialist thought that will ultimately dismember its own formal logic: while cultivation is the definitive marker of settled modernity, it is antithetical to the uprooting and relocation of population necessary for a colonial invasion. For this reason, Arabin's enthusiasm for mobility and the romance become equally problematic once he lands on Australian soil.

Placed so explicitly under Scott's imprimatur, *Arabin* might well be expected to follow the template of the Waverley novels through to its conclusion. Adhering to those genre norms would see the wavering Arabin cross the colonial frontier, partake in adventures, and immerse himself in indigenous society, before ultimately returning to civilization enriched with a sense of "luxurious, aestheticized melancholy" over his erstwhile hosts' impending extinction.[46] In contrast to these expectations, Arabin's adventures take place solely within the ambit of colonial society, and therefore foreground instead the kinds of questions that Wakefield raised about wandering and settled populations. Despite McCombie's overt criticism of Wakefield's theories in the novel, as also in the later *Essays on Colonization* (1850), the narrative's underlying entanglement with the spatial principles of systematic colonization is signaled by the "vast," apparently empty plains where Arabin is first glimpsed on Australian soil:

> They extend thirty miles from east to west, and twenty miles from north to south.... Far as the eye can wander, it rests on the silent, boundless plains; neither house nor living thing is visible, not even a bird: the traveller might be buried in the bosom of an African desert. There is, however, a grandeur present in the scene – a magnificence derived from its vast proportions: compared with it, the scenery of Britain is tame. (29–30)

The plains provide the geographical center of the novel; as Barry Argyle observes, "Australia's size is perhaps its most obvious quality; but McCombie was the first to note it in a novel."[47] Placing a romance-enthused protagonist within a stereotypical colonial waste land ensures that the formation of British subjectivity is framed in Wakefield's spatial terms. The novel asks if Arabin will, as it is put in *Letter from Sydney*, become subject to "concentration ... which in almost every thing is the essence of power," or remain "ever on the move ... unable to bring any

---

[46] Ian Duncan, "Primitive Inventions: *Rob Roy*, Nation, and World System," *Eighteenth-Century Fiction* 15, no. 1 (2002): 83.

[47] Barry Argyle, *An Introduction to the Australian Novel, 1830–1930* (Oxford: Clarendon Press, 1972), 59.

thing to perfection" (151, 155). Put more broadly, what is under examination is the ability for Victorian society to survive its translation to a colonial space.

The undoubted narrative awkwardness of *Arabin* usefully brings to light the uncomfortable common ground shared between the romantic urge to "behold strange lands," attributed to emigration, and the barbaric connotations of wandering that haunt Wakefield's vision of settlement. Arabin remains unsettled for most of the novel, disavowing colonial society in favor of a nomadic ethos that he associates with the indigenous population. "Rather than follow flocks of sheep," he claims, "I would wander the country with an erratic tribe of black men, and see one spot to-day, another tomorrow, and be untrammelled by the artificial rules of society" (74). This purported identification with the original "erratic" inhabitants of Australia is not taken very seriously in the novel, and ultimately not even by Arabin, but despite this his unwillingness to make a "settled" contribution to society remains striking. The novel presents the challenge of converting Arabin from a migratory to a settled state by mapping his movements between two contrasting settler households. Willis is a patient he is treating for melancholia, whose appearance is marked by a "peculiarly dark complexion, with wild, unsettled eyes" (85), and who lacks any settled dispositions: he is "labouring under mental derangement" (33) and "could not live without excitement" (199). In contrast to the erratic Willis is the prosperous and settled pastoralist, Butler, who is entirely satisfied with his prosaic colonial environs. "[I]t is very fine to move about, but very miserable, I am positive," he asserts: "Give me a comfortable home, plenty of money, and allow me to live comfortably" (68). Arabin's latent capitalist inclinations eventually take concrete form through the purchase of a nearby sheep station, and he soon after wins the hand of the beautiful and pure Martha, Butler's sister-in-law, who had previously and repeatedly rejected Willis's overtures. In domesticating and settling the migratory Arabin, the novel strives to follow the stadial teleology modeled by the Waverley novels by self-consciously sloughing off its initial fascination with the romance. As the narrator reflects, "The Colonies are the regions of stern reality; romance in the Colonies would not be tolerated; plain matter-of-fact is what the majority look to" (200). The concluding chapter accordingly uses Arabin's reformation as a pretext for offering sober advice to any "young adventurer" who contemplates following in his footsteps: "A Colonist must land with a determination to pursue an even, steady course; he must resolve that no temptation shall ever wean him from habits of industry. His aim must be to get a fair start" (225).

Pastoralism and regularity ultimately come into alignment, in a seeming triumph of the settled ethos of realism over the nomadic impulses of romance.

Arabin's creaky plotting and thin characterization have ensured its almost total critical oblivion, yet those structural problems also demonstrate compellingly that, from the outset of Victorian settler colonialism, conceiving of the colony as a settled space involved thinking in simultaneously novelistic and economic terms. This is most clearly on display a few chapters into *Arabin*, when the narrative comes to a sudden halt to offer an excursus on "a new order of beings," the Australian large-scale pastoralist or "squatter":

> The extent of the squatting interest may be conceived by the following table of the stock in the Colony of New South Wales.
>
> | Horses | . | . | . | . | 56,585 |
> |---|---|---|---|---|---|
> | Horned Cattle | . | . | . | . | 897,219 |
> | Pigs | . | . | . | . | 46,086 |
> | Sheep | . | . | . | . | 4,804,946 (55) |

What appears to be a clumsy suspension of novelistic narrative for the raw data of political economy is, seen from another perspective, a blunt yet necessary authenticity effect in service of cementing the stadial link between settler colonization and capitalist modernity. Sitting alongside the individualized tale of Arabin's settlement, the statistics work similarly to assert the possibilities of cultivation and private property at a broad societal level. Yet the uneven movement between plot and statistics also underlines the volatile relationship between Wakefield's stadialist vision of civilization and the Australian practice of pastoral squatting. After all, even before Wakefield began to outline his vision of a settler colony founded upon small-scale, intensive agriculture, Australia's economy was becoming dominated by a geographically dispersed, quasinomadic form of large-scale pastoralism.[48] As the term indicates, Australian squatters lacked tenure over the vast lands occupied by their flocks. To McCombie's narrator, as to Wakefield, such an unsettled form of society must inevitably produce unsettled dispositions:

> [T]hey do not cultivate the soil, because any person might go to the Government Office, and request that the station should be put up to auction…. On the contrary, however, if the Australian settler had fixity

---

[48] Peter Burroughs, *Britain and Australia, 1831–1855: A Study in Imperial Relations and Crown Lands Administration* (Oxford: Clarendon Press, 1967), 43.

of tenure, he would conjoin agricultural and pastoral pursuits; he would build a comfortable house, and eat his food independently of the land commissioners. (20)

Despite such qualms, Arabin's entry into the squatting class is cast as the endpoint of his wandering. The novel's vision of social stabilization and "domestic felicity," achieved without his securing title to the land he occupies, thus ends surprisingly far from the expectations of stadial theory. The formal difficulty of straightforwardly transplanting realism to the settler colony thus comes into focus as inseparable from a wider quandary of imagining character in stadialist terms, for the economic activity that McCombie presents as the bedrock of settled British society is defined precisely by those romance qualities and nomadic tendencies that it has so stridently sought to reject.

Arabin also illuminates with stark clarity the means by which indigenous populations are rendered invisible within the horizon of settled society demarcated by stadial theory. This operation proceeds by way of a double exclusion, whereby stadial logic first frames them in the premodern terms associated with the romance, before they are then expelled even from that formal domain as part of a project concerned exclusively with imagining the transplantation of British society to the antipodes.[49] At the time the novel was published, the Port Phillip District was far from pacified, let alone empty – in response to the settler invasion, "Aboriginal peoples resisted, and guerrilla warfare reached a peak … in the 1840s" – but the ongoing presence of the indigenous population is approached in the novel only in roundabout fashion.[50] McCombie's melancholic character, Willis, displays symptoms of madness in marked excess to their prosaic causes. While at times the novel ascribes his illness to Martha's rejection, and at other times invokes his alcoholism, when Arabin finds him stumbling around the streets he appears haunted by guilt: "It is a fearful thing to

---

[49] Along similar lines, Ivor Indyk describes a "double gesture" in colonial Australian pastoral poetry, "which recognizes the Aboriginal as the true pastoral subject only to have the figure superseded by that of the settler-farmer." Ivor Indyk, "Pastoral and Priority: The Aboriginal in Australian Pastoral," *New Literary History* 24, no. 4 (1993): 839.

[50] "By the 1840s, large numbers of settlers had arrived and rapidly outnumbered the Aboriginal population [in the Port Phillip District].... Aboriginal groups disrupted stock routes, broke the legs of sheep and cattle, and made surprise attacks on shepherds' huts and squatters' homes, sometimes burning them and taking their goods. They often killed hut keepers, especially those who were known to have abused Aboriginal women. European reprisals were often swift and vicious but carried out covertly." Jane Carey and Penelope Edmonds, "Australian Settler Colonialism over the Long Nineteenth Century," in *The Routledge Handbook of the History of Settler Colonialism*, ed. Edward Cavanagh and Lorenzo Veracini (London: Routledge, 2017), 375.

dwell with the shadows of night – the dark, dismal night, when the morning will never break…. Did you hear about it? …. The men I killed last night, and the wild animals" (90). No crime is ever directly attributed to Willis, yet he cannot escape this fear. Structurally disconnected from this inchoate settler guilt, yet strikingly similar to it in thematic terms, is a story recounted to Arabin of six Aborigines massacred by a group of drunk settlers – all the perpetrators flee the colony except one, who "ended his days in a mad-house" (76). At one further remove again is McCombie's "Essay on the Aborigines of Australia," published as an appendix to the novel, which refers to the murder of an indigenous woman in 1842 in the context of a broader discussion about the legitimacy of Australian colonization:

> I now arrive at a very important question – not merely important as far as regards the blacks personally, but important as regards civilisation and colonisation. The question is, – Has the Government of England a right to take possession of the country, and, without any consent from the original proprietors, sell the land, and make them amenable to the laws of Britain, of which they know nothing, and very likely could not be brought to believe that such a country was, or ever existed? (267–68)

McCombie's decision to "leave this question unanswered" is far less surprising than his willingness to describe the Aborigines as "the original proprietors" (and, in the next paragraph, "original owners") of the land. The essay's brief moment of candor breaks apart the iron logic of stadial theory – which denies proprietorship to nomadic populations – and throws into relief that such possibilities remain unacknowledged in the novel. This partitioned acknowledgment of Aboriginal property rights, bracketed outside of the narrative, helps frame Willis's insanity as a backhanded acknowledgment of the colonial violence and land appropriation occurring at the very moment of publication, and enabling the writing to take place at all, which the novel's focus on settler character is otherwise formally unwilling and unable to assert.[51]

---

[51] For the fate of indigenous property rights in Port Phillip in the 1830s and 1840s, see Henry Reynolds, *The Law of the Land*, 3rd ed. (Camberwell: Penguin, 2003), 179–90. In McCombie's later *Essays on Colonization* (1850), he reverts to a more orthodox stadialist view that posits hunter-gatherers as having no legitimate title to the land because their "erratic habits" preclude them from cultivating the soil: "The aborigines of the countries we have colonized had no laws, and they had no property in the soil in the shape of improvements, the work of labor. Priority of possession gave the indigenous races a moral right to the game on the land, but it conferred – according to the universally recognized opinion of modern nations – no privilege of holding, or transferring it against the right of a civilized nation." Thomas McCombie, *Essays on Colonization* (London: Smith, Elder, 1850), 46–47. As a colonial legislator, McCombie also laid the groundwork for the Aborigines

Extending the Borders of Britishness: *The Caxtons* and *David Copperfield*

Approached instead from a more broadly transnational perspective, systematic colonization and the "sufficient price" also brought metropolitan and colonial territories – and their British inhabitants – into a new conceptual alignment. In making this claim I have in mind something more than the influence that Wakefield's ideas had on the development of metropolitan political economy, whether as a bête noire of Karl Marx or as "the very backbone of Mill's colonial thought."[52] In *England and America*, Wakefield argues that the aims of colonization can be boiled down to a simple economic goal, "namely, an enlargement of the field for employing capital and labour."[53] Alongside the financial chicanery of systematic colonization, the Victorian renewal of settler colonialism also commenced an imaginative "enlargement" that paralleled its more tangible effects of financial and material extension. By presenting the kind of "abstract space" in the colonies that Mary Poovey finds emerging at the same time in Britain through the development of industrial capitalism, systematic colonization offered a means by which British society could be imagined beyond the borders of the nation. Wakefield put it thus: "In fewer words, every grant of land in these colonies would be an extension, though distant, of Britain itself," as if that new land was "removed miraculously to the coast of Lancashire."[54] In addition to the puffery that it undoubtedly is, the comment suggests the need to rethink the cultural dynamic of the Victorian settler empire, as not only extending Britain's reach but at the same time also bringing the colonies into previously unimagined proximity.

Protection Act (1869), which mobilized this logic as part of an attempt to centralize management of Victoria's missions and reserves: "McCombie argued for a thorough exception to the rights and entitlements of British subjecthood: freedom of movement, freedom of contract and the right to familial privacy should all be suspended for Aborigines in the liberal regime of protection, justified by an anthropological account of their incapacities and incompetencies." Leigh Boucher, "Victorian Liberalism and the Effect of Sovereignty: A View from the Settler Periphery," *History Australia* 13, no. 1 (2016): 46.

[52] Duncan Bell, "John Stuart Mill on Colonies," *Political Theory* 38, no. 1 (2010): 56. See also Katherine Smits, "John Stuart Mill on the Antipodes: Settler Violence against Indigenous Peoples and the Legitimacy of Colonial Rule," *Australian Journal of Politics and History* 54, no. 1 (2008); H. O. Pappe, "Wakefield and Marx," *Economic History Review* 4, no. 1 (1951).

[53] Wakefield, *England and America*, 508.

[54] Wakefield, *Letter from Sydney*, 164, 166. When first published in the *Morning Chronicle*, the former phrase was worded, "Thus … the progress of colonization would be … a progressive extension of old society." Edward Gibbon Wakefield, "Australia," *The Morning Chronicle*, October 6, 1829, 2.

What the novel relays more directly than political economy is that, while Wakefield's model of character formation was not readily translatable back from the colonies to metropolitan society, his underlying proposition that new settler colonies be seen as an extension of British society was far more widely influential in shaping Victorian thinking. The rhetoric of systematic colonization, that is, allowed the British settler to be increasingly imagined within what Elizabeth Deeds Ermarth describes as the "common horizon" of realist representation.[55] This new territorial and social bridging can be glimpsed in the fleeting portraits of English social restoration through Australian labor offered in works such as Edward Bulwer-Lytton's *The Caxtons: A Family Picture* (1849) and Dickens's *David Copperfield* (1849–50). *The Caxtons* offers the metropolitan novel's most direct portrayal of Wakefield-infused colonial thinking through its tale of a youthful protagonist, Pisistratus Caxton, and his immediate family, who fall upon difficult financial circumstances and are forced to relocate to his uncle's unproductive farm. The novel thus presents a twofold problem of character and society, for a lack of capital prevents the moribund family estate from being "redeemed" from a "dreary bleak waste," at the same time as Pisistratus is stymied by the dearth of opportunities for British subjects "not adapted for success in any of our conventional professions.[56] Indeed, as in the earlier *Arabin*, Pisistratus's unsettled character is explicitly articulated in stadial terms – his father describes him with the neologism "planeticose" ("disposed to roaming").[57] As the colonial plot enters the narrative, it is given moral and intellectual legitimacy through a paternalistic politician, Albert Trevanion, whose estate stands as a model of capital-infused productivity that diffuses broader social benefits. While Pisistratus has never before seen a landscape so "beautiful in its peculiar English character," it is a notably modern form of beauty: "It had none of the feudal characteristics of ancient parks ... the chief impression conveyed was that it was a new place – a made place" (1.200). These innovations have been spurred by a holy trinity of "improvement – energy – capital," and it is on the basis of these principles that the cultivating and cultivated Trevanion advises the unsettled Pisistratus to emigrate to Australia (1.201). The settler colony is no dumping ground, in

---

[55] Elizabeth Deeds Ermarth, *Realism and Consensus in the English Novel: Time, Space and Narrative* (Edinburgh: Edinburgh University Press, 1998), 21.

[56] Edward Bulwer-Lytton, *The Caxtons: A Family Picture*, 3 vols. (Edinburgh: Blackwood, 1849), 2.260, 2.293, 2.296. Hereafter cited in text.

[57] Ibid., 2.314. The definition is provided by Bulwer-Lytton in a footnote, and the *Oxford English Dictionary* cites this as the word's only usage.

other words, but is presented as a plausible extension – an "enlargement of the field" – of a conservative metropolitan vision for social regeneration.

Although Bulwer-Lytton departs repeatedly and self-consciously from the detail of Wakefield's colonizing script, his colonial solution to the Caxtons's metropolitan difficulties could nevertheless only be imagined in the wake of systematic colonization. The novel avoids endorsing any kind of formal colonizing organization or scheme, but Trevanion's letter urging Pisistratus to emigrate is motivated by the Wakefieldian idea of societal transplantation: "[N]ot turning a rabble loose upon a new soil," he avers, "but planting in the foreign allotments all the rudiments of a harmonious state, analogous to that in the mother country" (2.297). Indeed, a footnote later in the same chapter acknowledges the similarity between "the views here expressed" and "Mr. Wakefield's elaborate theory" (2.298). After ten years in the colony, where he has successfully invested in sheep, cattle, and land, Pisistratus not only possesses a large fortune but also feels able to return to Britain. Coral Lansbury notes that *The Caxtons* was met with "delight" by its Australian readers, "largely due to the relief that the colony was being regarded in literature as something more than a penal settlement."[58] Indeed, the settler colony is figured as a vital supplement to the continued health of metropolitan society. Upon his return, Pisistratus employs his colonial earnings to revive the moribund pastoral scene of his family's decline. Now "smiling cornfields replace the bleak dreary moors" on his uncle's estate, as its "domains ... are reclaimed, year by year, from the waste" (3.295). This ending, which hinges on reconciling capitalism with feudalism, and nationalism with imperialism, signals the broad perspectival change wrought by Wakefield's ideas, such that settler colonialism now appears capable of imaginative as well as financial alignment with fundamental principles of Victorian society and British political identity.

The uneven yet marked influence of systematic colonization on extending the global borders of British subjectivity and society is brought into sharper focus in *David Copperfield*, through the formal relationship between the major plot of David's maturation and the plot of reformation through emigration imposed upon a range of minor characters. Esty argues that through this geographic division of narrative labor, "the fulfillment of the protagonist's maturity interlocks with the reconsolidation of the national boundaries."[59] Indeed, although Dickens likely drew on

---

[58] Coral Lansbury, *Arcady in Australia: The Evocation of Australia in Nineteenth-Century English Literature* (Carlton: Melbourne University Press, 1970), 89.
[59] Esty, *Unseasonable Youth*, 50–51.

Bulwer-Lytton's novel for the emigration subplot, he only issues one-way tickets to Australia for the debt-ridden Wilkins Micawber, the fallen Emily, and an assortment of their relatives.[60] In the second-to-last chapter, Emily's uncle, Peggotty, returns briefly from the antipodes to regale David and Dora at their London fireside with the tale of their colonial redemption through agricultural labor:

> We haven't fared nohows, but fared to thrive.... What with sheep-farming, and what with stock-farming, and what with one thing and what with t'other, we are as well to do, as well could be. Theer's been kiender [*sic*] a blessing fell upon us ... and we've done nowt but prosper. That is, in the long run. If not yesterday, why then to-day. If not to-day, why then to-morrow.[61]

Esty rightly highlights how peripheral this settlement plot is to the main concerns of the bildungsroman, and for this reason it is typically read as little more than "a device to facilitate narrative closure."[62] Lansbury similarly argues that such Arcadian logic provided a "palliative, a means of solving social problems without disturbing existing society."[63] Yet this colonial addendum to *David Copperfield* also attests to a new ability to imagine British identity at the furthest reaches of the empire – a working out of Wakefield's claim that "these colonies would be an extension, though distant, of Britain itself." While the novel is amused by Mrs. Micawber's rhetoric, it is in complete agreement with her sentiment when she asserts to her husband, "You are going out, Micawber, to this distant clime, to strengthen, not to weaken, the connexion between yourself and Albion."[64] This testifies to the broadest impact left by systematic colonization upon Victorian culture – that the emigrant need no longer be thought of as lost to the body politic, or condemned to exist in a diminished affective, cultural, or patriotic relationship to it. By contrast, the theory of settler character formation that would contribute decisively to mid-century metropolitan ideas about British subjectivity derived from another source altogether.

Character in the Penal Colony: The Mark System

In 1836 – the year that the first attempt to enact the principles of systematic colonization began in the colony of South Australia – Captain

---

[60] Brantlinger, *Rule of Darkness*, 121.
[61] Charles Dickens, *David Copperfield*, ed. Jeremy Tambling (London: Penguin, 1996), 797.
[62] Moore, *Dickens and Empire*, 7.   [63] Lansbury, *Arcady in Australia*, 106.
[64] Dickens, *David Copperfield*, 742–43.

Alexander Maconochie resigned from his position as Professor of Geography at University College London, and moved with his large family to Van Diemen's Land. In taking up the position of private secretary to the colony's new lieutenant governor, the explorer Sir John Franklin, he had also been tasked by the Society for the Improvement of Penal Discipline with investigating the convict system. He was dismissed from his administrative role two years later when his critical views were widely shared in the colony, reverberating back from Britain where they had first been publicized by the recently formed Molesworth Select Committee on Transportation.[65] It was while unemployed that Maconochie first outlined the principles of his own theory of convict discipline, which he named the Mark System – originally published in Hobart as *Thoughts on Convict Management* (1838); quickly republished in London as *Australiana* (1839) – and he was soon given the chance to institute his ideas, as superintendent of the notorious Norfolk Island penal colony from 1840 to 1844. After he was also dismissed from this job, and recalled to England for good measure, Maconochie continued to publicize his Mark System, most prominently in his pamphlet, *Crime and Punishment: The Mark System, Framed to Mix Persuasion with Punishment, and Make Their Effect Improving, Yet Their Operation Severe* (1846). Historian of convict transportation Robert Hughes describes Maconochie as "the one and only inspired penal reformer to work in Australia throughout the whole history of transportation."[66] In a letter dating from mid-1846, Dickens would affirm this assessment: "I do not know of any plan so well conceived, or so firmly grounded in a knowledge of human nature, or so judiciously addressed to it ... as what is called Captain Macconochie's [sic] Mark System."[67] Far beyond the national horizons of the panopticon, the Mark System offered a means by which penal discipline might be brought into direct alignment with liberal reform. Reimagining the penal colony as "a school for the recovery of social weakness," Maconochie found settler colonialism offering new insights into the formation of responsible British subjects.[68]

Maconochie's interest in subject formation coincided with the emergence of a newly politicized understanding of character, as the extension of the franchise necessitated a cross-class model of political subjectivity. The figure of the criminal assumed theoretical and political prominence as a limit case to these endeavors, the embodiment of a failure of self-

[65] Hughes, *Fatal Shore*, 489–93.   [66] Ibid., 488–89.
[67] Dickens, *Letters of Charles Dickens*, 4.553.   [68] Maconochie, *Australiana*, 62.

character. At the same time, by proposing a path to reformation independent of any physical infrastructure, the Mark System offered a disciplinary mechanism that had the potential to be abstracted from a particular place.

Although Maconochie concurred with Wakefield in arguing that the laws of political economy could provide a structure capable of civilizing British subjects, he turned for inspiration to the temporality of bourgeois financial discipline rather than the spatial concerns of stadial theory. This provides the basis for his critique of a penal sentence defined solely in terms of temporal duration, and oriented solely toward a past crime, for it "leaves no choice of action, requires no virtue but obedience, affords no stimulus to exertion."[71] Maconochie instead proposed that habits of labor and self-discipline must be instilled through the same kind of mechanism that propelled middle-class success. The Mark System proposed that punishment instead be measured in terms of labor and good behavior, that this be quantified as a number of "marks" to be attained by the convict, and that marks function as a kind of currency that could be earned or lost on a daily basis. By "enlisting self-interest in the cause," the temporal stasis of a prison term was transformed into a developmental narrative. As demonstrated by the sample mark table in Figure 1.2, the marks accumulated in the prison ledger testify to the state of the individual's character and provide further incentive for its continued improvement. The convict's freedom thus hinged on internalizing the logic of making "proper calculations of long-run self-interest," learning to shape present actions in anticipation of future benefits:

> [T]he essential ingredient in moral Training ... is a limited amount of *free agency*, controuled [*sic*] and guided by *moral impulse* (prospective motive) .... Its domain is thus the future; — it looks to the future, — and operates by the future. It forms, consequently, a habit of resisting present impulses for the sake of consequent advantages, which, when confirmed, is just the result wanted, the precise form of social virtue which we wish to impress on our released criminals.[72]

Maconochie did not intend that his reformatory intervention would instill convicts with social mobility, but instead envisaged that they would

[71] Alexander Maconochie, *Crime and Punishment: The Mark System, Framed to Mix Persuasion with Punishment, and Make Their Effect Improving, Yet Their Operation Severe* (London: Hatchard, 1846), 43.
[72] Maconochie, *Australiana*, 97.

governance. Debates concerning penal reform therefore turned increas
ingly on questions of the criminal's interior state as the key to persona
improvement or even reformation. "It was less the actions than th
characters of offenders on which attention came to focus," notes Martii
Wiener, "crime was essentially seen as the expression of a fundamenta
character defect stemming from a refusal or an inability to deny waywarc
impulses or to make proper calculations of long-run self-interest."[69] O
those penal schemes, as Goodlad has argued, Benthamite panopticisn
was cemented by Foucault as the preeminent model for understanding
liberal subject formation in the Victorian era. Yet just as Bentham once
played off the Panopticon against the perceived inadequacies of convici
transportation ("characteristic feature of it, radical incapacity of being
combined with any efficient system of inspection"), so Maconochie
would in turn hold up the Mark System as an improvement on panopti-
cism's disciplinary effects. His short pamphlet, *Comparison between Mr.
Bentham's Views on Punishment, and Those Advocated in Connexion with
the Mark System* (1847), makes that contrast explicit: on the left of the
page are quotations from Bentham's writings on penal law; on the right,
Maconochie offers his own critical commentary. In the subsequent
discussion, Maconochie attacks the passivity of Bentham's techniques
of surveillance as likely to produce "only eye-servants" – that is, a mere
appearance of obedience – rather than any deeper and more long-lasting
reform of character:

> He considered them, as it were, objective agents, capable of being acted on
> to any extent by the external impulses which he proposed to bring to bear
> on them, rather than highly subjective agents, with strong wills and passions
> of their own, by which, like other men, they are always more immediately
> swayed.... [T]he means of gaining the permanent *will* of criminals have
> been subordinated to those of securing their temporary conformity to
> certain fixed regulations.[70]

While surveillance remained central to Maconochie's proposals, the Mark
System promised to peer beneath the observable surface of the subject,
and take hold of the internal domain of character. By shifting the focus
from punishment to reformation, and thus to the observation of change
over time, Maconochie also gave narrative shape to the production of

---

[69] Martin J. Wiener, *Reconstructing the Criminal: Culture, Law, and Policy in England, 1830–1914* (Cambridge: Cambridge University Press, 1990), 46.
[70] Alexander Maconochie, *Comparison between Mr. Bentham's Views on Punishment, and Those Advocated in Connexion with the Mark System* (London: Compton, 1847), 5, 6.

Date, or Prisoner's Number.	Previous Accumulation.	CR. EARNINGS.							DR. FORFEITURES.							
		Personal Demeanour.	Employments.					Total Earned.	Food.	Indulgences.		Punishments.				
			Kind of Employment.	Diligence.	Effect produced.	Chaplain's Report.	Schoolmaster's Report.			Kind of.	Charge for.	Offences.	Fines.	Imprisonments in days.	Total Forfeited.	Balance.
351	1440	3	D	5	5	2/4	3/3	25	5	V	5	B	7	„	17	8
	1448	3	D	5	5	2/4	3/3	25	5	L	2	C	11	„	18	7
	1455	3	D	5	6	2/4	3/3	26	5	L	2	„	2	„	9	17

Figure 1.2   A sample mark table published by Maconochie to illustrate a prisoner's progress toward completing their sentence under his system. The accrual of marks, based on detailed observation of character criteria, produces a developmental narrative of daily improvement.

become better fitted to the task of colonization. "[W]e must carefully copy the incidents of that frugal, honest, and laborious poverty to which we desire to restore our criminals," he argued, with the goal in mind of "constituting afterwards a good rural population."[73] Instead, it was the Mark System that became mobile, as a theory of subject formation proving able to be translated across boundaries of class and geography.

The scheme of "moral training" that Maconochie developed in the terrible clarity of the penal colony also put great weight on the potential for culture to instill settled dispositions in recalcitrant British subjects. As superintendent of the Norfolk Island penal colony, he undertook seemingly quixotic projects, such as establishing a library – including a set of the Waverley novels "to encourage national pride in Scottish convicts" – as well as forming Protestant and Catholic choirs and a band, "informed by the objective of using orderly, collective musicking to discourage both self-absorbed individualism, and politically-charged collective action."[74]

---

[73] Alexander Maconochie, *The Principles of Punishment on Which the Mark System of Prison Discipline Is Advocated* (London: Ollivier, 1850), 10; Maconochie, *Australiana*, 18.

[74] Hughes, *Fatal Shore*, 506; Alan Maddox, "On the Machinery of Moral Improvement: Music and Prison Reform in the Penal Colony on Norfolk Island," *Musicology Australia* 34, no. 2 (2012): 196.

In proposing that the individual might be reconciled to society through habits of labor and immersion in culture, Maconochie enters more directly onto a terrain more usually associated by Victorian studies with the political and philosophical calculus of liberal individualism. The reconciliation of individual will with social conformity is, after all, a "dilemma coterminous with modern bourgeois civilization":

> [I]t is not sufficient for modern bourgeois society simply to subdue the drives that oppose the standards of "normality." It is also necessary that, as a "free individual," not as a fearful subject but as a convinced citizen, one perceives the social norms as *one's* own. One must *internalize* them and fuse external compulsion and internal impulses into a new unity until the former is no longer distinguishable from the latter.[75]

If the most prominent formal resolution to this dilemma is offered by the bildungsroman, as Moretti argues, the Mark System stands as its colonial doppelganger. As Maconochie put it in *Crime and Punishment*: "The ultimate purpose of military discipline is, to train men to act together; but that of penal discipline is, to prepare them advantageously to separate."[76] This is not to say that the Mark System is exactly analogous to bildung, especially as it was articulated at mid-century by John Stuart Mill. Whereas Mill sought to shift the balance away from social conformity and toward individual variation – so that "free scope should be given to varieties of character, short of injury to others" – Maconochie's narrower, labor-based focus on habit, obligation, and duty aligned far more closely with the shared moral code that sustained mainstream understandings of character.[77] The homologies between the Mark System and the bildungsroman instead hinge, in addition to their similar assertions of individuation and socialization, on their shared interest in giving narrative form to an inner domain of character and the plotting of its formation across time. "*Aiming exclusively at the mind*," the ledger where the convict's marks were recorded promised to represent the state of the individual's will and offered a narrative structure by which an ideal form of character could be seen to take shape.[78]

---

[75] Moretti, *Way of the World*, 15, 16, original emphasis.

[76] Maconochie, *Crime and Punishment*, 29.   [77] Mill, *On Liberty*, 57.

[78] Maconochie, *Crime and Punishment*, 27, original emphasis. Mary Poovey draws attention to the sense of certainty instilled by the form of the ledger: "One of its *epistemological* effects was to make the formal precision of the double-entry system, which drew on the rule-bound system of arithmetic, *seem* to guarantee the accuracy of the details it recorded." Mary Poovey, *A History of the Modern Fact: Problems of Knowledge in the Sciences of Wealth and Society* (Chicago: University of Chicago Press, 1998), 30, original emphasis.

Charles Dickens and the Mark System: Urania Cottage, or the Home for Homeless Women

Maconochie's subsequent career exemplifies the global mobility of certain British subjects within the settler empire, and some of the means by which colonial ideas and narratives were inserted into metropolitan culture. Most readily legible is his institutional influence. Once he was relieved of his position on Norfolk Island, Maconochie returned to Britain, but was unable to take up any further roles in government service due to the "personal animosity of several key senior civil servants"; as a result, he instead worked on actively disseminating his ideas, through writing and personal advocacy.[79] Through this, he achieved his most discernible influence in the area of penal theory and reform. Maconochie was appointed as governor of the newly built Birmingham prison in 1849, but he was forbidden by the home secretary from implementing the Mark System as he once envisaged it: applying a modified version for incarcerated boys, where labor was mandated without being able to reduce the length of a sentence, he "found himself increasingly resorting to corporal sanctions to force them to work."[80] More successfully, elements of the Mark System were implemented in the Irish penal system in the 1850s, as part of Walter Crofton's innovative "Intermediate System"; Maconochie and Crofton's ideas were subsequently taken up in the United States, most directly in New York's Elmira Reformatory, which opened in 1876 and was for the next four decades "the most widely discussed and emulated prison in the world."[81] Yet Maconochie's return to Britain also demonstrates the power of more personalized networks that spanned the settler empire. Maconochie had first met Dickens just prior to his departure for Australia, and they renewed their acquaintance in March 1846, soon after his return to Britain – and two months before Dickens was approached by Baroness Angela Burdett-Coutts, then the richest woman in England, with the idea of founding a private home for the reformation of prostitutes. Dickens

---

[79] J. M. Moore, "Reformative Rhetoric and the Exercise of Corporal Power: Alexander Maconochie's Regime at Birmingham Prison, 1849–51," *Historical Research* 89, no. 245 (2016): 513.

[80] Ibid., 520.

[81] Robert G. Waite, "From Penitentiary to Reformatory: Alexander Maconochie, Walter Crofton, Zebulon Brockway, and the Road to Prison Reform – New South Wales, Ireland, and Elmira, New York, 1840–70," *Criminal Justice History* 11 (1991): 101; Elizabeth Eileen Dooley, "Sir Walter Crofton and the Irish or Intermediate System of Prison Discipline," *Modern Penal Practice* 7, no. 1 (1981).

proposed that the project be run in accordance with the principles of the Mark System, which he was by now very familiar with:

> I would carry a modification of this Mark System through the whole establishment; for it is its great philosophy and its chief excellence that it is not a mere form or course of training adapted to the life within the house, but it is a preparation ... for the right performance of duty outside, and for the formation of habits of firmness and self-restraint.[82]

Dickens immediately began to immerse himself in what Philip Collins describes as "the only charitable activity and institution to which he gave his consistent attention over a prolonged period (some ten or twelve years), and ... most of the ideas and their execution were of his devising."[83] With this scheme to reform the character of fallen women, in other words, Dickens essentially established a microcosm of Norfolk Island on the outskirts of London.

Urania Cottage, or the Home for Homeless Women, opened in Shepherd's Bush, London, in November 1847, and Dickens was involved in virtually every aspect of its planning and operation.[84] He chose its location and its name (after Aphrodite Urania, the pure goddess of love); appointed its staff; authored a tract to solicit inmates ("An Appeal to Fallen Women"); interviewed and admitted potential inmates; and even designed their uniforms ("I have made them as cheerful in appearance as they reasonably could be – at the same time very neat and modest").[85] In service of the "dream of returning to Society, or of becoming Virtuous Wives," the inmates were to be trained in a variety of virtues and skills deemed appropriate for domestic servitude, at the same time that the application of the Mark System instilled them with newly settled dispositions.[86] The categories of behavior that Dickens determined should be observed and assessed on a daily basis – "Truthfulness, Industry, Temper, Propriety of Conduct and Conversation, Temperance, Order, Punctuality, Economy, Cleanliness" – were shaped, as with Maconochie's original scheme, in accordance with a decidedly middle-class calculus.[87]

---

[82] Dickens, *Letters of Charles Dickens*, 4.554. Dickens had several of Maconochie's pamphlets in his library at Gad's Hill, and recommended *Crime and Punishment* to Burdett-Coutts in a letter dated October 5, 1846. Ibid., 4.523, 4.630.

[83] Philip Collins, *Dickens and Crime* (London: Macmillan, 1962), 100.

[84] The definitive history of Urania Cottage is Jenny Hartley, *Charles Dickens and the House of Fallen Women* (London: Methuen, 2009). See also Rosemarie Bodenheimer, *Knowing Dickens* (Ithaca: Cornell University Press, 2007), 135–42. Dickens's only public account of the project is his article, "Home for Homeless Women," *Household Words* 7, no. 161 (1853).

[85] Dickens, *Letters of Charles Dickens*, 5.185.   [86] Ibid., 4.554.

[87] Dickens, "Home for Homeless Women," 171.

Yet whereas Maconochie's marks merely imitated the financial system and never carried any real economic value, Dickens went further in choosing to give his marks a definite monetary worth. An inmate was able to earn a maximum of 6 pence daily, at a rate of 20 marks to 3 pence, so that good behavior was given a small yet tangible financial reward.[88] This simple decision literalized the relationship between character formation and bourgeois financial discipline that was only latent in Maconochie's writings: the earnings of the Urania Cottage inmates were not a reward for the actual labor of their "routine of household duties," but for the settled character traits that were revealed through it. That is, by translating his marks into Burdett-Coutts's money, Dickens aligned ideals of middle-class financial discipline more directly with those of middle-class character.

Dickens's vision of social reformation at Urania Cottage also extended the scope of the Mark System in its commitment to the idea of character's geographic mobility. One of the more notable ironies of the project is that it took the principles Maconochie had devised in Australia for the purpose of reforming British convicts, and applied them to women in Britain so they might become fit wives in Australia. Although emigration was in comparison only a "limited option" for inmates of a Magdalene house, Dickens's scheme was from the outset intended to culminate in a new life in a new place: "[W]e impress upon them that Emigration is an essential part of our compact."[89] During the 1850s, Dickens would also promote emigration to Australia in the pages of *Household Words*, publishing articles by the colonial booster Samuel Sidney and endorsing Caroline Chisholm's Family Colonisation and Loan Society. Nevertheless, Urania Cottage constituted his most active and personal role in that colonial endeavor.[90] Dickens's article on the project in *Household Words* claimed that just over half of the 56 inmates to date had already reached Australia, where they had "entered into good service, acquired a good character, and have done so well ever since as to establish a strong prepossession in favor of others sent out from the same quarter" – glossing over the "heavy disappointment and great vexation" he had felt in November 1849, for example, following news from the Bishop of Adelaide that five Urania Cottage alumni had

---

[88] In this regard Urania Cottage, which was entirely funded by Burdett-Coutts, diverged from the more well-known model of the Magdalene house. As a charitable organization that rarely raised enough money from donations to sustain its operations, the factory-like labor undertaken by inmates of a Magdalene house (generally sewing or laundry) was required to fund the institution. Linda Mahood, *The Magdalenes: Prostitution in the Nineteenth Century* (London: Routledge, 1990), 87–94.

[89] Ibid., 98; Dickens, *Letters of Charles Dickens*, 6.136.   [90] Moore, *Dickens and Empire*, 8–9.

"returned to their old courses & [were] totally unfit to be recommended as household servants" even before they disembarked in the colony.[91] Despite such setbacks, Dickens's translation of the Mark System from Australia to London allowed him not only to imagine character formation in a manner that aligned with political economy, but also to begin to envisage a self-governing British subject equally suited to liberal metropolitan society and the settler colonial frontier.

The Bildungsroman, the Mark System, and Metropolitan Character: *Great Expectations*

Each inmate of Urania Cottage was encompassed by narrative. On the one hand, the accumulation of marks related the story of her developing character in actuarial form; on the other, her detailed case history was also recorded, providing an "extraordinary and mysterious study ... interesting and touching in the extreme."[92] As Dickens wrote to Burdett-Coutts,

> I have provided a form of book, in which we shall keep the history of each case, and which has certain printed enquiries to be filled up by us, before each comes in, and a final blank headed its "Subsequent History," which will remain to be filled up, by degrees, as we shall hear of them, and from them, abroad.[93]

In one of the few critical discussions of the literary afterlife of the Home for Homeless Women, Jenny Hartley observes that these stories were "clearly a valuable resource for Dickens, a source of plots and narrative," and argues that its direct influence can be seen in his treatment of fallen women in a number of novels from that period.[94] The period of Urania Cottage was also bracketed by Dickens's two bildungsromans, *David Copperfield* (1850) and *Great Expectations* (1860–61), and I suggest that the formal contrasts between them can also be illuminated by that experiment in subject formation. One of these contrasts centers on the imperial scope of each character system. In the earlier text, it is only minor characters who seek a new beginning in the colonies, while David ultimately marries and establishes his career in London, but in the later novel it is Pip who emigrates, seeking to restore his financial and social standing, and to heal his damaged heart. A second difference is more psychological in nature. Martin Meisel's

---

[91] Dickens, "Home for Homeless Women," 169; Dickens, *Letters of Charles Dickens*, 5.637.

[92] Dickens, *Letters of Charles Dickens*, 5.178.   [93] Ibid., 5.186.

[94] Jenny Hartley, "Undertexts and Intertexts: The Women of Urania Cottage, Secrets and *Little Dorrit*," *Critical Survey* 17, no. 2 (2005): 65.

description of *Great Expectations* as a "Copperfield of the inner man" also highlights the greater interest of the later novel in probing its protagonist's interior constitution.[95] This simultaneous turn outward to the empire, and inward into Pip's character, represents perhaps the most obvious feature of the broader rethinking in *Great Expectations* of metropolitan subjectivity in light of the new perspectives offered by the Mark System. Tracing the linkages in the novel between acculturation and global movement, in relation both to Pip and Magwitch, puts in a new light a narrative that begins by highlighting the deleterious effects on character produced by centralized surveillance, before opening onto the kind of disciplines associated with the Mark System that appear able to produce a self-governing, reliably portable form of character.

Great Expectations begins early in the century, and this setting clarifies the sense that a pre-Victorian logic of character formation informs the panoply of malformed individuals and damaged social relations that dominate its first two volumes.[96] These accord with what might be termed a Benthamite understanding of social organization: an expectation that character is produced by surveillance and guaranteed by proximity. Pip's "first most vivid and broad impression of the identity of things" originates in his encounter on the Thames marshes with the escaped convict Magwitch, and their doubling in the novel is commonly remarked.[97] I wish to suggest that their respective qualities of pliability and recalcitrance are presented as mutually constitutive problems of character that prove equally threatening to personal selfhood and broader society. Most spectacularly, Magwitch's initial appearance as a figure of undefined yet seemingly limitless menace both leads to and is exacerbated by his transportation to Australia, which removes him from the social body. In associating his potential for violence, his unlocatability, and the unpredictability of his actions, the Gothicized portrayal of this "fearful man" (4) accords with Bentham's dismissal of the penal colony's reformatory potential due to its sheer distance: "Colonizing-transportation-system: characteristic feature of it, radical incapacity of being combined with any efficient system of inspection." Pip's childhood, however, is characterized by just such an "efficient system." He lives in a condition of constant observation, overseen by the domineering sister who raises him "by hand," as well as by her

---

[95] Martin Meisel, "Miss Havisham Brought to Book," *PMLA* 81, no. 3 (1966): 278.

[96] Jerome Meckier dates the beginning of the novel to 1812, in "Dating the Action in *Great Expectations*: A New Chronology," *Dickens Studies Annual* 21 (1992): 158.

[97] Charles Dickens, *Great Expectations*, ed. Charlotte Mitchell (London: Penguin, 1996), 4. Hereafter cited in text.

equally suspicious relatives and acquaintances (7). Constantly under their critical gaze, he also feels under constant accusation of criminal intent: "Even when I was taken to have a new suit of clothes, the tailor had orders to make them like a kind of Reformatory, and on no account to let me have the free use of my limbs" (23). This environment of carceral inspection notably fails to produce a self-governing subject, but instead divides his inner sentiments from his outer behavior and as a result brings about a kind of moral paralysis. This divided nature is evident from the outset, as Pip unhappily recalls, in his concealment of his assistance to Magwitch: "In a word, I was too cowardly to do what I knew to be right, as I had been too cowardly to avoid doing what I knew to be wrong" (41). Thus *Great Expectations* proceeds from the position that geographic distance and psychological interiority are equally problematic for a Benthamite understanding of character. For the novel to produce any "final resolution through an alignment between Pip and an English identity," it first needs to articulate an alternative understanding of how such an identity might be formed.[98]

As Pip leaves behind his working-class origins and expectations, first through the patronage of Miss Havisham and then as a result of his anonymous benefactor's largesse, he moves through further domestic spaces – Satis House, Little Britain – that continue to "bring out the worst" in him. That is to say that they notably fail to stabilize his improvident qualities, both financial and emotional, which stand in direct opposition to the developmental expectations of the bildungsroman. "What could I become with these surroundings?" Pip reflects on his time at Satis House: "How could my character fail to be influenced by them?" (96). In the midst of an environment that Susan Walsh describes as "economically barren," Pip becomes trapped in melancholy even as his social aspirations begin to rise.[99] This antidevelopmental state is exacerbated when Pip comes under the guardianship of Jaggers, the London criminal attorney who lives in close proximity to Newgate Prison and has essentially built a career around practices of surveillance. All who come within the orbit of Jaggers' home display violently fractured public and private selves: Wemmick's unflinching business persona contrasts sharply with his quasibucolic home life at Walworth; Molly, a former client accused of murder, is now a "wild beast tamed" under Jaggers's unflinching eye (202). The most

---

[98] Esty, *Unseasonable Youth*, 52.
[99] Susan Walsh, "Bodies of Capital: *Great Expectations* and the Climacteric Economy," *Victorian Studies* 37, no. 1 (1993): 60.

prominent figure within Jaggers's purview is Pip, and the continuing intensification of his internal contradictions and weaknesses further brings into focus the inability of culture – of bildung – to stabilize character within a framework of Benthamite principles. Having entered upon his great expectations Pip is not "designed for any profession," but he nevertheless commences a project of acculturation that will enable him to "'hold [his] own' with the average of young men in prosperous circumstances" (197). Even as his studies proceed, however, he becomes increasingly profligate and ungrateful for those who love him most. The coincidence of his accumulating debts and his expanding learning makes clear that the kind of acculturation able to be pursued under the auspices of Little Britain proves inadequate either for the tasks of unifying the public and private dimensions of character, or for making that character into a "self-governing," responsible citizen.

By the end of the second volume, Pip has notably failed to display the kind of social maturation expected of the bildungsroman. He instead displays the effects of a regime that, in Maconochie's terms, "weakens the springs of independent action, [and] makes at best only eye-servants." At this point, the novel effectively turns from Bentham to Maconochie, as it takes up the dual challenge of rethinking metropolitan character and reimagining the status and value of British subjects beyond the borders of the nation. Its improvident, unstable metropolitan protagonist desires the qualities that Maconochie had previously outlined as the goal of convict reformation, namely, "a limited amount of free agency, controuled [*sic*] and guided by moral impulse … and unfettered by direct present threat, or violence." At first glance, it might appear paradoxical that this new logic of character formation is inaugurated by Magwitch's ominous return, but I wish to suggest that the convict's renewed presence can productively be read not in the more literal (and anachronistic) terms of anxiety about returning convicts, but as signaling a turn to the colonial thinking associated with Maconochie. Upon their reunion, Pip is undoubtedly horrified by the thought of his filiation with the convict:

> [H]e … would stand before the fire surveying me with the air of an Exhibitor…. The imaginary student pursued by the misshapen creature he had impiously made, was not more wretched than I, pursued by the creature who had made me, and recoiling from him with a stronger repulsion, the more he admired me and the fonder he was of me. (339)

Yet while the reference to *Frankenstein* most directly implies the role of Magwitch's money in shaping Pip's social standing, it also suggests that

Pip's character might now be understood in what are essentially Australian terms. If Pip at this point is haunted by the sense that Magwitch's convict stain can never be concealed, within a few chapters he nevertheless appears to him "softened – indefinably, for I could not have said how, and could never afterwards recal [sic] how when I tried; but certainly" (377). Magwitch's restoration as a subject of sympathy is accompanied by his adoption of the name "Provis," which invokes the Latin for foresight or forethought. More directly, however, Dickens took the name from a governess working in the house of the Bishop of Adelaide, where emigrant women from Urania Cottage were first received upon their arrival in Australia.[100]

The transformations of Magwitch and Pip are precipitated by a single, seemingly insignificant act – the convict's recounting of the story of his miserable childhood. This biographical account, "put at once into a mouthful of English," as Magwitch describes it, mirrors the confessional practice that marked the inmate's entry into Urania Cottage (346). There, as Dickens explained in *Household Words*, "The history of every inmate, taken down from her own mouth ... is preserved in a book"; indeed, to enter the Home was, in his words, to be "booked."[101] Magwitch's story catalyzes Pip's confession of his own history to Miss Havisham and Estella, which marks the beginnings of his own reformation and development. The relation of his experiences and emotional life with them culminates in the declaration of his avowedly hopeless love for Estella – "The rhapsody welled up within me," Pip recalls, "like blood from an inward wound, and gushed out" (365) – so that his public speech for the first time accurately reflects his inner feelings. This confession immediately precipitates a display of newfound character qualities: Pip selflessly attempts to secure Herbert's partnership at Clarriker and Co., and begins to act with financial restraint for the first time by resolving to live within his means and not take any more of the convict's money. Moreover, this new form of character proves capable of reshaping and restoring the fraught network of Benthamite social relations centered on Little Britain. On the one hand, Pip's new mode of understanding proves superior even to Jaggers' own insight in solving the mystery of Estella's parentage; on the other hand, he alone is able to transcend the strict divide between public and private selves, with his appeal to Wemmick's "pleasant home" causing Jaggers to lapse, uncharacteristically, "into something like a smile"

---

[100] Hartley, *Charles Dickens*, 226.
[101] Dickens, "Home for Homeless Women," 170; Dickens, *Letters of Charles Dickens*, 5.504.

(412). That is to say that Dickens presents this new model of character formation as capable of reshaping metropolitan society, both in individual terms (honesty, self-discipline) and on a societal level (the reclamation of lost history). Nevertheless, the novel's work of personal development remains incomplete at this point. Pip is dramatically unsettled by news of Herbert's impending departure for the East – "as if my last anchor were loosening its hold, and I should soon be driving with the winds and waves" (416) – demonstrating his continued psychological vulnerability to changing circumstances.

According to the path charted by *David Copperfield*, the culmination of a metropolitan-centered process of acculturation should lead Pip inevitably to a stabilizing marriage. Indeed, following the death of Magwitch, Pip duly sets off to propose to the patient, dutiful, and thoroughly domesticated Biddy, in full expectation of "the change for the better that would come over my character" (477). Yet the novel is now operating according to a different social vision: this plan proves a catastrophic failure, and instead it is in another type of house altogether, and in a colonial location moreover – the Egypt branch of the merchants, Clarriker and Co. – that Pip is able to complete his apprenticeship in self-governance. That is, the ultimate stabilization of his character not only proceeds according to the twinned financial and psychological trajectories that Maconochie codified in the Mark System, but its success is also proved by the kind of imperial mobility that Dickens envisaged through Urania Cottage:

> Within a month I had quitted England, and within two months I was clerk to Clarriker and Co., and within four months I assumed my first undivided responsibility....
>
> Many a year went round, before I was a partner in the House; but, I lived happily with Herbert and his wife, and lived frugally, and paid my debts.... We were not in a grand way of business, but we had a good name, and worked for our profits, and did very well. (480)

If the compression of these events seems primarily driven by a desire to conclude the narrative, the encompassing of 11 years with so little drama also testifies to Pip's new ability to defer immediate pleasure for the sake of future financial rewards, and to a restoration of wider social bonds that accompanies this. If Pip's restorative time abroad offers a fleeting gesture toward the colonial origins of the Mark System, it also signals a geographic expansion of the ability to imagine a stable form of British character – especially in contrast to the pre-Victorian values that rendered Magwitch a Gothicized outcast. Yet whereas Maconochie had intended his reformed convicts to remain in Australia, only for Dickens's Urania Cottage scheme to further broaden this vision by enabling fallen women to leave Britain for a new life in the colonies, it is *Great Expectations* that ultimately envisages a normative British subject with sufficient character strength to move with freedom between the metropole and the imperial periphery.

Metropolitan Forms and the Networks of Empire

The fact that Pip's colonial profiteering proves more acceptable in the novel than the fruits of Magwitch's antipodean labors attests to the manner in which this newly delocalized understanding of British character might serve an expanding empire. Lesjak has noted that *Great Expectations* conveys the sense of an imperial economy increasingly blurring the distinction between Britain and its colonies:

> The notion of an "outside" to the system, or of margins opposed to centers, collapses as all spaces become equally rife for the market. This does not mean, of course, that the inequalities between margin and center disappear; rather the desire to maintain strict boundaries between them, or, more accurately, to keep those existing on the margins or in the periphery at (Botany) bay, becomes increasingly impossible as "peripheral" spaces and populations become central to Britain's development.[102]

Jonathan H. Grossman similarly argues that, by mapping the vectors of that globalizing system, the novel shows how developing nineteenth-century transport networks "made the unknown, simultaneous activity of ordinary people elsewhere synchronically consequential."[103] The offshore extension of what Benedict Anderson influentially described as the "homogeneous, empty time" of the nation depended, I suggest, not only on the physical infrastructure of transport networks, or the financial imperatives of trade and extraction, but also on the idea that British subjectivity could remain intact and legible – "consequential" – across vast distances. Dickens's acquaintance with Maconochie, and adaptation of his ideas in the Urania Cottage experiment, provided him with the conceptual tools to reimagine Britain's relationship with its empire in such terms. In this light, there is an unintended irony in Said's observation, regarding Pip's presence in Egypt, that such a colonial space "offer[s] a sort of normality that Australia never could." After all, the ability for Egypt to function as a space where Pip can

---

[102] Lesjak, *Working Fictions*, 110.
[103] Jonathan H. Grossman, "Living the Global Transport Network in *Great Expectations*," *Victorian Studies* 57, no. 2 (2015): 226.

work to restore his character originates in Maconochie's attempt to establish a "sort of normality" in the penal colonies of Australia, by way of Dickens's own attempt with Urania Cottage to establish such "normality" in the heart of Victorian Britain.

The series of material, ideological, and formal intersections that I have traced between Britain and the Australian colonies from the 1830s through the 1860s – spanning Wakefield and the theory of systematic colonization, Maconochie and the Mark System of convict discipline, and Dickens and the bildungsroman – attest to the extensive yet underacknowledged interpenetration of these two spaces. Specifically, these encounters suggest that the idea of the liberal subject's geographic mobility took on particular importance in light of the enthusiasm for Antipodean settlement – first sparked by Wakefield's colonizing schemes, and further inflamed by the discovery of Australian gold in the 1850s – because it offered a means by which Britain's imperial expansion might be made coterminous with the extension of Victorian capitalism. Nevertheless, Pip's enduring, melancholic fixation on Estella might seem to suggest that the affective dimensions of Victorian character remained firmly bounded by the nation at mid-century. Even though Pip's globetrotting in the service of Clarriker's restores his name and restructures his life, his refusal to marry demonstrates the lack of an equivalent degree of sentimental delocalization. "You have always held your place in my heart," he confesses to Estella (484). The mobility of sentiment instead plays out with the novel at a more material level: Dickens never visited the antipodes, although he flirted in the 1860s with the idea of a reading tour to Australia, but *Great Expectations* certainly did.[104] Tim Dolin's analysis of the colonial fortunes of the first three-volume edition – two copies of which arrived at the circulating library of the South Australian Institute, Adelaide, in October 1861 – stresses that the global circulation of the Victorian novel exacerbated a colonial double-consciousness on the periphery. "[T]he shipment of print products was largely one-way: it made one home – mid-Victorian Britain – more vitally present and real than the other, colonial Australia, which was either absent, hurried over, falsified, exoticised, or distorted."[105] This may be true, but this chapter has argued that to focus only on overt representations of coloniality is to tell only part of the story of the settler empire's role

[104] Freedgood, "Realism, Fetishism, and Genocide," 26–27. Two of Dickens's children, Alfred Tennyson and Edward Bulwer Lytton, also immigrated to Australia in the 1860s. See Mary Ellen Lazarus, *A Tale of Two Brothers: Charles Dickens's Sons in Australia* (Sydney: Angus and Robertson, 1973).

[105] Dolin, "First Steps toward a History," 277.

in the globalizing of Victorian culture. By broadening the critical horizons of Victorian studies to encompass the multiplicity of exchanges between Britain and its settler colonies, and being willing to consider their impact at the level of form as well as of content, what comes into focus is an exact reversal of Said's assessment of *Great Expectations*: what he describes as the appearance of "metropolitan space ... meticulously charted, spoken for, [and] inhabited by a hierarchy of metropolitan personages" proves to a significant extent to be a product of colonial thinking.

CHAPTER 2

Gold and Greater Britain
The Australian Gold Rushes, Unsettled Desire, and the Global British Subject

Our real state of nature consists not in the repression, but in the full development and satisfaction, of all those faculties of which our nature consists. Such a state is found, not in the poverty of the naked savage; but in the wealth of the civilized man.... Desires extend themselves with the means of gratification; the horizon is enlarged in proportion as we advance.

W. E. Hearn, *Plutology: Or the Theory of the Efforts to Satisfy Human Wants*

I am the least settled man in all the world.

Anthony Trollope, *John Caldigate*

The collapse of the stadial models underpinning the early Victorian novel and political economy began unobtrusively, in Australia, on February 12, 1851. On that day, Edward Hargraves – resident in Australia since 1832, and recently returned from the scene of the California gold rushes – discovered five specks of gold in Lewis Ponds Creek, New South Wales. Hargraves soon returned to Sydney, where he claimed a government reward for the first discovery of a payable goldfield; he also announced the location of his discovery in the local press, naming the region Ophir, and thus triggered the first Australian gold rush. An article published later that year in *Household Words* described how a prominent colonial newspaper, the *Sydney Morning Herald*, was transformed by this event "in a day" from its former "dull commercial routine" to an unswerving focus on "a single dazzling theme – changed from a leaden to a golden newspaper," with the writers finding in the colonial press "a distinctive and suggestive sign of the times in Australia."[1] Many more sensational discoveries would follow in the next year, both in New South Wales and the neighboring colony of Victoria – Clunes, Turon, Mount Alexander, Forest Creek, Ballarat, Bendigo – and as migrants began to pour into Australia from Britain, so

---

[1] J. Keene and W. H. Wills, "A Golden Newspaper," *Household Words* 4, no. 87 (1851): 208.

vast amounts of bullion began to flow in the opposite direction. Hence the
Times could report late in 1852:

> Yesterday three vessels arrived in the River Thames from Australia with the
> extraordinary quantity of upwards of seven tons of gold on board. One of
> the ships, the Eagle, was freighted with the largest amount of the precious
> metal ever known to arrive in one vessel, viz., 150,000 ounces (upwards of
> six tons), and of the value of more than 600,000*l*.... Great, however, as has
> been the wealth brought over by the Eagle, the ship Dido is expected in a
> few days, which will far surpass it, having on board 280,000 ounces, or
> about ten tons and a half of the precious metal.[2]

Between 1852 and 1861, the colony of Victoria alone received almost
300,000 emigrants from Britain; during that time, more than 28,500,000
ounces of gold were extracted from the continent as a whole; due to the
resulting economic boom, Australasia as a whole would absorb more than
30 percent of all British exports in the middle years of the decade.[3] Given
the scale of these events, they provide an exemplary test case for seeking
out what Dror Wahrman terms, skeptically, the hitherto invisible settler
"veins and sinews" of Victorian culture.[4] After all, of the three imperial
events that shook Britain in the 1850s – the Indian Rebellion, the Crimea
campaign, and the Australian gold rushes – the sensational discoveries at
the antipodes stand out, paradoxically, for their seemingly negligible
impact on Victorian literary culture. At the time, observers of popular
fiction could point to the "large ... Australian element ... gradually
working itself into our current literature," but in this chapter I argue that
the most wide-reaching impact of the gold rushes on Victorian culture was
not a brief flourishing of discussion about Australia.[5] Instead, events at the
antipodes played out in Victorian thinking through a network of mobile
writers – most notably Anthony Trollope and W. S. Jevons – who
registered their colonial experiences as challenges to the liberal narrative
of labor and land that underpinned early Victorian concepts of individual
character and societal development. Such concerns with British society and
identity, as well as the forms of political economy and the novel through
which they were articulated, came in the middle of the century to comprise

---

[2] "Seven Tons of Australian Gold," *The Times*, November 24, 1852, 7.
[3] Cain, "Economics and Empire," 35; Geoffrey Serle, *Golden Age: A History of the Colony of Victoria,
1851–1861* (Carlton: Melbourne University Press, 1977), 383, 390.
[4] Wahrman, "Meaning of the Nineteenth Century," 99.
[5] Frank Fowler, *Southern Lights and Shadows: Being Brief Notes of Three Years' Experience of Social,
Literary, and Political Life in Australia* (London: Sampson Low, 1859), 1.

the debatable common property of what C. W. Dilke influentially termed "Greater Britain."

The lack of critical discussion about the cultural impact of the gold rushes derives in part from the fact that, as a subject, they had a markedly uneven presence in metropolitan writing during the 1850s. In the period-ical press, Australia's gold and the ensuing tide of emigration it generated were regular subjects of discussion. Returning to *Household Words*, for example, George Augustus Sala's lead article in an issue from 1852 begins with a bravura sentence that spans the entire first column in an attempt to convey the scale of the recent population movements triggered by events in Australia:

> If I had not been in London within the last month, and seen the wondrous tide of emigration setting out from the Docks there; ... if I had not passed through the port of Southampton lately, and gazed upon the Hampshire folk singing loud emigratory pœans, and departing by whole tribes for the Diggings, with cradle, mattock, and spade; ... if I did not know that Plymouth, and Bristol, and Cork, yea, and the American seaboard far away (wheels within wheels) had each their exodus; ... if I did not know that ... wherever there were hearts to feel and tongues to express the fierce, raging lust for gold, the cry was, "Off, off, and away!" – if I did not know this, I say, I should be tempted to think that from Liverpool alone the great army of voluntary exiles was setting forth ... for, verily, all Liverpool seems to be off.[6]

In contrast to such energetic descriptions, gold and migration were not depicted directly or even acknowledged in the realist novel, but were confined to more popular genres such as Charles Reade's "Matter-of-Fact Romance," *It Is Never Too Late to Mend* (1856), or Mary Elizabeth Braddon's sensation novel, *Lady Audley's Secret* (1862). In both novels, the Australian subplot centers on the discovery of a freakishly large gold "nugget" (a word first used in this sense in Australia): in Reade, a "hundredweight of quartz and gold and beautiful as it was great"; in Braddon, a "monster nugget ... and ... a gold deposit of some magni-tude."[7] Such sensational scenes of fortune and fortuitousness, let alone the "raging lust" that produced them, could be taken to indicate that the gold rushes were unable to be comprehended by realist narrative. After all, their uncouth colonial settings and the sheer improbability of striking it lucky

---

[6] George Augustus Sala, "Cheerily, Cheerily!," *Household Words* 6, no. 131 (1853): 25.

[7] Charles Reade, *"It Is Never Too Late to Mend": A Matter-of-Fact Romance*, 2nd ed., 3 vols. (London: Bentley, 1856), 3.198; Mary Elizabeth Braddon, *Lady Audley's Secret*, ed. David Skilton (Oxford: Oxford University Press, 1987), 22.

clearly violate Scott's association of "civilized" narrative with plots that obey the "bounds of probability or consistency." "Don't be a fool," blurts one of Reade's characters, when another first hazards a guess at the possible size of their discovery, "there is no such thing in Nature."[8] Yet to focus on such spectacular scenes is to be distracted from the broader challenge that the gold rushes posed to the project of settlement and the narrative forms that gave it shape. The early Victorian revival of settler colonialism had been predicated on the basis that new, settled British societies could be reliably built upon the application of familiar Lockean and stadialist principles, which guaranteed that culture and capitalism could only be established upon a foundation of sedentary agricultural labor. Yet if character came from developing land with labor, as Locke had taught economists and novelists to assume, what happened to a society whose wealth came at random from holes in the ground?

"If Australia should ever become a great nation," the poet and prospector R. H. Horne could write only a few years after that first gold discovery, "we, the pick-and-shovel men, have dug out that nationality."[9] The simplicity of this equation between the labor of resource extraction and the formation of national identity belies the scale of the formal accommodations that Australia's gold-fueled boom demanded of the economic and literary principles informing the ideal of the settled society. In a moment of vatic flight at the beginning of the Australian section of *It Is Never Too Late to Mend*, Reade's omniscient narrator asserts that the transformations set in motion by the gold discoveries, spanning developmental time and imperial space, are a subject fit for "great epic":

> In the sudden return of a society far more complex[,] artificial and conventional than Pericles ever dreamed of to elements more primitive than Homer had to deal with; ...
>
> In the old barbaric force and native colour of the passions as they burst out undisguised around the gold,
>
> ...
>
> In the world wide effect of the discovery, the peopling of the earth at last according to heaven's long published and resisted design,
>
> Fate offered poetry a theme broad and high yet piquant and various as the dolphin and the rainbow.[10]

---

[8] Reade, *"It Is Never Too Late to Mend,"* 3.198.
[9] R. H. Horne, *Australian Facts and Prospects: To Which Is Prefixed the Author's Australian Autobiography* (London: Smith, Elder, 1859), 126.
[10] Ibid., 3.39–40.

The gold rushes meshed Britain and Australia together in an unprecedented fashion – through vast and sustained flows of emigrants, commodities, and bullion – yet Reade's enthusiasm begins to suggest how the distant view of these events afforded from Britain might at first have given the impression they were merely an acceleration of existing processes of British expansion through colonization. Closer proximity revealed a more troubling antithesis at work, between the primitive, nomadic behavior of British gold diggers and the explosive growth of the colonies' modern cities and consumer economies.[11] In particular, the formal challenges registered in the novel and political economy as a result of the gold rushes arose out of a distinct imperial "web" that emerged in the 1850s – a flow of "cultural traffic" arising from "institutions and structures [that] connected disparate points in space into a complex mesh of networks" – spanning the various goldfields, the quintessential boomtown of Melbourne and other urban centers in the affected colonies, and also distant Britain.[12] Moreover, that imperial web was unique for the extent to which it also set in motion a number of British writers, artists, and intellectuals. Whether Alfred Tennyson really "would have gone to Australia but for Mrs Tennyson," other literary figures who did reach the goldfields included the literary Jack-of-all-trades William Howitt, poet Richard Henry Horne, and novelist Henry Kingsley; perhaps the most iconic image of Victorian emigration, Ford Madox Brown's *The Last of England* (1855), was painted in response to the departure of Pre-Raphaelite sculptor Thomas Woolner; and political economists W. E. Hearn and W. S. Jevons were also drawn south by gold-related jobs.[13] At a textual level, economic historian Craufurd

---

[11] While the Australian gold rushes were directly preceded by similarly epochal discoveries in California, and there was considerable movement between the two frontiers, here I argue that the later discoveries had a distinct intellectual impact on Victorian culture because they occurred within the ambit of empire: "Suddenly, Britain had her own Eldorado. British colonies would now feel the golden spur of economic development; gold-seeking British emigrants could now travel to a British destination; the proceeds of the prospectors and miners would now flow directly into the imperial economy." Or, as the *Illustrated London News* reported on its front page, "If the Australians have not been playing a scurvy trick upon us, we have matched Brother Jonathan's auriferous region by discovering gold in Australia, as plentiful as it is beyond the Rocky Mountains." Robert A. Stafford, "Preventing the 'Curse of California': Advice for English Emigrants to the Australian Goldfields," *Historical Records of Australian Science* 7, no. 3 (1988): 216. "Another 'El Dorado,'" *The Illustrated London News* 19, no. 514 (1851): 273. For comparative accounts of Californian and Australian gold rushes, see Belich, *Replenishing the Earth*, 306–30; David Goodman, *Gold Seeking: Victoria and California in the 1850s* (St. Leonards: Allen & Unwin, 1994).

[12] Tony Ballantyne, "Race and the Webs of Empire," in *Webs of Empire: Locating New Zealand's Colonial Past* (Wellington: Bridget Williams Books, 2012), 44.

[13] Geoffrey Blainey, *The Rush That Never Ended: A History of Australian Mining*, 2nd ed. (Melbourne: Melbourne University Press, 1969), 37–38.

D. Goodwin describes how "recent travelers and old colonists alike issued a stream of publications which ranged from sensationalist pamphlets to detailed historical and statistical compilations prepared with colonial government sponsorship."[14] Nevertheless, the question remains whether Australia's gold rushes left any deeper mark on Victorian culture beyond the introduction into popular fiction of the new plot device of fortuitous enrichment through gold prospecting.

Operating alongside and in conjunction with vast movements of population and transfers of capital, the textual dimension of the Victorian settler empire in the era of the gold rushes is characterized by formal complexities arising from the intersecting and clashing of metropolitan and colonial concerns across discontinuous imperial spaces. This complexity can be readily glimpsed in the structure and concerns of the decade's "most influential single work" on the gold rushes, Howitt's travel narrative, *Land, Labour and Gold; or, Two Years in Victoria* (1855).[15] Howitt was established as a poet, journalist, and editor before he traveled to Melbourne in 1852, and his preface asserts a confident sense of the geographic and political distance between his British readership and his Australian subject matter: feeling a "great national duty" to recount the social and political consequences of the gold rushes, he nevertheless claims to have "no interest in the questions involved, – except such as are the interests of every British subject, – and no purpose to serve but a patriotic one."[16] This claim of an aloof metropolitan narrative perspective is, however, undermined from the start by the work's epistolary form, through which Howitt recounts his peripatetic and persistent search for colonial gold; even before he and his shipmates disembark in Melbourne, "Every soul is brimful of anxiety to learn what is the news about the Gold Fields" (1.4). The unfolding narrative also testifies to the inseparability of literary and economic domains in Australia. On the one hand, Howitt's primary category for assessing the suitability of the colony and the aptitude of its colonists is the picturesque, "the Englishman converting the wild forests of the most distant regions of the earth into homes of beauty and taste, and making them, as it were, a portion of the mother country" (1.34). On the other hand, Howitt's chosen title implies a different scale for measuring colonial quality, directly invoking the three factors of production – land, labor, and capital – that underpin classical political economy. Such worldwide

---

[14] Craufurd D. Goodwin, "British Economists and Australian Gold," *The Journal of Economic History* 30, no. 2 (1970): 406.
[15] Ibid.   [16] Howitt, *Land, Labour, and Gold,* 1.vii. Hereafter cited in text.

entanglements of form, materiality, and geography in works such as Howitt's affirm the most basic effect that the expanding settler empire had upon Victorian literary forms, which was for the economic, societal, and cultural questions at stake to bring to the fore the spatio-temporal underpinnings of genre. Subject to the additional pressures of hundreds of thousands of British migrants and millions of ounces of gold, the Victorian cultural forms explored in this chapter were extended beyond the borders of Britain to the antipodean limits of the empire, and in the process came to be characterized by an ongoing traffic between metropolitan cultural formations and the material conditions of the Australian discoveries.

What writers such as Howitt witnessed or even participated in was an event that dramatically challenged the pastoral narrative of Australasian colonization, and – more importantly – its underlying stadialist claim that capitalism and culture are equally grounded in a settled population. Textual responses to the gold rushes consistently foreground an apparent contradiction between the unsettled nature of gold mining and the undoubted spur it provided to the process of settler colonization, which they recur to by way of two thematic preoccupations: the nomadic and speculative figure of the gold prospector or "digger," and the explosive growth of urban settlement. The alluvial deposits that triggered the initial gold rushes were readily accessible to individual prospectors, who formed a "subculture of wandering men," and whose chances of success appeared to observers to depend less on steady labor over time than on random luck that resembled nothing so much as a form of gambling.[17] Furthermore, as Figure 2.1 suggests, in light of the developmental assumptions of stadialist theory and the expansion of pastoralism that had driven colonial economic growth over the previous decades, the forms of prospecting and digging associated with the early gold rushes seemed to belong to a premodern, precapitalist state outside any progressive sequence.[18] "Men had left their homes and families, and all the comforts and constraints of civilisation, for a wild life of wandering and seeking," David Goodman observes in his history of the Australian and Californian rushes: "It was difficult ... not to think of the activity of gold seeking as regressive, a return to an earlier, less

[17] Belich, *Replenishing the Earth*, 324.
[18] The alluvial deposits that triggered the initial gold rushes were readily located by individual prospectors and were accessible to diggers with minimal equipment – requiring "neither skill nor capital, but only strength and health" – in contrast to the more organized and capital-intensive mining operations that would later be required to exploit less-accessible forms of ore. Stafford, "Preventing the 'Curse of California,'" 224.

Figure 2.1   Edwin Stocqueler's painting illustrates the basic and haphazard nature of
life on the goldfields. The diggers' total focus on their labors is reflective of the
powerful desires that have removed them from the norms of settled society.

disciplined, and more primitive era."[19] In contrast to the pastoral model of
settled labor, the "uncertain, fluctuating, transient nature" of gold digging
generated a paradoxical understanding of the prospector as simultaneously
premodern, in his nomadic movements and squalid living conditions, and

---

[19] Goodman, *Gold Seeking*, xvii. As Goodman's observation suggests, and as the following analysis will
demonstrate, the gold rushes presented observers with a forceful expression of the tension that
Christopher Herbert has influentially described, "powerful and, in nineteenth-century Britain,
seemingly almost ubiquitous," between emergent ideas of culture and the "myth of a state of
ungoverned individual desire." The argument that follows deviates from Herbert's account in two
crucial ways: in focusing on events from the 1850s onward, it finds an anticipation of developments
in metropolitan ideas of the "culture concept" that are otherwise attributed to the "unravelling of
orthodox moral ideas which took place in and about the depression-stricken eighteen-seventies";
and in focusing on the seemingly unbounded desires of British subjects, it argues that observers
were forced to confront directly ideas of character and culture that were otherwise typically
displaced onto "that mythological creature or rhetorical figment who ... long dominated
Victorian cultural discourse, the passionate, uncontrollable savage." Christopher Herbert, *Culture
and Anomie: Ethnographic Imagination in the Nineteenth Century* (Chicago: University of Chicago
Press, 1991), 29, 65, 145.

Figure 2.2 A sketch of Melbourne in 1854 captures the rapid and vast extent of its growth under the impetus of the gold rushes. A solitary farmhouse in the foreground offers a reminder that stadialist expectations of colonial development have been completely sidelined.

ultramodern in his "fore-shortened, exaggerated experience of life ruled by somewhat serendipitous market forces."[20] Yet despite the seemingly anti-social propensities of these nomadic Anglo-Saxons, it was equally apparent to contemporary observers that their labors were dramatically accelerating the pace of colonization. In a dizzying contrary motion, that is, the goldfields scenes that Reade described (albeit at second hand) as comprising "elements more primitive than Homer had to deal with" were paralleled by the rapid emergence of towns and cities. The colony of Victoria exploded from 77,000 settlers in 1851 to 538,000 in 1861, eclipsing California in the process.[21] Henry Kingsley's invocation of "Marvellous Melbourne" – the emblem of settlement based upon gold – in his novel *The Recollections of Geoffry Hamlyn* (1859) is typical in its account of civilization's explosive emergence from the state of nature. What was two decades ago "the unbroken solitude of a primeval forest, as yet unseen by the eye of a white man" has become "a noble city, with crowded wharves, containing with its suburbs no less than 120,000 inhabitants."[22] Figure 2.2 captures something of the problematic nature of this transformation, for Melbourne's rapid growth short-circuited or even invalidated the stadial link between modernity and settlement, yet was too large and dramatic to simply be ignored. As such, the gold rushes posed a colonial problem of narrative form that played out in works by novelists and political economists seeking to account for such growth and what it might have to say about the nature of British subjectivity and society.

In this chapter, I trace the formal disruptions to the novel and political economy that were prompted by the gold rushes, first in Australia and subsequently in Britain, as writers grappled with newly emergent ideas about character and nation that took shape at the colonial interface between primitive accumulation and settled society. Because of its investments in the establishment of character and culture, colonial realism constituted ground zero for the conceptual challenge that the gold rushes posed to those early Victorian orthodoxies. Staged most explicitly in Catherine Helen Spence's *Clara Morison: A Tale of South Australia during the Gold Fever* (1854), the discoveries were figured initially as a clear yet manageable threat to social order and literary culture. In subsequent accounts of gold rush subjectivity and society, however, a more thoroughgoing challenge to

[20] Goodman, *Gold Seeking*, 113, 114.
[21] Belich, *Replenishing the Earth*, 307; Geoffrey Blainey, *A History of Victoria*, 3rd. ed. (Melbourne: Cambridge University Press, 2006), 48.
[22] Henry Kingsley, *The Recollections of Geoffry Hamlyn*, ed. Paul Eggert, J. S. D. Mellick, and Patrick Morgan (St. Lucia: University of Queensland Press, 1996), 281.

stadialist norms begins to emerge. In Howitt's *Land, Labour and Gold* (1855), the collapse of stadialist logic is foregrounded through the unsustainability of the opposition between the picturesque landscapes of successful settlement and the nomadic and antisocial behaviors of the diggers, but the new social vision emerging in the Antipodes was first given theoretical shape by colonial political economy. W. E. Hearn's *Plutology: Or, the Theory of the Efforts to Satisfy Human Wants* (1864), written in the gold colony of Victoria, proposed radically reorienting political economy away from production and toward a subject driven by "varied and insatiable desires," in keeping with the ethos of the unsettled society out of which it emerged.[23] From here, I follow the dissemination of these emergent ideas about character and nation into ostensibly metropolitan writing informed by significant encounters with Australian gold. W. S. Jevons's *The Theory of Political Economy* (1871) and Anthony Trollope's *John Caldigate* (1879) both offer narratives of delocalized and desiring metropolitan individuals, the former through extending Hearn's insights into a new "marginalist" conception of economic theory based on consumption rather than production, and the latter by aligning its protagonist's gentlemanly qualities with the romance-tinged scene of speculative colonial extraction. These examples demonstrate cumulatively the role of the settler empire's characteristic material and intellectual exchanges in helping catalyze developments within Victorian culture: Australia is revealed to be a waypoint in the transition to a consumer-driven model of economics, and the related reconceptualization of British identity in terms derived from the settler periphery. The settler colonial environment reveals and magnifies the global unconscious of metropolitan thought, with the gold rushes and the writing they generated helping reimagine the British subject as a more fully deterritorialized citizen of the world.

Settled Society and the Problem of the Gold Rushes: *Clara Morison*

At the beginning of the 1850s, immediately prior to the discovery of gold, the path taken by Australian colonization seemed to offer broad confirmation of the stadialist theory of societal development. This spatialized distinction between savagery and civilization had been imported wholesale into early Victorian economic and social thinking, and can be seen on full display in John Stuart Mill's essay, "Civilization" (1836):

---

[23] Hearn, *Plutology*, 21.

Whatever be the characteristics of what we call savage life, the contrary of these, or the qualities which society puts on as it throws off these, constitute civilization. Thus, a savage tribe consists of a handful of individuals, wandering or thinly scattered over a vast tract of country: a dense population, therefore dwelling in fixed habitations and largely collected together in towns and villages, we term civilized. In savage life there is no commerce, no manufactures, no agriculture, or next to none: a country rich in the fruits of agriculture, commerce, and manufactures, we call civilized.[24]

The contrast in Australia between the civilizing power of the settlers' burgeoning agricultural economy and the "savagery" of the continent's indigenous populations, deemed neither willing nor able to cultivate the land, could be held up, with a reasonable degree of confidence, as a case study of such linear developmental progress. By then, the continent was supplying almost 50 percent of Britain's wool, and pastoralism was visibly driving the spread of settlement: behind the continual expansion of the frontier by squatters, seminomadic pastoralists who dominated the wool trade, "a more *intensive* process of settlement (largely urban based) proceeded gradually in the settled districts, where 70 percent of the colonial population lived in 1850."[25] As Goodman observes, the development and expansion of agrarianism in the Australian colonies further reinforced the connection between civilization and cultivation by replicating long-standing Western traditions of virtuous rural productivity:

The colony of Victoria, in particular, was appropriated to agrarianism and [the genre of] pastoral; it was celebrated as a scene of cultivation or of grazing, a garden and a farm, in which the labour of humankind was necessary, morally as much as horticulturally, gently to tend the *almost* spontaneously fruitful soil. It was into this idyllic environment ... that the gold rush erupted.[26]

It was the sharpness of this contrast between the pastoral logic of settlement and the spontaneity of discovering mineral wealth – "the tension between Arcadia and El Dorado, the tension between the life of cultivation of the soil and that of extraction from it" – that ensured that the gold rushes were the cause of an intellectual as much as a societal crisis for colonial and metropolitan observers alike.[27]

[24] John Stuart Mill, "Civilization," in *Essays on Politics and Society*, ed. J. M. Robson, Collected Works of John Stuart Mill (Toronto: University of Toronto Press, 1977), 120.
[25] Philip McMichael, *Settlers and the Agrarian Question: Foundations of Capitalism in Colonial Australia* (Cambridge: Cambridge University Press, 1984), 101, 122.
[26] Goodman, *Gold Seeking*, 107, original emphasis.   [27] Ibid., 106.

The claim that capitalism and culture were equally grounded in a settled population, and the challenge consequently posed to it by the discovery of gold, were accordingly presented earliest, and with greatest force and clarity, in South Australia, the continent's only colony founded on Wakefield's stadialist principles of systematic colonization. This perspective was intensified further when goldfields were discovered in neighboring Victoria that could be reached on foot in three weeks, which precipitated an exodus of male settlers and a debilitating currency shortage in the colony. This calamity for the social fabric of South Australia is taken up directly in the novel regarded as the first Australian example of domestic realism, Catherine Spence's *Clara Morison: A Tale of South Australia during the Gold Fever* (1854).[28] Spence directly links settler literacy with agricultural production and pits both in opposition to the widespread antisocial behaviors prompted by the gold rushes, thus framing the latter as a threat to settled society that is equally economic and literary in nature. The "eclipse" of South Australia by Victorian gold, as the novel puts it, is focalized through the refined Clara Morison, whose "journey from governess to domestic servant to genteel wife … [is] made possible through an extended marriage plot that hinges on the hero and heroine's shared love of British literature."[29] The orphaned Clara is forced to emigrate from Edinburgh by her guardian because she is unable to sing, play the piano, or draw – "without one accomplishment that had any marketable value," as her unsentimental uncle puts it – but she is at the same time distinguished by her love and knowledge of literature:

> [S]he read aloud with exquisite taste; her memory was stored with old ballads and new poems; she understood French, and was familiar with its literature, but could not speak the language; she could write short-hand, and construe Caesar's Commentaries…. In her father's lifetime, Clara had been the general referee at home on all miscellaneous subjects. She knew what book such a thing was in, what part of the book, and almost at what page.[30]

The encyclopedic Clara is discomforted to learn that her lack of accomplishments also render her unemployable as a governess in South Australia, but her literary taste and discernment nevertheless remain central to her

[28] Pike, *Paradise of Dissent*, 442–60. Spence was born in Scotland in 1825, and her family chose to emigrate to Adelaide, South Australia, in 1839 following a disastrous speculation by her father in foreign wheat. See Susan Magarey, *Unbridling the Tongues of Women: A Biography of Catherine Helen Spence* (Sydney: Hale & Iremonger, 1985), 29–35.

[29] Janet C. Myers, "'Verily the Antipodes of Home': The Domestic Novel in the Australian Bush," *Novel: A Forum on Fiction* 35, no. 1 (2001): 117.

[30] Catherine Helen Spence, *Clara Morison: A Tale of South Australia during the Gold Fever*, 2 vols. (London: Parker, 1986), 1.2. Hereafter cited in text.

status as the novel's heroine.[31] Indeed, her significance as a bearer of culture is heightened by the contrast with the bad readers who surround her in the colony, notably the flirtatious Miss Waterstone, who "considered herself, in her own phrase, a *well-read woman*; but whatever she read she made a point of forgetting," and the formidable Miss Withering, who only reads for "information" (1.33–34, 1.123, original emphasis). Clara soon makes an impression on the refined Charles Reginald, who shares her tastes, seeking out "the newest works of Dickens, Bulwer, and Thackeray," and is proprietor of the Taringa sheep station (1.34). Thus from the outset, the marriage plot is strongly aligned with the stadialist logic that locates settled agriculture as the basis of capitalism and culture.

Clara and Reginald's relationship is, until the advent of the gold rushes, characterized by an eventlessness that is one of the aesthetic signatures of agriculture-based settlement narratives. In this staid colony, the epicenter of banality is Reginald's sheep station, a "dull place" with a "middling" climate, where he leads a "sort of vegetable life" that is closely paralleled by his taste in literature (2.210). Reginald finds Walter Scott to be "much more healthy" than Byron, especially in his portrayal of "middling" characters, and as the novel proceeds, the lovers are also required to adjust their personal horizons to a similarly "middling" level. Reginald must rid himself of his early and unwise engagement to the beautiful but "restless" Julia Marston, who has so far refused to emigrate to join her fiancé in colonial obscurity because she "like[s] nothing so well as variety" (1.48). Clara's enforced domestic servitude as she struggles to earn a living meanwhile fits her to be a more "useful" member of society, as much by expanding her sympathies as by instilling some practical aptitudes:

> [I]t is not merely the things I am learning to do, useful as they undoubtedly are, but the new thoughts and feelings which my present employments awaken, which will benefit me much. I have hitherto lived too much in books, and thought them all-important; now I see what things fill the minds of nine-tenths of my sex – daily duties, daily cares, daily sacrifices. I see now the line of demarcation which separates the employers from the employed; and if I ever, by any chance, should again have a servant under me, I shall surely understand her feelings, and be considerate and kind. (1.93)

---

[31] For a discussion of the status of reading in *Clara Morison*, see Myers, "Domestic Novel," 55–57. A South Australian Literary Association was first formed in 1834, and the South Australian Mechanics' Institute opened in 1839 for members to borrow books and hear lectures. Spence's family belonged to the Mechanics' Institute, and its library allowed her to supplement her early reading of Scott with the works of contemporary British authors. Derek Whitelock, *Adelaide: A Sense of Difference* (Kew: Arcadia, 2000), 259; Magarey, *Unbridling the Tongues of Women*, 51.

Yet while the protagonists are in the midst of these slight adjustments to their sensibilities, the social, cultural, and economic bases of their world are suddenly and spectacularly imperiled by the discovery of gold in the neighboring colony.

Immediately prior to the commencement of the gold rushes, Clara had relocated to the household of her cousins, the Elliots, and this allows *Clara Morison* to further differentiate the agricultural and auriferous modes of settler colonization in gendered terms. The Elliot brothers, George and Gilbert, and their friend Henry Martin feel they have little option but to join the mass exodus for Victoria; their departure leaves the household in possession of Margaret and Annie Elliot, as well as Clara, and consequently the gold rushes are framed from the outset as an antisocial, masculine form of nomadic adventure. As Annie Elliot recounts in a letter to a friend, the "all-engrossing gold-fever" has transmuted a settled society into a wandering state:

> The clerks out of employment, supernumerary shopmen, failing tradesmen, parasol-menders, and piano-tuners, went first; but now everyone is going, without regard to circumstances or families. Married and unmarried, people with lots of children, and people who have none, are all making up their minds and their carpet-bags for Mount Alexander. Those who are doing nothing here fancy they will do something at the diggings, and those who are doing something are sure they will do more; so that there is no security against any one's leaving dear South Australia. (1.219)

In this account, the gold rushes are figured as a Wakefieldian nightmare of population dispersal. In Adelaide, "you hear men in knots talking of going … and the words nuggets, ounces, gold-dust, cradles and diggings, are in everybody's mouth": "The chief streets are full of a most unsettled-looking population; but the outskirts of Adelaide are greatly thinned, and the villages round about are almost deserted" (1.222).[32] All is not lost for those left behind, however, as the "feminine heterotopia" that emerges in the home of Clara and the Elliot sisters "allows the denaturalisation, under the guise of social and economic necessity, of the role of colonial middle-class women in the household," as they continue to pursue their

---

[32] The novel thus reflects something of the widespread social and economic upheaval wrought by the gold rushes: "For most colonists the years of gold were years of anxiety. They were short of coin and labour, and prices rocketed. Early in 1852 meat rose from a penny a pound to eightpence; bulkier goods that depended on cartage became almost unprocurable.... Little was done to help public servants and others with fixed incomes. Some resigned, and more were sacked as the business of their departments dwindled.... In Adelaide one house in five was empty." Pike, *Paradise of Dissent*, 455–56.

accomplishments and their intellectual studies alongside the daily house-hold chores.[33] In contrast to this quasi-utopian restructuring of the scene of domestic realism, the novel turns to the romance to portray the masculine realm of the goldfields and the speculative logic that it gives rise to at the levels of character and society.

More than simply providing a metaphor for the excitement of the gold rushes, the genre of romance provides a formal means for Spence to comprehend the gold rushes as a threat to the stadialist alignment of settlement with culture and cultivation. "Now, Reginald, don't you envy me?" the stolid and stay-at-home sheep farmer is taunted by one of his friends: "There you are, tied to a parcel of sheep, and unable to pursue adventure at the mouth of a hole" (2.55). In *Clara Morison*, "adventure" encapsulates qualities of economic speculation, spatial mobility, and unsteadiness of character that are all equally antithetical to the South Australian project of pastoral settlement. One of the Elliots' male acquaint-ances asserts, as he proposes to leave his job and the colony, "Why, even if my salary were ten times what it is, I should want to see the gold fields just the same. It shows a great lack of spirit to stay quietly boxed up in an office, when all the adventurous young men in the colony are camping at Mount Alexander!" (2.31). The novel's keenness to show its male charac-ters' enthusiasm for quick and spectacular enrichment is matched only by its determination to show the futility of that desire. Despite their strenuous labors, as recounted by Henry Martin in his first letter to the sisters, he and the Elliot brothers have little to show for their efforts:

> It is a perfect lottery here; we have sunk nine holes already, and have got nothing, while from holes close by us fellows have taken pounds upon pounds of gold. I saw one party take eighteen pounds' weight of gold from a hole that touched ours, in a day and a half. We can only say, "Better luck next time".... Here have we paid two months' licence – that is nine pounds for three – we have worked like slaves, and send you five and a half ounces of gold, worth here only two pounds fifteen per ounce. (2.39)

Describing the labor of the diggers as a "lottery" was a common response to the gold rushes, but in Spence's novel it serves as the leading edge of a critique aimed at an entire colony characterized by various forms of mobility. The nomadic existence of the gold diggers is seen to be of a piece with the new lability of social distinctions in the city of Melbourne, and in both environments steady labor has been disconnected from

[33] Rosalind Smith, "*Clara Morison*: The Politics of Feminine Heterotopia," *Southerly* 61, no. 3 (2001): 44.

financial reward. Gilbert Elliot, writing from his luckless claim, reflects that he "cannot make a home in this sort of vagabond life at the gold diggings," and contrasts this to colonial farmers who, in "making the value of their land ten times greater by their labour, have a much stronger attachment to the soil" than those who "are not connected with the land at all" (2.47, 2.48). Reflecting on the characteristics of Melbourne, one character laments that "vulgar wealth is so completely in the ascendant, and ... talents, education, and refinement are trodden under foot," while another anathematizes it as the scene of the "universal overturn of society" (1.246, 2.94). In other words, Spence's deployment of the genres of the romance and domestic realism serves to rearticulate the familiar Wakefieldian opposition between antisocial wandering and Lockean settlement in the new characterological and societal contexts of the gold rushes. Written in the earliest years of the gold rushes, and understanding the challenge that they pose to be equally social and formal, *Clara Morison* responds from its colonial fringes by imagining gold to be a temporary aberration from the laws of civilizational development that can and must be overcome as those principles reassert themselves in due course.

The possibility of reestablishing the pastoral basis of British society in Australia, and with it rejecting the wandering and speculative behaviors of the gold rushes, is symbolized in *Clara Morison* by the marriage of Clara and Reginald. "Carlyle says: – 'Find your work, and do it,'" Clara observes in the middle of the novel, and goes on to wonder what her own "proper work" might be, to which Margaret responds, somewhat dismissively, "Your vocation is marriage.... You are formed to make some good man very happy.... All your little talents are pleasure-giving; you have feeling, and taste, and tact, and I can fancy your husband finding new charms in you every day" (2.17). Clara's marriage and relocation to the Taringa sheep station reasserts the alliance of pastoralism, culture, and capital. Indeed, at the novel's conclusion, the new bride is seen wasting no time in domesticating the scene of her husband's Lockean striving:

> [W]hitewash and paper-hangings had quite divested Taringa of the gloomy appearance Reginald used to ascribe to it. It was really a cheerful, pretty place; the garden was thriving, and ... the sheep-station began to look like a comfortable farm-house....
>
> All his vague wishes were satisfied, and he rested in the consciousness of entire happiness. Margaret thought his life was too inactive, and his ambition too low; but it suited Clara, though it would not have suited her. (2.271)

In recounting this private triumph of pastoral banality over the lottery of the goldfields, the novel does not abandon its broader interest in the progress of settlement. Switching focus from the scene of Clara's "inactive" domestic bliss to the overtly political concerns of her cousin, Margaret, it appears that stadialist order might also be reestablished across the colonies:

> She ... is in hopes that the Victoria gold fields will soon yield nothing more than good wages for hard work; so as to offer no very powerful inducement for South Australians to desert their agricultural and mechanical pursuits. Even Victoria is getting into a wonderfully orderly state; and Margaret's alarm about the demoralization of the colonies has greatly subsided. (2.272)

Simon During has argued this conclusion marks Spence's abandonment of "literary terms" for "political, economic and governmental ones," and is testament to her realization that "the colony's project of democratic nation building cannot place literary styles of life and literary values at its core since they lead to the privatization and domestication of subjectivity and perpetuate traditional gender inequities."[34] Yet the alignment between literary cultivation and the cultivation of the soil that the novel has asserted from the outset suggests that Margaret and Clara's divergent endings in fact offer complementary endorsements of the settled vision of society mapped out decades earlier in Wakefield's repurposed stadial theory. The news of Clara's successful domestication, after all, coincides with the equally domestic (if nonreproductive) vision of Margaret "settled ... down with her brother in their cottage," where she studies "with all the energy of her active nature" and he, newly restored to settled society, is now "as industrious and methodical in his own business, as any member ... of any service, public or private, in the colony" (2.271, 2.272). Published in London in the early years of the gold rushes, *Clara Morison* stands as the high-water mark of that stadialist consensus, and also signals its impending colonial dissolution: the Lockean narrative of land and labor could no longer be applied straightforwardly to the project of replicating Victorian society in Australia without also reckoning with the forms of sociality emerging on and through the goldfields. Subsequent literary and economic responses to the gold discoveries would increasingly portray the social order they produced as normative and long-lasting rather than atypical

---

[34] Simon During, "Out of England: Literary Subjectivity in the Australian Colonies, 1788–1867," in *Imagining Australia: Literature and Culture in the New New World*, ed. Judith Ryan and Chris Wallace-Crabbe (Cambridge: Harvard University Press, 2004), 18.

and fleeting, signaling with increasing urgency that new narratives of British character and society would be needed. Those revised narrative forms would now have to center precisely on "the restless desire of our population" that *Clara Morison* hoped to dismiss (1.208).

The Aesthetics and Economics of Extraction: *Land, Labour, and Gold*

Despite the inability of *Clara Morison* to imagine the compatibility of literary culture with the act of digging for gold, the growth of Melbourne into a city during the 1850s was paralleled by its emergence as the hub of an imperial literary network, as impoverished British writers and intellectuals sought to try their luck on the goldfields.[35] One such figure, William Howitt, provides particularly clear insight into the pressures shaping the formal reorganization of both the novel and political economy during this time because his quixotic attempt to restore his family's finances on the goldfields came in the wake of an unremunerative career as a Romantic chronicler of the English countryside and its rural culture. Howitt would draw on his Australian experiences in two novels – *A Boy's Adventures in the Wilds of Australia, or, Herbert's Notebook* (1854) and *Tallangetta, the Squatter's Home: A Story of Australian Life* (1857) – but it is in the epistolary travel narrative, *Land, Labour, and Gold; or, Two Years in Victoria* (1855), that he reluctantly yet definitively acknowledges the need to rethink the relationship between British political identity, the landscape, and economics in the gold rushes' febrile atmosphere. Howitt appears determined at the outset of *Land, Labour, and Gold* to offer a conservative critique of the colony similar to that of *Clara Morison*, viewing what he calls the "gold fever" as antithetical to British subjects and society because it ruptures the relationship between labor, private property, and culture (1.13). Yet his garrulous, opinionated, and occasionally witty account largely eschews pastoral spaces and themes in favor of mapping the complex array of Victoria's goldfields and their spatial and economic relationship to the booming city of Melbourne. After landing in Melbourne, he and his companions soon leave for the Ovens (Beechworth) goldfields, a distance of 150 miles that took two months to cover on the colony's rudimentary roads; after a month without success, they begin

---

[35] See, for example, Jason R. Rudy, "On Literary Melbourne: Poetry in the Colony, ca. 1854," *BRANCH: Britain, Representation, and Nineteenth-Century History*.

prospecting elsewhere and discover "abundant signs of gold" several miles away, in an undisturbed portion of the Yackandandah Creek (1.191). After digging there for two months, they return to Melbourne before undertaking a tour of the other goldfields: McIvor (Heathcote), Bendigo, the Ovens again – because of "curiosity," and due to the irresistible temptation of "creeks beyond that on which we had so successfully worked, that we had not thoroughly prospected" (2.70) – before returning to Bendigo, then on to Mount Alexander (Castlemaine) and Ballarat. As even this schematic account begins to suggest, the decidedly nonlinear movements traced in *Land, Labour, and Gold* operate at a formal level to undermine the stadialist model of development by connecting the capitalist frenzy of urban Melbourne and the nomadic characteristics of frontier primitive accumulation. That ideological pressure is further intensified by Howitt's self-conscious portrayal of his own active and sustained participation in the gold rushes, and his sense of personal culpability in destroying the kind of picturesque landscape that he so fervently maintains should anchor a stable British population.

Howitt arrived in Australia especially sensitized to picturesque rural landscapes and committed to the idea that they ought to provide the basis of a healthy national culture.[36] As Judith Johnston observes, "It is the English rural landscape, the vision of an unsullied and beautiful countryside ... with which the Australian scene is overlaid."[37] Howitt most clearly established his baseline for colonial comparison in *The Rural Life of England* (1838), a Romantic paean to the rural traditions, occupations, and landscapes that he believed offered a window into the origins of national culture. The picturesque is at the center of this project, providing Howitt with an aesthetic shorthand for his broader stadialist vision of culture and production. When he frames the emergent manufacturing economy of Lancashire in terms of "the vast difference between the character and habits of the working class, and the character and habits of the pastoral and agricultural districts," the contrasting lack of picturesque qualities in the modernizing landscape function synecdochally to convey a wider set of economic, social, and historical differences:

[36] Paul Carter places Howitt in a wider tradition of picturesque thinking in Australia in *Road to Botany Bay*, 230–60.
[37] Judith Johnston, "William Howitt, Australia and the 'Green Language,'" *Australian Literary Studies* 29, no. 4 (2014): 40.

We have no longer those picturesque villages and cottages half buried in their garden and orchard trees; no longer those home crofts, with their old, tall hedges; no longer rows of bee hives beneath their little thatched southern sheds; those rich fields and farm-houses, surrounded with wealth of corn-ricks, and herds and flocks. You have no longer that quiet and Arcadian-looking population.... Over these naked and desolate hills are scattered to their very tops, in all directions, the habitations of a swarming population of weavers; the people and their houses equally unparticipant of those features which delight the poet and the painter.[38]

Howitt's critique of nascent industrial modernity, though far from unique in its sentiments, usefully conveys the means by which he would assess the progress of Australian colonization. On the one hand, *The Rural Life of England* suggests that the successful establishment of British society in Australia will be predicated upon recapitulating stadial theory's creation myth of capital and culture, that is through agricultural productivity, a settled population, and a picturesque rural scene. "Nothing can be more consonant to nature, nothing more delightful, nothing more beneficial to the country, or more worthy of any man," Howitt avers, "than the georgical occupations which form so prominent a feature in the rural life of England."[39] On the other hand, the sight of a "swarming" colonial populace and a "desolate" rural landscape would constitute an almost inconceivable disjunction in the progress of societal development, resembling most closely a state of society associated with the degradations of modernity brought about by the encroachments of urbanization. Informed by this deeply aestheticized, nationalist commitment to a harmonious rural concatenation of land and labor, Howitt's *Land, Labor, and Gold* is therefore able to present with unique clarity the overwhelming of those stadialist norms as the gold rushes played out across New South Wales and Victoria.

The picturesque remains Howitt's aesthetic and cultural touchstone throughout his time in Australia, and he repeatedly draws attention to landscapes that fulfill its qualities. Shortly after his arrival in Melbourne, where he is confronted by the sight of the Canvas Town slum – "A balder and more unattractive scene cannot meet the eye of man" – Howitt and his companions seek aesthetic relief in the neighboring countryside (1.15). There they find reassuring evidence that the establishment of a colonial British society might indeed be able to proceed along the expected rural lines:

[38] William Howitt, *The Rural Life of England*, 2 vols. (London: Longman, Orme, Brown, Green, and Longmans, 1838), 1.286.
[39] Ibid., 1.69.

> On this side of the river, lying within a sweep, are two farms, one called
> Abbotsford…. They both had a very pleasant, home-like look; both were
> one-storey houses, surrounded by their green enclosures and large gardens
> and vineyards, with cattle and horses grazing, and children at play. A mass
> of weeping willows near the river gleamed out like a mass of sunshine, from
> the lively green of their foliage amid the dusky hues of the native trees.
> (1.30)

This picturesque antipodean Abbotsford – "its proprietor, of course, a
Scotchman" – gestures both to the Scottish Enlightenment roots of
stadial theory and to the colony's amenability to literary representation
(1.30). In colonial Australian texts, Paul Carter argues, the picturesque
offered "a traveller's viewpoint, a possible stopping place, a punctuation
mark, an opportunity to reflect on the future."[40] Howitt's observation
and praise of such vistas constitutes a lingering faith that the new
British society must necessarily be built upon a settled, rural point of
origin. Accordingly, he finds it desirable that "intellectual men" immigrate to take up land in the countryside, for they not only "love
country life, and are capable of cultivating cheap land of their own,"
but are also able to "breathe a soul through the brute mass, [and] shed
refinement and intelligence around them" (2.113–14). Cultivation,
both agricultural and intellectual, is also the standard against which
Howitt proposes to judge the social and physical landscapes produced
by the gold rushes.

Howitt's critical portrayals of Melbourne and the goldfields are united
by their emphatic lack of picturesque qualities and social virtues. It is
Melbourne's suburbs, springing up rapidly on the outskirts of the city,
which first attract his attention upon arrival:

> A balder and more unattractive scene cannot meet the eye of man. Every
> single tree has been levelled to the ground; it is one hard bare expanse, bare
> of all nature's attractions, a wilderness of wooden huts of Lilliputian
> dimensions…. There is not the trace of the idea of a garden amongst the
> whole of them. (1.15–16)

The suburban environment turn out to be a preface for the goldfields, for
the qualities of disproportion, ugliness, and impermanence that Howitt
finds so abhorrent are replicated there at far larger scale. Howitt's scathing
description of the Spring Creek diggings provides a typical example of the
frontier vistas presented throughout *Land, Labour, and Gold*:

---

[40] Carter, *Road to Botany Bay*, 254.

[N]o scene can be more revolting to an eye that is accustomed to the beautiful. No scene would be pronounced more horrible by English ladies, if they could see it; no scene is less characterized by an air of wealth than a gold-digging. The tents have a wretched, rag-fair appearance, and they stand on a field composed of holes and clay and gravel heaps. Every tree is felled; every feature of Nature is annihilated. (1.252)

Gold diggers are "a race without a spark of the picturesque or of the perception of beauty in their souls," and this failure marks them in Howitt's eyes as bad colonists, constitutionally incapable of adequately reshaping the frontier into an image of British society (2.144). In contrast to an idealized, leisurely process of "converting the wild forests ... of the earth into homes of beauty and taste, and making them ... a portion of the mother country," the gold rushes demonstrate a dramatically accelerated and visibly destructive form of colonization (1.33). Indeed, Howitt comments frequently on the "velocity" of the gold rushes, referring both to the populations they set in motion and the speed of the resultant transformations of the landscape (2.48). Yet in contrast to *Clara Morison*, which framed such movements as temporary aberrations within an overarching stadialist narrative of pastoral settlement, the awkward alignment of colonization and geographic mobility is so visible, widespread, and central to *Land, Labour, and Gold* that it must be acknowledged and accommodated at a formal level in some other way.

One strategy employed in *Land, Labour, and Gold* to manage the unsettling developmental implications of the gold rushes is to simply excise the digger population from membership in civil society. Surveying the wreckage of the picturesque across the colony, Howitt links the squalid character of the diggings, the powerful desires produced by gold, and the extreme mobility of the digging population, all qualities associated with stadialism's lowest developmental level. Tracing the fortunes of the "ever-pouring crowd of immigrants" from their disembarkation at Port Phillip Bay, some of his most persistent themes are their highly transient nature as a population and their "wild, nomadic life" on the goldfields (1.16, 1.113). Governed by their speculative desires, gold seekers live constantly in an "uneasy state": "wonderful rumours are afloat on all sides, and everywhere the diggers are ready to run after them" (1.185). Howitt often notes the melancholy sight of anonymous settler graves, in the midst of goldfields or scattered along the rough tracks that link them, and stresses the precariousness of "a rude, wild sort of life, which no one can realize to himself without seeing it," one lived in "tents and nondescript huts" and surrounded by "ravaged and desolated woods" (2.72). Howitt's dissatisfaction with this miserable colonial population is heightened by its implicit resemblance to the indigenous population. Aborigines have only a fleeting presence in his narrative, and he readily fits their nomadic qualities into a stadialist framework. Asserting that "the hunter races are but the precursers [*sic*] of the sons of Japhet, who till the soil and build cities," the first tribal grouping he encounters leads him to confidently assert they can neither survive nor adapt to the pressures of colonial modernization: "They see fields tilled and yielding abundance of food, yet they do not cultivate; they see houses rise full of comfort and plenty, yet they raise none, but still crouch under the miserable gunyah, or mimi of withered boughs; they see the white man ride on horses, but they still wander on foot" (1.257, 1.258). Although in *Land, Labour, and Gold* they are never explicitly likened to each other, the nomadic diggers and indigenous populations are united nevertheless by what Howitt perceives to be their shared incapacity to found or belong to a settled society. Such straightforward conclusions about the path to civilization are destabilized, however, by the presence of "Marvellous Melbourne," a hub of frenetic commercial activity virtually adjacent to the primitive Victorian goldfields.

Melbourne's growth appeared to observers to be as contrary to the norms of a settled society as the gold diggings. When Howitt turns his attention from the diggings to Melbourne, he finds the streets are "mottled with the people and costumes of nearly all nations" (1.285), and life there is characterized by the same qualities of speed and unconstrained desire that trouble him in the hinterland. The "extravagance of all sorts" that characterizes digger behavior is writ large in Melbourne's atmosphere of speculative mania (1.62), and comes to exemplify the financial irrationality that governs the colony:

> [T]he Melbournians, from some cause or other, have shown themselves from the beginning of their brief history, a most mercurial race, – the maddest speculators in the world.... They disdain everything but the most lunatic prices and profits. To all warnings, "The gold! the gold!" is the answer, and the assurance that this outrageously unnatural rate of property will last for ever. They might as well expect pyramids to stand on their points. It is contrary to all the laws of specific gravity. The value is not in the things, and, therefore, it cannot remain. (2.277–78)

Melbourne and the goldfields therefore constitute the two poles of a single, spectacular divergence from stadial norms. The apparent paradox that Howitt confronts is that the most modern of imperial cities might be founded on the regression of British settlers to a primitive state and the rupturing of the Lockean equation of labor and private property. Yet despite his discomfort with this developmental trajectory, Howitt is forced to acknowledge grudgingly that the sheer numbers of immigrants and the collective wealth generated by the gold rushes have nevertheless successfully catapulted Melbourne to the forefront of modernity. "The diggers are styled 'The New Aristocracy'; and the shopkeepers flatter them with the title in their advertisements," he notes in a suggestive blending of tradition and commercialism, before proposing that they might better be called a "*hairystocracy*, – for hairy enough they are in all conscience" (1.62–63). Here again *Land, Labour, and Gold* seems at first to follow *Clara Morison* in dismissing the sociality of the gold rushes – suggesting that the gold colony is a realm of romance rather than realism, where "Arabian Nights' fables" (1.169) attract immigrants and drive speculation – yet Howitt cannot so easily dissociate his own narrative from romance's unsettling formal taint.

Hedged around by restless and apparently unproductive social formations, *Land, Labour, and Gold* yearns to reassert the validity of stadial theory and its agricultural model of British societal emergence, yet this is decisively short-circuited by Howitt's account of his own participation in the gold rushes. At a formal level, the narrative is marked throughout by the qualities of romance. Recounting his party's movements across the colony in search of gold, in an episodic and erratic mapping of the colony whose interest arises in large part from picaresque anecdotes and encounters – impassable roads, the persecutions of flies and mosquitoes, a broad range of rogues, and "Lignum, the Irish Giant" (2.81–82) – Howitt and the reader are enfolded within a "locomotive" romance of primitive accumulation (2.67). Moreover, through his active participation in the gold rushes, Howitt is self-consciously complicit in the destruction of the picturesque. This is brought to the fore most dramatically after his party strikes gold along a previously undisturbed section of the Yackandandah Creek. Despite having crossed the globe in the hope of just such a moment, the beginning of the letter that recounts the commencement of their digging is notably sober, in sharp contrast with Howitt's usual tones of detached amusement or scandalized outrage. Indeed, it is one of the few times in the text where Howitt actively identifies himself with the nomadic digger population:

> Upper Yackandanda [*sic*], Feb. 28th. 1853.
> We have begun to destroy the beauty of this creek. It will no longer run clear between its banks, covered with wattles and tea-trees, and amongst its shallow parts overgrown with foreign-looking shrubs, flags, and cypress-grass. A little while, and its whole course will exhibit nothing but naked-ness, and heaps of gravel and mud. We diggers are horribly destructive of the picturesque. (1.205)

In *The Rural Life of England*, Howitt had employed a collective "we" to invoke a Romantic sense of national identity, so that "our British literature" could serve as the medium through which "the admiration of nature is diffused as one great soul";[41] now, by contrast, his affiliation with the digger embodies a new, more developmentally regressive understanding of collective British identity. As he goes on to recount in subsequent letters from the same location, Howitt's success soon triggers a rush from the neighboring diggings, directly exacerbating the "velocity" of colonization. Within days, he observes "crowds which every day oppress ... the diggings, grow[ing] constantly and rapidly" (1.227), and returning to the scene a few weeks later, Howitt is incredulous at the changes he has precipitated:

> But now, we had no longer, as in coming up, to make our way through the untracked bush. It was tracked to some purpose. The diggers who had followed on our course were thousands. They had settled along these creeks for miles; and the extent of ground that they had turned up was surprising. We were astonished at the population that we found where, at our coming, it was an untracked desert. (1.247–48)

In contrast with the arm's length treatment of gold in *Clara Morison*, the episode on the Yackandandah temporarily yet powerfully effaces the distance between Howitt, standard-bearer for the picturesque, and the nomadic settlers who are his ostensible subject. With this moment, moreover, *Land, Labour, and Gold* arrives at the conclusion that narrating the formation of British society, and accounting for the British subject who might achieve that task demands a different form than the stadial model of cultivation, culture, and capital is able to offer.

The sheer vigor of Melbourne, and Howitt's own exploits as a digger, lead him to agree reluctantly that the gold colony of Victoria might not be just a temporary deviation from a universal pattern of development whereby agricultural settlement demarcates the threshold of civilized forms of society. Not only does Howitt recognize that the discrete colonial spaces of city and frontier are united by the shared character trait of speculative desire, but he also comes to see metropolitan Britain and the Australian colonies defined by similar social and economic pressures. Reflecting on the sheer number of diggers seeking gold, he reflects, "Here, at the ends of the earth, the struggle is as fierce and discouraging as it is in London"

---

[41] Howitt, *Rural Life of England*, 2.16, 2.26.

(1.298). Melbourne's bustling transport arteries also draw direct comparison with the heart of the empire:

> The ships lying in the bay; the crowded forest of smaller craft blocking up the river for miles; and the bustle of loading and unloading at the quays; the piles of goods of all sorts; the clamour, and stir of hundreds of porters and wharf-labourers, mark the seat of an astonishing commerce. The streets are thronged with a busy press of people; and the carriages, omnibuses, and cabs are plying as actively as in London; and in all the great highways leading to the city, long trains of loaded drays, smart equipages, people hastening along on horseback and on foot, announce a numerous and a prosperous population. (2.309–10)

Ultimately for Howitt, however, the gold rushes remain a problem to be solved, and his preferred solution is along the same lines that Spence envisaged, imagining the ultimate settling of Australian society through the widespread establishment of agricultural small-holdings. It is on that premise that he perseveres until the end in trying to shoehorn the social upheavals brought about by the gold rushes into a teleological narrative of colonization. "England, in fact, is here re-producing herself on a larger scale," he concludes in the last pages: Australia's future holds a "glorious vista of progressing certainties" (2.397). Yet this conclusion is undercut entirely by Howitt's prior assertion of an intrinsic relationship between the nomadic sociality of the diggings and the capitalist excesses of Melbourne, precisely because it short-circuits the developmental logic of stadialist history and the rhetoric of settled economic behavior and cultural production that it supports.

In writing from the diggings rather than the farm, Howitt lays bare the inadequacy of stadial theory's developmental equation of cultivation, culture, and capital to account for the emergence of British subjectivity and society. In the domain of economics, *Land, Labour, and Gold*'s increasingly normative juxtaposition of gold with land and labor ultimately signals the radical disruption of classical political economy's theoretical model of societal formation by a society whose accelerating development is propelled by the anomic force of acquisitive, wandering desire. At the same time, Howitt also usefully demonstrates the interpenetration of economic and literary domains in the settler colonial environment, for the dismantling of classical political economy in *Land, Labour, and Gold* is of a piece with its laying waste to the picturesque as a guarantor of culture's origins. In finding the settler colony's originary scene of extraction to be devoid of the picturesque, yet entirely (if uncomfortably) compatible with his own literary subjectivity, Howitt signals the foreclosure of stadialist theory in

Australia and points to the need for a new vocabulary to describe the settler-colonial project and the perspective that it implicitly affords onto British subjectivity and society.

Unsettled Desire in Political Economy: *Plutology*

The story I wish to tell of the emergence in Australia of a new economic and literary means of imagining British society and subjectivity begins in 1854, when the young Irish political economist W. E. Hearn was appointed as a foundation professor in modern history and literature, logic, and political economy at the University of Melbourne. The Legislative Council of Victoria had resolved to establish the university only a few years previously, in the hopes that "higher education might help to counteract uncivilizing aspects of mounting gold fever," but at the time of Hearn's arrival it amounted to little more than "a few buildings in a paddock along the dusty Sydney Road taken by the amateur miners on their way to the diggings."[42] Hearn's *Plutology: Or, the Theory of the Efforts to Satisfy Human Wants* (1864), the first work of political economy published in Australia, was based on the lectures he gave in those unassuming environs in the late 1850s and early 1860s, and it bears numerous traces of the febrile atmosphere of gold-rush Melbourne.[43] At a surface level, Hearn takes frequent recourse to analogies and examples drawn from the diggings: the vigor of the colonial miner, "working on his own account in a payable claim," is contrasted favorably to the sloth of Italians employed by the state to excavate the Roman Forum; at a later point, there is an extensive discussion of the progression of the gold-mining industry in Victoria.[44] Beyond merely using colonial scenarios to add local color, *Plutology* undertakes a more thorough antipodean reimagining of some of the fundamental principles of political economy. Ricardo's understanding of natural agents, for example, is held to be fatally limited by being "constructed solely in reference to countries long previously settled,"

---

[42] Craufurd D. W. Goodwin, *Economic Enquiry in Australia* (Durham: Duke University Press, 1966), 568; Gregory C. G. Moore, "The Anglo-Irish Context for William Edward Hearn's Economic Beliefs and the Ultimate Failure of His *Plutology*," *The European Journal of the History of Economic Thought* 18, no. 1 (2011): 38, 39. If Hearn's working conditions left something to be desired, his remuneration was presumably more satisfactory: the £1,000 salary he was offered eclipsed the £150 he had been earning teaching Greek at Queen's College, Galway. Thomas A. Boylan and Timothy P. Foley, "'Tempering the Rawness': W. E. Hearn, Irish Political Economist, and Intellectual Life in Australia," in *The Irish-Australian Connection*, ed. Seamus Grimes and Gearóid Ó Tuathaigh (Galway: University College Galway, 1989), 94.

[43] Moore, "Anglo-Irish Context," 39.   [44] Hearn, *Plutology*, 43, 112–13. Hereafter cited in text.

for "its author had not that familiarity with a different state of facts which only residence in a new country still in course of settlement can give" (113). Yet the most significant consequence of Hearn's located thinking occurs at the level of form, in the "unusual narrative order" of *Plutology*, which jettisons the orthodoxy of stadial theory and the factors of production – land, labor, and gold – in favor of a new, sweeping account of the generative powers of individual consumer appetite.[45]

Plutology amounts to a sustained argument that political economy need no longer conceive of society as settled to imagine the emergence of economic activity and culture. Instead of beginning with the familiar stadialist narrative of the historical emergence of the laboring Lockean subject, it proffers an ahistorical account, derived from Darwinian biology, of an individual defined by their unpredictable and insatiable appetites. "Not merely is the amount of human desire indefinite," Hearn argues, "but the modes in which desire in many different individuals is manifested, are equally without any practical limit" (18).[46] Labor and production, so central to classical political economy, are now displaced in favor of desire and consumption. Thus, while the opening sections reiterate political economy's familiar investment in differentiating civilization from savagery, their merging of Darwinian theory with utilitarianism leads to the startling claim that it is not diligent and disciplined labor but the continued expansion of appetite that performs the "moral function" of driving the civilizing process:

> Our real state of nature consists not in the repression, but in the full development and satisfaction, of all those faculties of which our nature consists. Such a state is found, not in the poverty of the naked savage; but in the wealth of the civilized man. It is the constant and powerful impulse of our varied and insatiable desires, that urges us to avoid the one state, and to tend towards the other.... Desires extend themselves with the means of gratification; the horizon is enlarged in proportion as we advance. (21)

Hearn's formulation deliberately scrambles the most pressing social and cultural connotations of stadialist theory by dissociating unbounded and settled forms of desire from their accustomed level of civilizational development. The spatialized logic of "proportion," for example, which appears

---

[45] Moore, "Anglo-Irish Context," 42.

[46] Hearn was predisposed to make this turn away from the rhetoric of production as a result of his training at Trinity College Dublin, where Richard Whately and Mountifort Longfield had been questioning labor-based definitions of value since the 1830s. Gordon Bigelow, *Fiction, Famine, and the Rise of Economics in Victorian Britain and Ireland* (Cambridge: Cambridge University Press, 2003), 114–15.

to echo Wakefield's earlier commitment to an "imaginary standard of elegant proportion" as a guarantor of class structure and values, is now infused with the speculative and irrational behaviors of Melbourne's successful diggers.[47] Through this Hearn begins to propose a striking answer to the questions raised in *Land, Labour, and Gold* about how to comprehend the societal lessons of the gold rushes.

This is to say that Hearn's vision of proliferating individual desire, while presented in the guise of an ahistorical abstraction, resembles closely the world of gold-era Melbourne as recounted by Howitt and other visitors to the colony. When Hearn dwells on the "great diversity" of human desire, and finds it shaped by "differences of climate, age, sex, and other considerations" such that "in the desires which are peculiar to man, we seldom find agreement," he translates into the realm of political economy the economic frenzy that surrounded him (18). Howitt, for instance, frequently emphasizes the multinational heterogeneity of the digger population – "Turks, Lascars, Negroes, and black natives, and many other strange races, in strange costumes, are all in quest of gold, along with Englishmen, Frenchmen, Germans, Poles, Swedes, Danes, Spaniards, Californians, Yankees, and men of still other nations" (1.286) – and finds this intimately associated with the sheer commercial vigor of Melbourne's consumer economy, "which every day becomes more droll – actually that is the only phrase for it – droll in its extravagance of all sorts" (1.62). Yet whereas Howitt views Melbourne's bustle with suspicion because of its speculative origins and propensity to overturn social hierarchies, Hearn consciously abandons a moralistic stance toward desire and seeks instead to accurately describe its workings and effects. "We pass no judgment upon the character of the want, or upon the manner in which it should be regulated," he maintains: "We have to deal with them merely as forces, without any other estimate of their characters than the intensity with which they are felt by the persons who experience them" (22–23). By displacing the rational and laboring subject of stadial theory with the "varied and insatiable desires" of the nomadic gold diggers of Victoria, *Plutology* marks a striking colonial departure from metropolitan political economy, and demonstrates the unfolding settler project's ability to catalyze the revaluation of mid-Victorian narrative models.[48]

---

[47] Merivale, *Lectures on Colonization*, 1.84.

[48] Such a reading contrasts with the claim that Hearn's "experiences and observations in Australia … had merely reinforced the ideas formed in his Anglo-Irish youth," that is, that society's path to progress is defined by evolution toward an English market economy. Moore, "Anglo-Irish Context," 45.

Colonial Gold and the Form of Metropolitan Economics: Jevons's *Theory of Political Economy*

But what of the impact of such thinking, if any, upon metropolitan culture? After all, *Plutology* was a "dismal failure" when reprinted in Britain.[49] The question can be approached initially through two brief testaments to Australian gold's global transit in the years after the rushes began. First, in political economy: R. H. Patterson's heterodox *The Economy of Capital, or, Gold and Trade* (1865), which opens in Australia with the discovery of "one of the richest 'placers,' or gold-beds, even of that most auriferous country."[50] Imagining its hazardous excavation and eventual transfer to Britain, Patterson finds the volatile qualities of gold permeating the metropolitan economy and the civilization it supports: "The City of Gold [i.e., London] is based upon gold: and the foundation is found to be pre-eminently unstable and perilous.... It rises and falls, expands and contracts, and sometimes seems to slip away from beneath the City altogether."[51] Second, in the novel: Mary Elizabeth Braddon's *Lady Audley's Secret* (1862), which commences with its protagonist, George Talboys, en route to Liverpool with £20,000 to his name after three years' labor on the goldfields of Victoria. While that colonial fortune proves surprisingly peripheral to the novel's sensational economy, its relocation nevertheless prefaces a thorough reappraisal of the settled nature of British society and the countryside:

> We hear every day of murders committed in the country.... [S]udden and violent deaths by cruel blows, inflicted with a stake cut from some spreading oak, whose very shadow promised – peace.... No crime has ever been committed in the worst rookeries about Seven Dials that has not been also done in the face of that sweet rustic calm which still, in spite of all, we look on with a tender, half-mournful yearning, and associate with – peace.[52]

By the 1870s, Patterson and Braddon's accounts suggest, Australian gold was generally available as a sensational trope that licensed the questioning of societal norms. Yet for metropolitan authors with experience of Australia, the settler colony prompted a more thoroughgoing – yet still sensationalized – reconsideration of Victorian society. In W. S. Jevons's *Theory of Political Economy* and Anthony Trollope's *John Caldigate*, forms of

---

[49] Ibid.

[50] R. H. Patterson, *The Economy of Capital, or, Gold and Trade*, Amended ed. (Edinburgh: Blackwood, 1865), 1.

[51] Ibid., 168.   [52] Braddon, *Lady Audley's Secret*, 54.

colonial thinking afforded by the settler empire play out in accounts of metropolitan individualism no longer anchored by specific territory or even the wider nation.

W. S. Jevons is remembered as the British instigator of political economy's "marginal revolution," or the theory of diminishing marginal utility. "[T]he proposition that millions of students have since learned, indeed still learn," John Kenneth Galbraith observes of the ongoing significance of his insights, is that "the utility of any good or service diminishes, all else equal, with increasing availability; it is the utility of the last and least wanted – the utility of the marginal unit – that sets the value of all."[53] Put in terms more aligned with the concerns of the current argument, Jevons's *Theory of Political Economy* "stands at the very juncture at which classical political economy transmuted into neoclassical economics," marking the turning point from the former's focus on labor value to the latter's concern with consumption, and doing so on the basis of a new methodological emphasis that "imparted far more momentum to the shift to mathematical economics than any other economist" of the period.[54] Jevons was aged 19 and had studied chemistry and mathematics, but not political economy, at the point when he arrived in Sydney in 1854 to take up a position as assayer at the new branch of the Royal Mint, which had been established specifically to facilitate the export of Australian bullion to Britain. To ask whether his five-year colonial sojourn might have shaped his subsequent thinking about economics is to grapple with the challenge that the networks of the settler empire pose to the nation-based imaginary that still largely informs Victorian studies. Recent discussions of Jevons's place within Victorian culture by Regenia Gagnier, Catherine Gallagher, and Mary Poovey all pass over his time in Australia in silence, in keeping with what Levine describes as a "logic of autochthony" that instinctively restricts Victorian studies within a national horizon.[55] The resulting picture of Jevons's

---

[53] Credit for initiating the marginal revolution is usually shared between Jevons and the European economists Carl Menger and Léon Walras, who published similar theories independently of each other in the early 1870s. John Kenneth Galbraith, *A History of Economics: The Past as the Present* (London: Hamilton, 1987), 108.

[54] Margaret Schabas, *A World Ruled by Number: William Stanley Jevons and the Rise of Mathematical Economics* (Princeton: Princeton University Press, 1990), 9, 140.

[55] Caroline Levine, "From Nation to Network," *Victorian Studies* 55, no. 4 (2013): 649. See Regenia Gagnier, *The Insatiability of Human Wants: Economics and Aesthetics in Market Society* (Chicago: University of Chicago Press, 2000), 19–60; Catherine Gallagher, *The Body Economic: Life, Death, and Sensation in Political Economy and the Victorian Novel* (Princeton: Princeton University Press, 2005), 118–55; Mary Poovey, *Genres of the Credit Economy: Mediating Value in Eighteenth- and Nineteenth-Century Britain* (Chicago: University of Chicago Press, 2008), 219–83. Historians of economic thought have sporadically attempted to assess the long-term significance of Jevons's time

political economy reflects an underlying assumption that colonial experience is incommensurable with forms of thinking undertaken in Britain. Such a stance is in marked contrast to the evidence of Jevons's own archive, which readily presents Britain and Australia as a unified field of interest and attachment.

Writing prior to his departure from Australia in 1859, Jevons acknowledged the "considerable advantages" that had accrued to him in the previous five years, including "a small capital ... [and] my mind well-formed and its direction clearly determined, with a good many years *colonial experience* of the world which will be equal to double as much *home experience*."⁵⁶ In material terms, the settler empire's networks of global commodity exchange were at the core of Jevons's work at the Sydney Mint, and replicated in miniature in his remission of his salary to London to support his two unmarried sisters. At a conceptual level, Jevons used his ample free time to undertake an extensive reading program in political economy and other social sciences, and his budding economic and scientific interests displayed a markedly sociological character, expressed most notably in an abortive and unpublished social survey of Sydney that combined statistical analysis with participant observation.⁵⁷ Jevons also made extensive tours of goldfields in New South Wales and Victoria, and if he found them "almost entirely devoid of any picturesqueness," he saw them nevertheless as being "surrounded with extreme interest in both a scientific and social aspect."⁵⁸ In marked contrast to Howitt's conclusions about the antisocial qualities of the diggings, Jevons stresses the rapid emergence of economic and social order out of inchoate frontier environments. Rather than highlighting vagrancy and disorder, he notes "[t]housands of very sturdy independent diggers ... rapidly adopting fixed habits, manners, and appearance," and his description of New Rush Back Creek (Talbot) conveys wonder at a capitalist economy's spontaneous emergence:

---

in Australia, but their emphasis on what he was reading there differs from my stress on the generative nature of the social and economic environment he encountered. See, for example, John Andrew La Nauze, *Political Economy in Australia: Historical Studies* (Melbourne: Melbourne University Press, 1949); Michael V. White, "Jevons in Australia: A Reassessment," *Economic Record* 58, no. 1 (1982).

56 William Stanley Jevons, *Papers and Correspondence of William Stanley Jevons*, ed. R. D. Collison Black and Rosamond Könekamp, 7 vols. (London: Macmillan, 1972–1981), 1.110, original emphasis.

57 Schabas, *World Ruled by Number*, 15–16; La Nauze, *Political Economy in Australia*, 33–37.

58 Jevons, *Papers and Correspondence*, 2.370.

Here some 30,000 diggers had literally rushed together in the space of a
month or six weeks in consequence of rich new discoveries of gold just
made. To describe the appearance of the mushroom town of canvas thus
suddenly created among the ancient (and we may poetically imagine)
terror-stricken gum-trees, would be impossible in a moderate-sized letter.
There were full two miles of regular canvas streets, densely set with every
kind of shop.... There were photographers, doctors, dentists, lawyers,
apothecaries, bankers, watchmakers, laundresses, libraries, in addition to
every common kind of trade. I have an advertising newspaper published in
the place within the first few weeks of its existence.[59]

There is no record that Jevons and Hearn ever met in Australia, yet any
claim for a direct connection between Jevons's colonial experience and his
subsequent metropolitan writing nevertheless hinges on Hearn's *Plutology*,
which he first praised in an anonymous review in *The Spectator* several
years after his return to Britain. Finding Hearn's work "in many respects in
advance of the treatises of the day, including on certain points even Mr.
J. S. Mill's great work," Jevons concluded that "there is something in the
development of a colony that nourishes studies of the kind."[60] A decade
later, at the conclusion of his own pathbreaking work, *Theory of Political
Economy*, Jevons would recur to the theme of the productive novelty of
Hearn's colonial thinking: "I have the more pleasure and confidence in
putting forward these somewhat heretical views concerning the general
problem of economics, inasmuch as they are nearly identical with those
arrived at by Professor Hearn, of Melbourne University."[61] While not
diminishing the significance of other influences on Jevons's thinking, these
colonial considerations must nevertheless be reckoned as vital to an economic theory that enabled the divergent developmental states of Britain
and its settler empire to be embraced within a single, ahistorical
framework.

Positioning Jevons's *Theory of Political Economy* as a response to the
material circumstances of settler colonization may appear counterintuitive,
given its foundational role in the marginal revolution – that is, in directing
economics away from social considerations of production and toward
abstract mathematical models of consumption. The appeal of the "relative
simplicity" of marginalist thought, Gagnier argues, arises precisely because

---

[59] Ibid., 2.370, 2.371.
[60] William Stanley Jevons, review of *Plutology; or, the Theory of the Efforts to Satisfy Human Wants*, by
W. E. Hearn, *The Spectator* 37, no. 1862 (1864): 276. Jevons's authorship is identified by Moore,
"Anglo-Irish Context," 46.
[61] William Stanley Jevons, *The Theory of Political Economy*, ed. R. D. Collison Black
(Harmondsworth: Penguin, 1970), 258–59. Hereafter cited in text.

it offers a vision of an economic science "stripped of epistemological, psychological, and social complexities."[62] Gallagher also asserts the deculturated quality of Jevons's work, stressing its basis in the universal "biological facts" of bodily sensation.[63] This apparent disavowal of the social nevertheless bears a settler imprint, for Jevons follows Hearn in centering *Theory of Political Economy* on the idea of an individual defined primarily by the capacity for desire. The significance of this shift becomes more apparent in comparison with the claims of a proponent of classical political economy such as J. R. McCulloch. Working within a stadialist framework that praised production and associated it with the virtues of settlement, McCulloch argued that the duty of the political economist was to consider only "man in the aggregate, not the solitary individual."[64] By contrast, in maintaining that the "general forms of the laws of economics are the same in the case of individuals and nations," Jevons now posits that society is best construed simply as "multitudes of individuals" (86). This atomized vision remains circumscribed by an implicit racial logic for, as Kathleen Frederickson points out, Jevons attributes lesser temporal awareness to the savage than the civilized individual, and, consequently, less willingness to labor and accumulate for long-term purposes, so that *Theory of Political Economy* remains oriented toward the description of a British economic subject.[65] What emerges within these racialized parameters is a profound challenge to the territorial logic that continued to underpin discussions of liberal individualism. Elaine Hadley asserts the "deeply identical" relationship between landed proprietorship and citizenship that persisted into the 1870s, and argues that continued imperial expansion posed fundamental questions of "just what *grounds* of connection ... to civil society and society more generally a liberal individual can establish."[66] The response offered by *Theory of Political Economy* is a deterritorialized British subject, who can now be comprehended across imperial space, and who is equally legible in divergent stages of societal development.

Alongside the contribution made by Jevons's economics to the imperial project of imagining the Victorian settler empire as a coherent space, a more unsettling taint of gold persists in its goal of rationalizing political economy as a mathematical science. Furthering Hearn's dismantling of the

---

[62] Gagnier, *Insatiability of Human Wants*, 42.   [63] Gallagher, *Body Economic*, 127.

[64] McCulloch, *Principles of Political Economy*, 17.

[65] Kathleen Frederickson, "Liberalism and the Time of Instinct," *Victorian Studies* 49, no. 2 (2007): 308–10.

[66] Elaine Hadley, *Living Liberalism: Practical Citizenship in Mid-Victorian Britain* (Chicago: University of Chicago Press, 2010), 264, original emphasis.

early Victorian alignment of economics, territory, and labor, *Theory of Political Economy* offers in its place a statistical account of consumer appetite, equally applicable to metropolitan space and the frontier town of the antipodean goldfields.[67] "We shall never have a science of economics," Jevons maintains, "unless we learn to discern the operation of law even among the most perplexing complications and apparent interruptions" (150). Yet desire remains a persistently unruly presence in this borderless account of the liberal individual. Offering a utilitarian model of individual motivation, Jevons doubts the possibility of ever "measuring directly the feelings of the human heart," yet argues that individual experiences of pleasure and pain can instead be deduced from economic activity: "[I]t is the amount of these feelings which is continually prompting us to buying and selling, borrowing and lending, laboring and resting, producing and consuming; and *it is from the quantitative effects of the feelings that we must estimate their comparative amounts*" (83, original emphasis). Concerned with the "lowest rank of feelings," regarding matters of "moral indifference," Jevons follows Hearn in positing an ostensibly value-neutral approach, where "*to maximize pleasure*, is the problem of economics" (93, 101, original emphasis). In this formulation, the stadialist paradox posed by the goldfields – that a civilization might be built by vagrant subjects and their undisciplined appetites – is recapitulated as a central aporia of marginalist thought: a "purely mathematical" economics is claimed to be founded upon the measurement of individual sentiment, yet "the numerical expression of quantities of feeling seems to be out of the question" (78, 84). In response to the persistent vagaries of individual desire, *Theory of Political Economy* proposes a "Fictitious Mean" that will enable their abstraction into a more stable form, in full awareness that such "numerical results ... do not pretend to represent the character of any existing thing" (136). Put another way, Jevons's theory is oriented around a fictional individual whose representative status, as he subsequently explained more fully in *The Principles of Science* (1874), "enabl[es] us to conceive in a single result a multitude of details" through a "hypothetical simplification

---

[67] In the later *Money and the Mechanism of Exchange* (1875), Jevons argues that money is a universal aspect of human society – "It is entirely a question of degree what commodities will in any given state of society form the most convenient currency" – and goes on to hypothesize that even hunter-gathers, embodying "the most rudimentary state of industry," derived a form of currency from "the proceeds of the chase." William Stanley Jevons, *Money and the Mechanism of Exchange*, 13th ed. (London: Kegan Paul, Trench, Trubner, 1902), 19–20.

of a problem."[68] The installation of this statistical fiction at the center of Victorian political economy marks the transit of the unsettled individual from the Australian colonies to the metropolis, silently naturalizing a settler-colonial hermeneutic as a means of understanding Britain's society and economy.

Colonial Gold and the Form of the Metropolitan Novel: *John Caldigate*

The imperial breadth latent in Jevons's account of fictionalized individual desire is taken up and expanded in the novel, which in the hands of Trollope becomes newly capable of using such a gold-driven figure to imagine Britain as coterminous with its settler-colonial periphery. Trollope's wide first-hand experience of the empire, unparalleled among the period's canonical writers, was especially intense and personal in the case of Australia. As Trollope recounted in his *Autobiography* (1883), his second son, Frederic James Anthony, had "very early in life gone out to Australia, having resolved on a colonial career when he found that boys who did not grow so fast as he did got above him at school"; after returning to Britain in 1868, Frederic took £6,000 of his father's earnings back with him to Australia the following year, which he used to purchase a 27,000 acre sheep station in New South Wales.[69] The Trollopes visited their son "among his sheep" in 1871 – the year that Jevons's *Theory of Political Economy* was published – as part of a wider tour of the Australasian colonies, during which Trollope felt he "succeed[ed] in learning much of the political, social, and material condition of these countries."[70] It was the impending failure of the colonial pastoral dream that prompted Trollope's return to the continent in 1875, where Frederic was struggling to remain solvent; despite maintaining that his son's ruin would mean he could "no longer believe in honesty, industry, and conduct," Trollope ultimately lost most of his money early the following year after the sheep station was sold for only £1,400.[71] In *Australia and New Zealand* (1873), Trollope's record of his extensive first visit, he reflects at length on the gold rushes and their ongoing physical and social impact. While ceding that the sheer labor involved in mining has a "certain redeeming manliness," Trollope concurs

---

[68] William Stanley Jevons, *The Principles of Science: A Treatise on Logic and Scientific Method*, 2nd ed. (London: Macmillan, 1913), 363.
[69] Anthony Trollope, *An Autobiography*, ed. Frederick Page and Michael Sadleir (Oxford: Oxford University Press, 1980), 326.
[70] Ibid., 348.   [71] N. John Hall, *Trollope: A Biography* (Oxford: Clarendon Press, 1991), 402.

with previous commentators in his skepticism toward the individual and collective value of the pursuit of gold.[72] This stance is articulated through, yet also complicated by, his attention to the gentrified settler and the potential of goldfields privation to dissolve class identity. Trollope's anxiety regarding the fragility of traditional forms of British culture and society overlays a more fundamental concern regarding the inability to maintain a distinction between gentility, primitive accumulation, and speculation. The juxtaposition of such oppositions – gambling and industry, gentility and privation – and their concentration around the figure of the gentlemanly digger begins to convey a sense that Britishness requires redefinition, even to the point of rethinking it in Australian terms.

While Trollope's retrospective criticism of *Australia and New Zealand* was reasonably accurate – "dull and long"; not readable "in the proper sense of that word" – it nevertheless stands out for the melancholic conclusions about British identity that it draws from the goldfields.[73] Focusing on a series of gentlemen that he meets in his travels, Trollope finds their actions and motivations revealing of instabilities in class and character that cannot be attributed solely to the colonial environment. If such conclusions are somewhat surprising, it is in part because of a critical orthodoxy that Trollope's travel writing as a whole is premised upon a sense of English racial identity as stable, homogeneous, and impervious: "The boundary that matters in Trollope's travels is … the seal around the moving traveler: the portable boundary of a racial identity that Trollope very much wanted to believe determined his values, his outlook, his way of life, and was proof against alien infiltration."[74] In *Australia and New Zealand*, however, the British imprint being left upon Australia – by settlements and by settlers – frequently proves disappointing. Whereas, as Paul Delany asserts, the "continuity of landed property is the foundation of Trollope's social myth," the British presence in Australia appears defined instead by impermanence.[75] Sparsely populated country towns, laid out in Wakefieldian grids in anticipation of future growth, display "an apparent mixture of pretension and failure" that "creates a feeling of melancholy sadness in the mind of a stranger" (1.247). The highly

---

[72] Anthony Trollope, *Australia and New Zealand*, 2nd ed., 2 vols. (London: Chapman and Hall, 1873), 1.426. Hereafter cited in text.

[73] Trollope, *Autobiography*, 349.

[74] James Buzard, "Portable Boundaries: Trollope, Race, and Travel," *Nineteenth-Century Contexts* 32, no. 1 (2010): 9.

[75] Paul Delany, "Land, Money, and the Jews in the Later Trollope," *Studies in English Literature* 32, no. 4 (1992): 765.

transitory nature of many of the goldfields towns leaves an even worse impression: Currajong (Parkes) seems "the most hopelessly disappointing place I had visited in the colonies" (1.292); Edwards Reef is "a miserable melancholy place" (1.439); Matlock is "the most wretched place I ever saw" (1.441). Gold diggers, particularly those from upper-class backgrounds, provoke similarly grim reflections. In Queensland, Trollope stumbles upon one "who had been at school with my sons, and had frequented my house": "He had been softly nurtured, well educated, and was a handsome fellow to boot; and there he was eating a nauseous lump of beef out of a greasy frying-pan with his pocket-knife" (1.90). In finding such social levelling to be characteristic of the goldfields, Trollope is concerned not only because of the individual's abandonment of their class status but also because of the challenge it poses to the very concept of gentility:

> [T]hey [i.e., diggers of different classes] dress very much alike, work very much alike, and live very much alike. And, after awhile, they look very much alike.... The "gentleman," even though in the matter of gold he be a lucky gentleman, gets a corresponding fall. He loses his gentility, his love of cleanliness, his ease of words, his grace of bearing, his preference for good company, and his social exigencies.... [G]entility itself, – the combination of soft words, soft manners, and soft hands with manly bearing, and high courage, and intellectual pursuits, – is a possession in itself so valuable, and if once laid aside so difficult to be regained, that it should never be dropped without a struggle. (1.85–86)

While *Australia and New Zealand* makes this initial, melancholy acknowledgment of British settlers' innate susceptibility to speculation and desire, it is in the later *John Caldigate* – Trollope's "most wholehearted and accomplished attempt at a sensation novel" – that Trollope employs the subject of Australian gold to explore the inadequacy of the Lockean conception of the individual in the face of a globalized British population.[76]

Trollope's decade of investment and travel within the Victorian settler empire was bookended by *John Caldigate*, a novel that reflects that world of global mobility in its assertion of commonalities of British identity across its disparate settings. *John Caldigate* is in many ways a rewriting of Trollope's first Palliser novel, *Can You Forgive Her?* (1865), which was published immediately prior to Frederic Trollope's emigration to New South Wales, and the structural differences between the two texts offer a

---

[76] P. D. Edwards, *Anthony Trollope, His Art and Scope* (New York: St. Martin's Press, 1978), 216.

first clue as to the impact on the novel of Trollope's encounter with gold and settler colonialism. The two novels are Trollope's only works set largely in Cambridgeshire, in rural settings so firmly associated by his narrators with qualities of stability and sobriety that they serve as almost parodic exemplars of stadial principles. Far from being picturesque, however, the Cambridgeshire of *Can You Forgive Her?* is ugly to the extent that any trace of culture appears to have been entirely sundered from aesthetics:

> I believe it is conceded by all the other counties, that Cambridgeshire possesses fewer rural beauties than any other county in England. It is very flat; it is not well timbered; the rivers are merely dikes; and in a very large portion of the county the farms and fields are divided simply by ditches – not by hedgerows. Such arrangements are, no doubt, well adapted for agricultural purposes, but are not conducive to rural beauty.[77]

In the later novel, the Caldigate estate of Folking produces an even more dismal impression, "a place [not] having many attractions of its own, beyond the rats," and "bisected by an immense straight dike ... which is so sluggish, so straight, so ugly, and so deep, as to impress the mind of a stranger with the ideas [*sic*] of suicide."[78] The protagonists that emerge from these similarly unspectacular points of origin, both named John, diverge over the markedly different forms of gentlemanly character they embody. In *Can You Forgive Her?*, the drably named John Grey lives a settled life amidst the "desolate calmness" of his country house, eschewing London society and politics to spend time reading in his library and cultivating his extensive gardens.[79] The woman he falls in love with, Alice Vavasor, is at first repelled by this rural scene and instead contracts a disastrous engagement to her cousin, the "wild man" George Vavasor, only to ultimately yield to Grey's "imperious ... tranquillity" at the novel's conclusion.[80] By contrast, the likeable but undisciplined John Caldigate rapidly gets into debt while studying at Cambridge; excited by news of the gold discoveries in Australia, he subsequently emigrates in the hope of redeeming his fortunes. Whereas Grey doggedly pursues his erstwhile fiancée across Europe, Caldigate is still en route to Sydney when he abandons his commitment to the beautiful Hester Bolton to become engaged to an actress, Euphemia Smith. When Caldigate returns to Britain as a wealthy man and marries Hester, Euphemia follows and

---

[77] Anthony Trollope, *Can You Forgive Her?* (London: Oxford University Press, 1973), 100.
[78] Anthony Trollope, *John Caldigate*, ed. N. John Hall (Oxford: Oxford University Press, 1993), 3–4. Hereafter cited in text.
[79] Trollope, *Can You Forgive Her?*, 111.   [80] Ibid., 356.

accuses him of bigamy, leading to a sensational court case. These global movements of characters and capital already begin to indicate the novel's interest in thematizing Britain's imbrication in its settler empire, as the Caldigate estate and title are both strengthened and threatened by Australian gold.

In the earlier *Australia and New Zealand,* Trollope cast gold as a seductive and socially disruptive force, and characterized the quest for it as an irrational, speculative behavior contrary to the tenets of civil society. The possibility of primitive accumulation creates a "fury in the minds of men compelling them to search for it, let the risk, the danger, the misery, the probable losses, be what they may," as the thought of such "haphazard" mineral wealth "overcomes the imagination of the unconscious thinker, and takes possession of his heart and brain" (1.283). The translation of these sentiments into *John Caldigate* is enabled by the formal vocabularies of the romance, which Trollope typically invokes in his fiction to demarcate attitudes and territories that lie outside the norms of bourgeois sociality.[81] Australian gold is accordingly figured in the novel as "an article which adds fervour to the imagination and almost creates a power for romance" (106), capable of overwhelming rationality and self-discipline: "There is a curse about it, or a blessing, – it is hard to decide which, – that makes it almost impossible for a man to tear himself away from its pursuit when it is coming in freely" (122). Yet not all aspects of Trollope's on-the-ground conclusions about gold are imported straightforwardly into the novel. Despite having previously expressed distress at the thought of a "man I loved working in a gold-mine," and feeling even greater concern if he were to "see him successful," due to the mental disturbances that gold can provoke, Trollope's protagonist is strikingly impervious to the dangerous romance of gold, especially in light of his scapegrace past, and instead seems at first to affirm the enduring power of Lockean individualism (1.86). After only five weeks' labor at the fictional Ahalala diggings, Caldigate and his two companions hit pay dirt, which ultimately causes the ruin of his alcoholic fellow miners but marks the beginning of his own prosperity. Caldigate eventually graduates from mining this individual claim to managing a large commercial goldmine, the Polyeuka. The reformative effects of this colonial labor are first displayed in a letter to his estranged father, which strikes a tone of "sober, industrious determination," initiating their personal rapprochement and

[81] Walter M. Kendrick, *The Novel-Machine: The Theory and Fiction of Anthony Trollope* (Baltimore: Johns Hopkins University Press, 1980), 62–82.

suggesting that he has become fit to assume his inherited role as a member of the gentry (117). Caldigate ultimately sells his stake in the mine and returns to Britain, where he is able to repurchase the entail on the family estate; he soon marries Hester – his "second Ahalala" – and fathers a son, assuring the family succession and the continuation of tradition (134). Now prepared to contribute to wider society as well, he "surprised both his friends and his enemies by the exemplary manner in which he fulfilled his duties as a parish squire," and attends church "very regularly" (211). Yet at the same time as this act of reverse migration promises a close and stable relationship between Britain and Australia, Trollope deploys another form of narrative desire from the colony – erotic romance – to disrupt metropolitan society and its expectations of gentlemanly character.

At first, the immediate impact of Australian gold in *John Caldigate* appears entirely positive, and thus in marked contrast to Trollope's quasiproverbial observation, in *Australia and New Zealand*, "The Phoenix who has made his fortune at the diggings, and kept it, is a bird hardly to be found on Australian ground" (1.91). Standing again on his ancestral lands, Caldigate confidently narrates his colonial endeavors as a Lockean triumph of private property accumulation and character formation: "If a man will work steadily, and has backbone to stand up against reverses without consoling himself with drink; and if, when the gold comes, he can refrain from throwing it about as though it were endless, I think a man may be tolerably sure to earn something" (166). Caldigate's relationship with Euphemia Smith, which will detonate the sensation plot that shatters his gentlemanly facade, seems at first incommensurable with his disciplined success as a miner, yet his wayward passion is entirely in keeping with the unsettled ethos of appetite and desire that defines the goldfields. His susceptibility to romance is cast as a failure of character – "he ... was, within his own mind, conscious of his lack of all purpose, and very conscious of his folly" – but the novel does not portray Caldigate as simply having been degraded by his exposure to a colonial zone of primitive accumulation (66). Instead, *John Caldigate* suggests that this underdeveloped environment reveals a form of volatility already inherent in gentlemanly character. Drawing on the vocabulary of desire and chance that animates responses to the goldfields from Howitt to Jevons, the novel goes further to foreground the contingency inherent in class and racial identity. Reflecting on the contrasting fates of himself and his fellow migrant, the alcoholic Dick Shand, Caldigate comes to believe that his success is due to luck rather than strength of character:

> I am sometimes aghast with myself when I think of the small matter which, like the point on a railway, sent me running rapidly on to prosperity, – while the same point, turned wrong, hurried him to ruin… . It was something nature did for me rather than virtue. I am a rich man, and he is a shepherd, because something was put into my stomach capable of digesting bad brandy, which was not put into his. (136)

That is, instead of reaffirming the stability and global translatability of British identity by aligning it with inherent values of gentility, the novel attributes Caldigate's social and financial success to individual circumstances of biology as random as striking gold. Tracking its gentlemanly protagonist from his family estate to Australia and back again, *John Caldigate* asserts the surprising compatibility of Australian gold, and the unsettled qualities of character that it foregrounds, with an ancestral connection to land that remained the mythical heart of liberal individualism's sense of political agency.

"I am the least settled man in all the world" (143), Caldigate claims upon his return from Australia: spoken to parry to the maneuverings of a prospective mother-in-law, his words also reflect the novel's determined troubling of the stadial equation of territory and civic identity. The ostensibly settled world of Cambridgeshire is sensationally disrupted by Euphemia's accusation of bigamy, Caldigate's subsequent trial, and his ultimate conviction, with the salacious details of his life on the goldfields adding to the "romance of the occasion" (398). His conviction and the consequent delegitimation of his son might appear to suggest that the social disorder of the goldfields and the bullion extracted there are equally antithetical to British society, before the metropolitan status quo is ultimately restored with the discovery of new evidence that sanitizes Caldigate's colonial past and leads to a Queen's pardon. Yet the novel's ongoing refusal to fully disavow the settler colony, and the insights that it affords, is evident in the striking contrast between the fate of Caldigate's gold and the outcome of the archetypal Victorian narrative of scandalous Australian wealth, *Great Expectations*. In Dickens's novel, the introduction of Magwitch's money into British society immediately produces social upheaval, and Pip eventually refuses the convict's wealth on the way to strengthening his own character. By contrast, Caldigate's wealth not only remains untouched throughout the course of the novel, but he also acknowledges that his traditional world is inextricably linked to the wider settler empire: "I should not have done very well here unless I had been able to top-dress the English acres with a little Australian gold" (217). Caldigate's unapologetic stance earned a reproach from the *Saturday Review*, which complained that Trollope "so far excuses him under the circumstances that ... he never inflicts on him the novelist's true punishment – the disapproval of the honest conscientious characters of the story."[82] The ongoing continuities between Cambridgeshire and Australia are further underscored by the fact that Caldigate's pardon does not erase the original conviction. As is spelled out to him in a letter from the Home Office, "[W]e have but this lame way of redressing a great grievance. I am happy to think that in this case the future effect will be as complete as though the verdict had been reversed" (587). With the original bigamy conviction thus lingering as a ghostly presence in the novel, its happy ending ultimately remains dependent merely upon the legal classification of Caldigate's Australian romance rather than its absolute disavowal.

Trollope's protagonist's limited yet successful reintegration within British society occurs on the back of the novel's amalgamation of the colonial romance with the realism of the provincial novel, a formal rapprochement that signals the growing interpenetration of the disparate spaces of the Victorian settler empire. In keeping with these expanded horizons, *John Caldigate*'s dissolution of the intrinsic relationship between territoriality and its protagonist's character leads by the concluding chapter to an ongoing traffic between Britain and the settler colonies. The minor civil servant in the Post Office whose detective work uncovered the fraudulent nature of Euphemia Smith's evidence is temporarily posted to New South Wales, ostensibly to reform the Sydney office, but he instead facilitates a minor act of colonial knowledge transfer when he "bring[s] home with him ... a newly-discovered manner of tying mail-bags" (611). At the same time, while the dissolute Dick Shand remains unfit for metropolitan society, he is enabled to participate in the imperial economy after Caldigate bankrolls him to take a stake in a Queensland sugar company, a fusion of character and capital brought about by the continued circulation of Australia's gold within the settler empire. It is the sheer normality with which these continuing colonial exchanges are portrayed that is ultimately, and paradoxically, one of the novel's most striking features.

Bridging Metropolitan and Colonial Space

The reformulation of British identity and its relationship to land and labor prompted by the Australian gold rushes coincided with movements toward

---

[82] Quoted in Donald Arthur Smalley, ed. *Trollope: The Critical Heritage* (London: Routledge, 1969), 456.

the rethinking of liberalism and liberal subjectivity occurring in other colonial contexts at this time. Elaine Hadley argues that debates about Irish tenancy and the codification of "occupancy" as the basis of rights in the Irish Land Act of 1870 produced an emergent sense of "landed localism," instantiating a liberal nationalism that "problematizes the universalism of the liberal subject and its capacity to relocate its 'connection' beyond national boundaries."[83] Along related lines, Andrew Sartori maintains that discussions over tenancy and custom in Bengal meshed with those concerning Ireland to form a "crucial field in which metropolitan intellectuals could work out their own anxieties about the status of property as a normative foundation of liberal polity."[84] Charting the colonial and metropolitan responses to the Australian gold rushes brings to light a different liberal dynamic: the emergence into public prominence from the 1870s onward of an ideological terrain capable of sustaining the idea of a "Greater Britain" as a racially homogeneous, worldwide political formation.[85] Duncan Bell's history of the vigorous movement for a political federation of Britain and its settler empire that took shape during this time stresses its dependence on a distributed notion of British identity and the concomitant reimagination of metropolitan space in global terms. As he spells out, J. R. Seeley's *The Expansion of England* (1883) had made explicit that a "shift in political – as well as spatiotemporal – consciousness" was a necessary precursor to any closer imperial connection: "The first and most important step on the road to building Greater Britain was a cognitive one, involving a transformation in the way that people imagined the empire. 'If Greater Britain in the full sense of the phrase really existed,' insisted Seeley, 'Canada and Australia would be to us as Kent and Cornwall.'"[86] Seeley's formulation illuminates a new efficacy of imagining the political equality of metropolitan and settler colonial spaces, and highlights its dependence on the production of patriotic and racial sentiment capable of traversing imperial space.

At the same time, Seeley's ongoing subordination of the colonies through the language of provincialism is in contrast to the colonial origin of Trollope and Jevons's attempts to imagine the translatability of a recognizably British subject across imperial space. In this light, *John Caldigate* stages a different kind of imperial thinking to the period's most

---

[83] Hadley, *Living Liberalism*, 287.   [84] Sartori, *Liberalism in Empire*, 29.

[85] Belich observes of the state of Greater Britain at the turn of the twentieth century, "It had no formal shape, no federal constitution, yet it was an important economic and cultural reality." Belich, *Replenishing the Earth*, 460.

[86] Bell, *Idea of Greater Britain*, 9.

prominent manifestoes for the geopolitical revaluation of the settler empire, C. W. Dilke's *Greater Britain: A Record of Travel in English-Speaking Countries during 1866 and 1867* (1868) and J. A. Froude's *Oceana, or, England and Her Colonies* (1886). These works are also organized around an individualized and geographically mobile narrative perspective, a choice that enables Dilke and Froude to present their personal journeys through the settler empire as metonymies for the imperial sentiments and related political innovations they were seeking to describe and advance.[87] Yet both Dilke and Froude break off their narratives at the point of their return by steamship to Britain, reasserting the primacy of metropolitan space in a manner that lays the foundation for the asymmetric understanding of imperial portability that I argued in the Introduction animates current criticism. The gold-inflected accounts of empire offered by Trollope and Jevons stand out by contrast for their willingness to reimagine metropolitan space and subjectivity in colonial terms: their revaluations of the civilizing power attributed to land and labor, prompted by the dramatic events in Australia, helped bridge the Victorian settler empire in new ways by reconceiving the modern British individual as a powerfully mobile yet unpredictably volatile property.

---

[87] For the "world-making" intent of Dilke's *Greater Britain*, see Anna Johnston, "'Greater Britain': Late Imperial Travel Writing and the Settler Colonies," in *Oceania and the Victorian Imagination: Where All Things Are Possible*, ed. Richard D. Fulton and Peter H. Hoffenberg (Farnham: Ashgate, 2013).

CHAPTER 3

Speculative Utopianism
Colonial Progress, Debt, and Greater Britain

In the colonies everything is brand new. There you have the most
progressive race put into circumstances most favourable to progress.
They have no past and an unbounded future.

J. R. Seeley, *The Expansion of England*

There is probably no Colony of the British Empire which, relatively,
has enjoyed so uninterrupted and important a flow of British capital
to its shores as New Zealand.... [N]ot merely thousands, or even
hundreds of thousands, but millions are annually flowing into the
Colony to fertilise and develop its resources.

Falconer Larkworthy, *New Zealand Revisited*

The dissolution of the territorial basis of British subjectivity and sociality,
charted in the previous chapter, provided the foundation for a wide-
ranging reimagination of imperial territory and identity that constituted
"one of the most audacious political projects of modern times" – the
movement for a federation of Britain and its settler colonies, most commonly known as Greater Britain.[1] With the novel and political economy
bringing into focus a new sense of equivalency between British subjects in
the metropolis and the settler colonies, Britain's relationship with its settler
empire was increasingly able to be understood in terms of its geopolitical
value. Rather than being shaped by a straightforward sense of ethnic
identity, however, the imperial connection was characterized by a mutually
constitutive yet persistently unstable relationship defined along two intersecting axes: one defined by the poles of cultural commonality and
financial investment; the other, by competing principles of spatial homogeneity and temporal difference. Those spatiotemporal tensions, which
colored all matters of culture and finance, are clearly on display in J. R.
Seeley's popular and influential imperial history, *The Expansion of England*
(1883). Looking forward to the possibility of an imperial federation, based

[1] Bell, *Idea of Greater Britain*, 11.

on the belief that a unified British identity might transcend distance, Seeley's vision is expressed in markedly territorial terms: "If Greater Britain in the full sense of the phrase really existed, Canada and Australia would be to us as Kent and Cornwall."[2] Yet when he thinks about the political cultures of Britain and the settler colonies, Seeley instead turns to temporality: "In the colonies everything is brand new.... They have no past and an unbounded future."[3] Rather than posit the settler colony as backward, underdeveloped, or premodern, advocates of Greater Britain typically engaged in speculative visions of this kind, locating its fullest value in its future potential. The discussion that follows centers on the fact that the settler colonies became a key site for theorizing the progressive evolution of Britishness and British society at the same time that they were also seeking to attract unprecedented levels of investment from the metropole. The instability of this imperial conformation of culture and capital, freighted with the logic of past and future, played out most dramatically during the last decades of the century in one of the smallest and most obscure corners of the empire, in the developing relationship between New Zealand and Britain, where assertions of its British qualities were inextricably linked to discussions of its unprecedented levels of debt. I shall return to the largely forgotten debate surrounding New Zealand's debt, and treat it alongside the similarly unfamiliar tradition of colonial utopian writing, because in combination they demonstrate that the debate concerning Greater Britain was not simply a matter of metropolitan rhetoric imposed upon a willing colonial periphery. Instead, the enthusiasm for imperial federation prompted active manipulation of those rhetorical formulations and identity claims by settler novelists, politicians, and financiers, revealing the colonial determination to "leverage" British identity for local ends.

The metropolitan and settler writing discussed in this chapter demonstrates an imbrication of literary form, global political debates, and financial investment that challenges recent accounts of the transnational circulation of the Victorian novel. Historians have tended to discuss Greater Britain within several discrete frames – as a political movement for imperial union; as a proto-globalized zone of imperial trade and economic activity; as the global dissemination of British culture – and literary critics, concerned with the last of these, have generally posited the novel as a metonymic repository of Englishness, impervious to colonial appropriation or contamination. The "textual boundaries" of the novel, James Buzard argues, are "stand-ins for the boundaries of the culture or

---

[2] Seeley, *Expansion of England*, 75.   [3] Ibid., 204.

nation."[4] Extending this analysis, John Plotz maintains that these boundaries remain largely impermeable even as narratives are disseminated throughout the empire:

> [T]he problem of "staying English" within the wider realm that Dilke in 1868 called "Greater Britain" is addressed in novelistic representations of implicitly and explicitly *national* portable property. It is the existence of Greater Britain that requires not just a notion of portable cultural objects, but also of *asymmetry* in portability, so that the flow of culture-bearing objects from core to periphery is not counterbalanced or interrupted by a flow in the opposite direction.[5]

This model of a "pure asymmetry" of representational flow is concerned with the deployment of British cultural forms as a means to "protect Englishness," simultaneously denying the autochthony of indigenous cultures and asserting in the face of racial difference colonists' "psychic distance from one's actual site of residence."[6] But such a model has little to say about the potential for asymmetries to also exist within the Victorian settler empire's sphere of ostensible cultural and ethnic homogeneity. That is, a more complex model of literary exchange is required to allow for the possibility that settler populations might also appropriate and deploy forms of Britishness, not only to assert the kind of differences that contribute to the subjugation of indigenous populations, but also to assert the kind of commonalities that would allow metropolitan privileges to be turned to their advantage.

The asymmetries that I am highlighting within the settler empire in the last quarter of the century collide with greatest intensity in the various forms of utopian speculation associated with the idea of the colony, all of which hinged on imagining its future in positive terms. In the domain of finance, as Audrey Jaffe points out, the act of speculation – "identified as the placing of money in the service of risky projects" – is synonymous with "terms like 'optimism,' 'hope,' and 'bubble.'"[7] Optimistic visions of the cultural and political future are also the domain of utopian writing, and as Lyman Tower Sargent observes, "settler colonies have produced a rich harvest of utopian literature and projects," especially envisaging "new or

---

[4] James Buzard, *Disorienting Fiction: The Autoethnographic Work of Nineteenth-Century British Novels* (Princeton: Princeton University Press, 2005), 43.
[5] Plotz, *Portable Property*, 2, original emphasis   [6] Ibid., 22, 50.
[7] Audrey Jaffe, "Trollope in the Stock Market: Irrational Exuberance and *The Prime Minister*," in *Victorian Investments: New Perspectives on Finance and Culture*, ed. Cannon Schmitt and Nancy Henry (Bloomington: Indiana University Press, 2009), 151.

revised social and political institutions and economic patterns."[8] The most powerful and persistent variant of utopianism associated with the settler colony, however, was defined since Edward Gibbon Wakefield by the intersection of these financial and cultural modes of thought: deficient in capital in the present moment, but rich in British values, its social plenitude is offered as a promissory note for financial investment. Put another way, in the settler colonies, the cultural realm was uniquely able to overlap and impinge upon the domain of economics. "Being seen to be British paid dividends," because identity functioned as a de facto form of security for investors faced with a paucity of information about the myriad available opportunities for overseas investment:

> The underlying message seems to be that the dominions were regarded as "safe" precisely because the British investor knew what type of behavior to expect from both the borrowers and the state apparatus that ultimately guaranteed their capital's security.... [I]t was this perception of themselves, and by extension those in their colonies, that influenced, at both the conscious and sub-conscious levels, the attitudes of investors.[9]

Mary Poovey has described how ideas of character emerged alongside instruments of financial credit in the eighteenth century, and this impulse is writ large in the project of settlement, where portrayals of the colonies as spaces where British character and institutions could flourish proved integral to the financial mechanisms driving imperial expansion. As a result, I am suggesting that virtually all writing about the British qualities of the settler empire carried a burden of financial significance, but this played out especially in the blurring of generic boundaries between financial debates about colonial investment and utopian narratives of settlement. At the same time, however, additional formal tensions are generated in these texts by the discontinuities of imperial power, as the financial stakes of genre are further stratified by the political differences between metropole and periphery.

The narration of utopian speculation became an increasingly fraught act in New Zealand from the 1870s onward, as its reputation as the most British of all the settler colonies was complicated by the unprecedented amount of borrowing undertaken by its government and private sector.

---

[8] Lyman Tower Sargent, "Colonial and Postcolonial Utopias," in *The Cambridge Companion to Utopian Literature*, ed. Gregory Claeys (Cambridge: Cambridge University Press, 2010), 202.

[9] Magee and Thompson, *Empire and Globalisation*, 212–13, 214. In the analogous case of Australia, note P. J. Cain and A. G. Hopkins, "kinship offered the British a sense of security about … investment which meant that the colonies could often borrow when foreign supplicants were frowned upon." Cain and Hopkins, *British Imperialism*, 220.

Throughout the writings of this period Australasia is routinely observed to be the most "intensely English" part of the empire, and New Zealand in particular is singled out as a potent symbol of the possibilities of the settler project to replicate an ideal version of British society.[10] "Closely resembling Great Britain in situation, size, and climate," C. W. Dilke observed, "New Zealand is often styled by the colonists 'The Britain of the South.'"[11] Yet such sanguine observations were paralleled by a darker strain of commentary concerned with the state of the colony's accounts. "The most striking fact connected with the financial affairs of New Zealand and the Australian states is the enormous size of their public debts," begins an article in *The Journal of Political Economy* in 1909, which concludes that the "ease with which the government has been able to borrow has been a temptation to extravagance which it has been unable to resist."[12] This persistent anxiety about New Zealand debt and the susceptibility of metropolitan lenders originated with a vast borrowing scheme launched there in 1870 by the colonial treasurer (and later premier) Julius Vogel. Following a decade of costly colonial warfare and economic stagnation, Vogel proposed to borrow 10 million pounds in London to stimulate settlement through investment in infrastructure, especially railways, and assisted immigration. "Vogel had insisted on the urgency of attracting British immigrants and capital to ward off stagnation and regression," observes Darwin: "He saw that New Zealand must compete with many other calls on British investment and grasped (although not the first to do so) that its special claim must be based on assertions about its likeness to Britain."[13] Vastly exceeding its initial goals, the colony succeeded in obtaining almost £20,000,000 over the course of the decade, and this vast sum was further supplemented by the success of similarly expansive private investment schemes seeking to profit from swathes of land suddenly made valuable by proximity to the new railways. Remarkably, New Zealand was the destination for almost 9 percent of Britain's export capital in the period 1875–79, despite its population of only 250,000 at the beginning of the decade.[14] The scale

---

[10] William Clarke, "An English Imperialist Bubble," *The North American Review* 141, no. 344 (1885): 69.

[11] C. W. Dilke, *Greater Britain: A Record of Travel in English-Speaking Countries during 1866 and 1867* (London: MacMillan, 1868), 1.334.

[12] James Edward Le Rossignol and William Downie Stewart, "The Public Debt of New Zealand," *The Journal of Political Economy* 17, no. 8 (1909): 509, 526.

[13] Darwin, *Empire Project*, 172.

[14] W. J. Gardner, "A Colonial Economy," in *The Oxford History of New Zealand*, ed. Geoffrey Rice, 2nd ed. (Auckland: Oxford University Press, 1992), 71; Magee and Thompson, *Empire and Globalisation*, 174; Belich, *Making Peoples*, 359–60.

and audacity of the borrowing policy, often attributed (partly for anti-Semitic reasons) to Vogel's "strong and even over-mastering imagination," made him an intensely polarizing figure in the colony and beyond. As one colonial commentator reflected in the middle of the borrowing spree,

> But one thing is certain – whether he be a clever rogue or a heaven-sent statesman – he has been by far the most prominent man in the Colonies for the last five years. His name is deeply carved for weal or woe in the annals of this country, and future historians will mark as the one solitary figure which stood out in bold relief in New Zealand during the last five years the figure of Julius Vogel.[15]

Vogel's New Zealand critics accused him of being a "rogue" for advancing a reckless economic populism that threatened to plunge the colony into long-term debt or even bankrupt it entirely. British skeptics were equally askance at Vogel's ability to garner such vast metropolitan support for such a risky colonial venture. Both perspectives were unified by an awareness that the yoking of imaginative and financial forms of speculation, and their application to the settler colony, had produced financial, political, and cultural effects that seemed little short of intoxicating.

The complex questions of agency brought to light through the transfer of such substantial amounts of capital to the antipodes are captured in Belich's description of it as a "New Zealand-led New Zealand-British financial system."[16] Crucially, these flows were accompanied and enabled by settler endorsements of Greater Britain as a political project based on the successful global transfer of British character and values. Vogel's public pronouncements also illuminate the significance of this representational domain. As a self-described "ardent advocate" of a political union between Britain and the settler colonies, his defense of imperial lending within the empire was consistently founded on appeals to the British qualities of the settler population.[17] Writing on "The Finances of New Zealand," in *Fraser's Magazine* in the mid-1870s, he argued:

> [F]ar above climate, soil, and mineral and other capabilities, the strength of New Zealand depends on its people.... Upon its people depends a

[15] W. L. Rees, *The Coming Crisis: A Sketch of the Financial and Political Condition of New Zealand, with the Causes and Probable Results of that Condition* (Auckland: Reed and Brett, 1874), 14, 19.

[16] Belich, *Making Peoples*, 360.

[17] Julius Vogel, *New Zealand and the South Sea Islands, and Their Relation to the Empire* (London: Edward Stanford, 1878), 3.

ists of New Zealand have those virtues of
ʒy which ensure success and happiness to

ioneer traits might be regarded as
typical of the Greater Britain
ʿe immediate context of New
ᴐveals a more highly charged,
ᴖs of British character. Vogel's
debt and colonization, suggests why
ᴄ homogeneity or otherwise of Greater
ᴗ battlegrounds over the nature, location, and

ᴗ ᴗws, I argue that during the era of enthusiasm for Greater
ᴄne common ground shared by claims of British identity and
ᴩpeals for British investment was actively contested by settler and metropolitan writers through a form of writing that I term speculative
utopianism. In advance of New Zealand's expansion of imperial
borrowing, Samuel Butler's nonfictional *A First Year in Canterbury Settlement* (1863) and the genre-bending utopia *Erewhon, or, Over the Range*
(1872) signaled the emergence of speculative utopianism as a future-
oriented mode that constructs the settler colony as a British space of
guaranteed returns on metropolitan investment. The political stakes of
speculative utopianism in the 1870s can best be glimpsed in Julius Vogel's
essays, which seek to justify New Zealand's enormous borrowings in
London by positing the British character of settlers as the ultimate ground
of safe investment. The leveraging of the rhetoric of Greater Britain as a
means of stimulating investment was increasingly contested following the
collapse of New Zealand's credit in the late 1870s, most strikingly in
Trollope's *The Fixed Period* (1883). This dystopian narrative imagines a
future South Pacific settler colony ruled by a Vogel-like demagogue, and a
plot centered on its policy of compulsory euthanasia allows Trollope to
position the rhetoric of colonial futurity and progressiveness as a cultural
aberration rather than a source of value. In the final decade of the century,
New Zealand writers and politicians responded to such metropolitan
skepticism with narratives that raised the stakes of locating British values
in the settler colony. Speculative fictions such as Vogel's *Anno Domini
2000; or, Woman's Destiny* (1889) and Henry Crocker Marriott Watson's

[18] Julius Vogel, *The Finances of New Zealand by the Premier of the Colonial Government* (London:
Longmans, Green, 1875), 20.

The Decline and Fall of the British Empire, or, the Wi
plot the future subordination of the metropolis to the c
time as asserting their common Britishness, at a moment v
geopolitics were redefining the settler empire as a resourc
continued global security.

Culture, Investment, and Utopia: *A First Year in*
Canterbury Settlement and *Erewhon*

The idea of a delocalized and mobile British subject was fundame
to the movement for an imperial federation of Britain and its sett
empire. Advocates for a "Greater Britain" based their arguments for the
political homogeneity of imperial territory on claims of its equally
homogeneous racial and cultural makeup. This tendentious confidence
in British identity's iterability at unprecedented scale is spelled out in
one of the movement's two urtexts, C. W. Dilke's *Greater Britain:
A Record of Travel in English-Speaking Countries during 1866 and 1867*
(1868), a travel narrative that doubles as a manifesto for reimagining
empire's political utility by demonstrating the commonalities of "race"
across globally dispersed British spaces. "In 1866 and 1867," Dilke
begins, "I followed England round the world: everywhere I was in
English-speaking, or in English-governed lands. If I remarked that
climate, soil, manners of life, that mixture with other peoples had
modified the blood, I saw, too, that in essentials the race was always
the same."[19] Dilke's ability to narrate such a journey in itself constitutes the main evidence for Greater Britain as an emerging political
entity and, despite including India and Ceylon in his itinerary, his
argument coheres most fully around the settler colonies: Lydia Wevers
describes his account as "a series of iterations of upper-class, white,
male England and Englishness."[20] Concluding his extensive discussion
of Australia with a general reflection on the value of Britain's colonies,
he maintains that their cultural benefits will be most manifest
when there is a relationship of political equality between metropolis
and colony:

> It may, perhaps, be contended that the possession of "colonies" tends to
> preserve us from the curse of small island countries, the dwarfing of mind

[19] Dilke, *Greater Britain*, 1.v. Hereafter cited in text.
[20] Lydia Wevers, *Country of Writing: Travel Writing and New Zealand, 1809–1900* (Auckland: Auckland University Press, 2002), 136.

ake us Guernsey a little magnified…. That which
ncialism of citizenship of Little England is our
Saxondom which includes all that is best and
-37)

assertions of the global spread of "English
1otes that such claims are comparatively
lonies presented as being "unproblematic-
' whereas they become fraught "as soon as
portion of the globe that is both under British political
control and populated by blood English."[21] Despite his critique of Dilke's "conceptually confused" notion of race, Plotz nevertheless follows his lead in also concentrating on racial difference (exemplified by India) as the sole challenge to Victorian faith in "cultural portability."[22] I will suggest, however, that the presence of "white Britons" could also challenge such notions of one-way cultural flow, as growing affiliation to the settler colony spurred contestations of metropolitan cultural primacy.

Alongside the rhetoric of racial and cultural solidarity, Britain and the settler empire were also connected by flows of trade and finance, as "the colonies became part of the 'invisible' financial and commercial empire which had its centre in the City of London."[23] Yet in both of these domains – the cultural and the financial – structural distinctions between metropolis and colony were preserved and remained influential. This seeming paradox plays out in the second urtext of the imperial federation movement, J. R. Seeley's *The Expansion of England* (1883), where such differences are foregrounded even in the act of positing a "homogeneous" global territory across which Englishness – as a population and as a cultural heritage – is evenly distributed and readily comprehended. That is, despite claiming that "settlement colonies should be seen as an organic extension of Britain," Seeley reinforces key spatial and temporal distinctions between imperial core and periphery.[24] "If Greater Britain in the full sense of the phrase really existed," he claims, "Canada and Australia would be to us as Kent and Cornwall."[25] While the analogy might seem to imagine these discrete polities on equal terms, likening the colonies to provinces reinforces the asymmetrical primacy of the metropole over the periphery.

[21] Plotz, *Portable Property*, 66.   [22] Ibid., 68.
[23] P. J. Cain and A. G. Hopkins, *British Imperialism, 1688–2000*, 2nd ed. (Harlow: Longman, 2002), 214.
[24] Darwin, *The Empire Project*, 147.   [25] Seeley, *Expansion of England*, 75.

A similar tension is on display when *Expansion of England* settler empire in temporal terms:

> In the colonies everything is brand new. There you have the most ̶ sive race put into circumstances most favourable to progress. They h̶ past and an unbounded future. Government and institutions are all u̶ English. All is liberty, industry, invention, innovation, and as yet tranqu̶ lity. Now if this alone were Greater Britain, it would be homogeneous, all of a piece; and, vast and boundless as the territory is, we might come to understand its affairs.[26]

By figuring the colony as the fulfilment of a liberal progress narrative, Seeley effectively frames the periphery as the apotheosis of Britishness. Out of the temporal gap that consequently opens between colony and metropole emerges the rhetorical potential for settler writers to "leverage" the concept of British identity for colonial ends.

In New Zealand, I will argue, such claims about the progressive future of British identity were redeployed to authorize financial investment. This potential can be glimpsed at the outset of the era of Greater Britain in the works that Samuel Butler produced out of his experiences as a settler pastoralist in the south of New Zealand, first the nonfictional *A First Year in Canterbury Settlement* (1863), and later the genre-bending utopia, *Erewhon, or, Over the Range* (1872). Compiled from Butler's letters and journal entries and published in Britain while he was still in the colony, *First Year in Canterbury Settlement* is essentially a narrative of metropolitan investment: it recounts his voyage to New Zealand in 1859, along with £2,000 of his father's money and a promise of a further £3,000, and his efforts to cash in on the colony's booming pastoral economy by locating and purchasing grazing land.[27] Butler's family connections within the Anglican church smoothed the process of his relocation to Canterbury, for it had been founded in 1850 by the Church of England as the last and most developed of Wakefield's schemes of systematic colonization, with its initial cohort of settlers comprising "the nearest approximation to a 'Wakefield' colonial nucleus in both homogeneity and numbers."[28] The settlement of Canterbury had been prefaced by the dubious purchase of 20 million acres of land by the Crown from the Ngai Tahu tribe and their

---

[26] Ibid., 204.

[27] Peter Raby, *Samuel Butler: A Biography* (London: Hogarth, 1991), 67–68. See also Belich, *Making Peoples*, 340–45.

[28] Gardner, "Colonial Economy," 62. For the background to Butler's decision to emigrate to New Zealand, see Raby, *Samuel Butler*, 62–63.

relegation to a series of reserves.[29] By the time Butler arrived, the vast expanse of the Canterbury plains appeared virtually empty of Māori and thus fully available for settler appropriation.

The actions of the colonial government and Wakefield's Canterbury Association in the decade prior to Butler's arrival therefore underpin his initial impressions of the colony, which stress its cultural and scenic likeness with Britain. He finds that the "conversation was English in point of expression," and that the surrounding landscape is reminiscent of Cambridgeshire.[30] Venturing into the hinterland for the first time, an encounter with two farmers provides a rare opportunity in the text to register the prior presence of Ngai Tahu, but also signals how peripheral this knowledge is to the colonists' current concerns:

> These men were as good gentlemen, in the conventional sense of the word, as any with whom we associate in England – I daresay, *de facto*, much better than many of them. They showed me some moa bones which they had ploughed up ... also some stone Māori battle-axes. They bought this land two years ago, and assured me that, even though they had not touched it, they could get for it cent. per cent. upon the price which they then gave. (38)

The passage asserts a strict temporal distinction between Māori, who are fixed in the archaeological past, and the future-focused concerns of Butler's gentlemanly settlers. Their plans hinge on the transformation of the land into a particular kind of "no-place," or utopia. Disconnected from present-day questions of sovereignty and dispossession, the land's value is instead located entirely in the future, when it will provide a return on their initial investment.

The farmers' confident expectations of increasing land value are, for Butler, a synecdoche for the colony as a whole, which he finds to exist solely for the provision of a return on British investment. "The fact is, people here are busy making money," he observes; "that is the inducement which led them to come in the first instance, and they show their sense by devoting their energies to the work" (50). Butler includes himself in this assessment: after spending considerable time puzzling over what to do with his father's capital, he decides to search out unclaimed pasture in the hinterland, and stock it with sheep. This project immerses Butler in

[29] Ann Parsonson, "The Challenge to Mana Māori," in *The Oxford History of New Zealand*, ed. Geoffrey Rice, 2nd. ed. (Auckland: Oxford University Press, 1992), 179–81.
[30] Samuel Butler, *A First Year in Canterbury Settlement*, ed. A. C. Brassington and Peter Bromley Maling (Auckland: Blackwood & Paul, 1964), 35, 37. Hereafter cited in text.

the landscape, and it requires him to view it in different terms to those instilled by his earlier training in landscape painting. He distinguishes these competing perspectives as "scenery" and "country" (63). To view the colony as "scenery" is to prioritize its noneconomic values, and to approach it through categories such as the picturesque and the sublime, whereas to regard it as "country" is to engage in an act of utopian speculation that overlays the visible landscape with a vision of future returns it promises to provide. Butler's own view of the land as "country" is realized most tangibly not through narrative description but through detailed tabular calculations that plot the growth that might be expected from an initial purchase of five hundred ewes (40):

	Ewes	Ewe Lambs	Wether Lambs	Ewe Hoggets	Wether Hoggets	Wethers	Total
1 year old January, 1860	500	—	—	—	—	—	500
,, 1861	500	100	100	—	—	—	700
,, 1862	500	100	100	100	100	—	900
,, 1863	600	120	120	100	100	100	1,140
,, 1864	700	140	140	120	120	200	1,420
,, 1865	820	164	164	140	140	320	1,748
,, 1866	960	192	192	164	164	460	2,132
,, 1867	1,124	225	225	192	192	624	2,582

This utopian flock is immediately converted into a predicted return on investment:

			£	s.	d.
January, 1861 .	.	2s. 6d. per head	62	10	0
,, 1862 .	.	. . .	87	10	0
,, 1863 .	.	. . .	112	10	0
,, 1864 .	.	. . .	142	10	0
,, 1865 .	.	. . .	177	10	0
,, 1866 .	.	. . .	218	10	0
,, 1867 .	.	. . .	266	10	0
Total wool money received	.	. .	£1,067	10	0
Original capital expended	.	. .	£625	0	0

At first glance these tables resemble those colonial novels discussed previously that supplement their plots of settlement with occasional turns to political economy. In those cases, recourse to numbers affirmed the settled state of the colony by attesting to its viability as a space of labor and accumulation. By contrast, Butler's tabular acts of utopian speculation aren't simply one component of his account, but instead provide its underlying logic of narrative progression, and through this the means by which the text comprehends the colony. Orientated entirely toward the future, the colony's primary interest now lies in its capacity for delivering a reliable and significant return on investment.

If *First Year in Canterbury Settlement* defines the settler colony as the destination of metropolitan capital, Butler also suggests that this financial flow is crucially enabled by its status as a recognizable, if reduced, version of Britain. At the beginning of his first journey, he describes traveling to a sheep station homestead on the very edge of settlement, "*bona fide* beyond the pale of civilisation" (48). There, rather than finding the colonists degraded by the privations of their environment, Butler observes the pragmatism demanded by frontier life to be surprisingly balanced with the social and intellectual trappings more commonly associated with metropolitan society:

> The men are all gentlemen and sons of gentlemen, and one of them is a Cambridge man, who took a high second-class a year or two before my time…. He regarded me as a somewhat despicable newcomer (at least so I imagined), and when next morning I asked where I should wash, he gave rather a French shrug of the shoulders, and said, "The lake." … Under his bed I found Tennyson's *Idylls of the Kings*. So you will see that even in these out-of-the-world places people do care a little for something besides sheep. (49)

Crucially, the presence of high culture at the furthest extent of the frontier is not presented to critique the colonists, or to perform the ideological conversion of the land back from "country" to "scenery." (Simon During maintains that through colonial experience, Butler "declassed himself, even if without removing himself from the social recognition and privilege attached to gentility.")[31] Instead, even such a refined text as *Idylls of the Kings* helps enable the farming economy by demonstrating that the settler frontier is a space that can sustain British culture and identity. Concluding this episode with a general reflection on colonial character – "Men are as

---

[31] Simon During, "Samuel Butler's Influence," in *A History of New Zealand Literature*, ed. Mark Williams (Cambridge: Cambridge University Press, 2016), 47.

shrewd and sensible, as alive to the humorous, and as hard-headed" as in Britain (50) – Butler brings into even closer alignment the values of metropolitan culture and the principles of colonial investment.

Writing with the dual purpose of justifying his use of his family's capital, and offering advice and encouragement to other potential emigrants, Butler's anecdote of discovering Tennyson in the shepherd's hut provides a form of security for his various metropolitan readers: it underwrites a potentially risky venture by domesticating and rendering familiar this foreign space. After all, around the same time Walter Bagehot was writing with alarm in *The Economist* of the heedless risks taken by imperial investors due to their inability to imagine cultural difference:

> Many persons have not a distinct perception of the risk of lending to a country in a wholly different state of civilization. They can hardly imagine the difficulties with which such a country struggles, and the dangers to which it is exposed. They forget that national good faith is a rare and recent thing, and they expect to find it where the condition of its existence cannot be found.[32]

In this formulation, where the security of imperial investment rests on the intangibles of "national good faith," the impossible need for familiarity with distant and unknown locations places great weight upon British "character" and culture as proxies for knowledge of the actual investment. Bagehot concludes, "We lend to countries whose condition we do not know, and whose want of civilization we do not consider, and, therefore, we lose our money."[33] The straightforward narrative of *First Year in Canterbury* seeks to assuage anxieties such as these, offering a first-hand account of a colony where nothing is unsettling from a metropolitan perspective. It thereby anticipates the metropolitan view of Greater Britain, soon to be popularized by Dilke and Seeley, as a unified political entity demarcated by common bonds of culture and identity. Indeed, Butler's subsequent colonial career only lends weight to such claims. Within fifteen months of his arrival in New Zealand, he had secured leasehold rights over a 40,000-acre sheep station, which he named Mesopotamia and stocked with 2,000 sheep. At the point he chose to return to Britain, in mid-1864, Butler was already financially independent after almost doubling his money.[34]

---

[32] Walter Bagehot, "The Danger of Lending to Semi-civilised Countries," in *The Collected Works of Walter Bagehot*, ed. Norman St. John-Stevas (London: Economist, 1978), 419.

[33] Bagehot, "Danger of Lending," 423.

[34] Raby, *Samuel Butler*, 84, 95–96. On leaving the colony, Butler chose to reinvest his money there, where it promised to keep earning a high rate of interest. Eventually calling in his New Zealand investments, Butler then invested in a range of colonial speculations, only to lose most of his money in early 1874. Resolving to attempt to improve the fortunes of the Canada Tanning Extract

Butler was living off his New Zealand earnings in London when he began to revisit the settler colonial scene in the narrative that would become *Erewhon*. Indeed, its intellectual origins are also firmly located in New Zealand, for its "first published nucleus" had been published in the Christchurch *Press* in 1863, one of a series of articles Butler had written in response to reading *Origin of Species* while living at Mesopotamia.[35] James Smithies argues that such an early engagement with Darwin attests that "the cultural relationship between Victorian England and its antipodes during the mid-nineteenth century appears to have been basically synchronous," yet synchronicity does not amount to homogeneity.[36] *Erewhon* registers the complexity of these imperial textual and financial exchanges in presenting the settler colony as a space for the revaluation and appropriation of Britishness. *Erewhon* opens in 1868 with the arrival of its protagonist, Higgs, in an unnamed settler colony that closely resembles Canterbury, determined to secure financial success; like Butler, he is set on "finding, or even perhaps purchasing, waste crown-land suitable for cattle or sheep farming, by which means I thought that I could better my fortunes more rapidly than in England."[37] Unlike Butler, Higgs eventually succumbs to the temptation to regard the landscape as "scenery," and his quest for unclaimed land develops into a quest to explore the mountain ranges that dominate the view from the plains, a hazardous journey that he undertakes with the assistance of a shiftless Māori guide, Chowbok or Kahabuka. After Chowbok abandons him, Higgs continues on alone at great personal risk, eventually scaling the mountain range and crossing over into the land of Erewhon. There he discovers a quasimetropolitan society where, as Sue Zemka puts it, "Victorian institutions and cultural beliefs ... [are] ineluctably reproduced across temporal and spatial divisions" while its inhabitants nevertheless remain "insistently a different people."[38] As a consequence, the idea of Greater Britain is brought into play in *Erewhon* at the same time as destabilizing its underlying assumptions. On the one hand, the settler empire provides a clear overarching

Company, "the one business out of all his investments that looked salvable," he was placed in charge of the company by the board of directors; after living in Montreal in 1874–75, he ultimately resigned from his position, and it collapsed shortly after. Ibid., 142–49.

[35] Ibid., 89, 116.

[36] James Smithies, "Return Migration and the Mechanical Age: Samuel Butler in New Zealand 1860–1864," *Journal of Victorian Culture* 12, no. 2 (2007): 220.

[37] Samuel Butler, *Erewhon, or, Over the Range*, ed. Peter Mudford (London: Penguin, 1970), 39. Hereafter cited in text.

[38] Sue Zemka, "*Erewhon* and the End of Utopian Humanism," *ELH* 69, no. 2 (2002): 441.

geographic and cultural framework for the novel, first in bringing Higgs to
the colony for the purpose of investment, and then through the consistent
ability of Erewhonian social norms to collapse the distinctions between
metropolis and colony. On the other hand, the version of Britishness that
Higgs discovers in the settler colony is actively disaggregated from its
metropolitan equivalent through the portrayal of character and class traits.
Beneath this uncanny vision of Britishness as both sameness and difference, *Erewhon* enacts a more profound conceptual shift – especially in
comparison to *First Year in Canterbury Settlement* – in articulating those
categories of collective and individual identity from the perspective
afforded by the frontier.

Over the course of Higgs's time in Erewhon, metropolitan notions of
Britishness are repeatedly scrutinized and destabilized through the
uncanny encounter with a society that seems familiar yet disconcertingly
strange. His initial impressions of Erewhon are presented as identical to the
unsettling feelings he had previously experienced on his arrival in the
colony, which arose from the paradoxes of antipodean colonial Britishness.
This produces a recursive layering of comparisons, as what Zemka calls the
"uncanny echoes of Victorian life" in Erewhon are comprehended through
the similar-yet-different contrast between Erewhon and the settler colony,
which in turn is simultaneously shown to be like-yet-unlike Britain.[39] "It
was not at all like going to China or Japan," Higgs reflects soon after his
arrival in Erewhon, "where everything that one sees is strange":

> The more I looked at everything in the house, the more I was struck with its
> quasi-European character…. Yet everything was slightly different. It was
> much the same with the birds and flowers on the other side, as compared
> with the English ones…. [N]ot quite the same as the English, but still very
> like them – quite like enough to be called by the same name. (74–75)

The unsettling effect of viewing Britishness from a different part of the
world is encapsulated in the anagrammatic, implicitly antipodean, inver-
sions that Butler employs to name the new land – Erewhon (Nowhere) –
as well as its inhabitants, such as Senoj Nosnibor (Jones Robinson), and its
social classes, notably that of Ydgrun (Grundy). This sense of inverted
familiarity is taken furthest in Butler's extensive reflections on the Erewhonian understanding of crime and of illness: the former is viewed as the
product of misfortune that requires medical treatment, while the latter is
punished for criminal carelessness in accordance with the severity of the

case. In the case of bad luck, which is considered a form of crime rather than something to be met with sympathy, Butler's unsettling of metropolitan norms is further informed by ethnographic knowledge gleaned from his time in the colony: "Among foreign nations Erewhonian opinions may be still more clearly noted.... [T]he New Zealand Maories [*sic*] visit any misfortune with forcible entry into the house of the offender, and the breaking up and burning of all his goods" (103).[40] This translation of the Māori custom of *muru* into Butler's inverted account of Victorian society marks with particular intensity the spatial breadth of the cultural imaginary encapsulated in *Erewhon*. Simon During describes the novel as "an adventure into a place where society turns away from orthodoxy – like Māori lifeways and also like the early settler colony as Butler experienced it."[41] Colonial knowledge and insights into Britishness are here directed back toward the metropolis, such that *Erewhon* essentially offers a literary map of Greater Britain with its zero meridian centered on the antipodes.

The recentering of the settler colony in *Erewhon* as a place from which to rethink British identity and sociality is inseparable from the way it strengthens the speculative utopianism previously gestured at in *First Year in Canterbury Settlement*. Butler's utopianism is distinct from "the classic utopianism of a radical political and philosophical tradition, where certain buried or occluded potentials of humanity are imagined as 'shattering' social and economic structures that repress them."[42] It also diverges from the more specific utopianism typically associated with the metropolitan advocates of Greater Britain, who invoked it as "a positive ideal, an inspirational model of the future necessary to crystallize transformative action in the present."[43] In contrast to both these possibilities, Butler's recourse to utopian form allows him to define a link between the dual conceptions of futurity that together classify the settler colony as a particular type of speculative zone: what might be called a cultural utopianism, which posits the colony as the site of a future apotheosis of British identity, is aligned with a financial utopianism that trades on the colony's Britishness to assert its suitability for investment. The unstable temporal difference between Erewhon and Britain – its population exists in an idealized semifeudal state while being advanced enough to have also experienced a Victorian-like machine age several centuries previously – provides a

---

[40] Joseph Jones details the ethnographic texts that influenced Butler in *The Cradle of Erewhon: Samuel Butler in New Zealand* (Austin: University of Texas Press, 1959), 145–50.

[41] During, "Samuel Butler's Influence," 49. [42] Zemka, "End of Utopian Humanism," 439–40.

[43] Bell, *Idea of Greater Britain*, 19.

foundation for its portrayal of the Erewhonian gentleman as legible in British terms yet also distinctively colonial:

> Being inured from youth to exercises and athletics of all sorts, and living fearlessly under the eye of their peers, among whom there exists a high standard of courage, generosity, honour, and every good and manly quality – what wonder that they should have become, so to speak, a law unto themselves....
>
> [T]hey were more like the best class of Englishmen than any whom I have seen in other countries. (157–58)

Simon During accordingly finds the "most important" value asserted in *Erewhon* to be "male physical grace."[44] This linking of an ideal gentleman-liness with colonial physicality also occurs in *First Year in Canterbury Settlement*, which praises "healthy clear-complexioned men, shaggy-bearded, rowdy-hatted, and independent, pictures of rude health and strength" (33). But whereas in the earlier text questions of physical appearance remain peripheral to the utopian speculations centered on the future growth of the colony's flocks, *Erewhon* now foregrounds these qualities of settler masculinity as central to the future value of Erewhon.

Erewhon's charting of the intersection between cultural and financial speculation, embodied in its account of gentlemanliness as a colonial resource, therefore complicates Paul Cain and P. J. Hopkins's "gentle-manly capitalism" thesis of imperial expansion. Cain and Hopkins observe that "the export version of the gentlemanly order" that dominated the City of London was manifested as a sense of imperial mission, and that "Britain's representatives abroad shared the social origins and values of their counterparts in the metropole."[45] In contrast to this sense of gentle-manliness anchored in Britain, the value ascribed by Butler to settler gentlemanliness establishes it as a primary form of security for British speculative investment. The intersection between cultural and financial speculation is ultimately brought together in the novel's conclusion, following Higgs's escape from Erewhon and return to London. There he proposes to profit from his experiences through the formation of a joint-stock company, the Erewhon Evangelisation Company, to "convert the Erewhonians not only into good Christians but into a source of considerable profit to the shareholders":

> We should begin by representing the advantages afforded to labour in the colony of Queensland, and point out to the Erewhonians that by

---

44 During, "Samuel Butler's Influence," 49.   45 Cain and Hopkins, *British Imperialism*, 47–48.

emigrating thither, they would be able to amass, each and all of them, enormous fortunes....

Should we be attacked, our course would be even simpler ... we should be able to capture as many as we chose; in this case we should feel able to engage them on more advantageous terms, for they would be prisoners of war....

[W]e could go backwards and forwards as long as there was a demand for labour in Queensland, or indeed in any other Christian colony, for the supply of Erewhonians would be unlimited, and they could be packed closely and fed at a very reasonable cost. (256–57)

This ironic proposal is responding most immediately to the Australian practice of "blackbirding," or forced indenture of Pacific Island laborers, as well as invoking Britain's recent military incursions into the indigenous heartland of New Zealand's North Island. Nevertheless, it also underscores the new sense that the quasisettler population of Erewhon is central to conceptions of the colony's "commercial value." That is, it reveals that by the beginning of the 1870s, when New Zealand's borrowing began with earnest, metropolitan investment could already be seen to be dependent upon, and therefore able to be influenced by, assertions of settler character emanating from the colony.

Borrowing on British Character: New Zealand's Debt

Butler's speculative utopianism highlights an emergent settler ability to make claims on and for British identity that was further heightened in New Zealand in the 1870s, where the tactical usage of the rhetoric of Greater Britain was spurred by the colony's unprecedented efforts to borrow money in London to accelerate the progress of settlement. As one London-based New Zealand financier observed in later years, "There is probably no Colony of the British Empire which, relatively, has enjoyed so uninterrupted and important a flow of British capital to its shores as New Zealand."[46] The broad contours of this rhetorical effort can be seen in the *Official Handbook of New Zealand* (1875), edited by the indefatigable Julius Vogel, which was intended to appeal to prospective settlers. The immigrant is promised, upon arrival in New Zealand, to be "surrounded by numbers of his own countrymen ... dressed like himself," as well as being encompassed by the broader trappings of Victorian social infrastructure, "those institutions of social life that in England are the outcome of

---

[46] Falconer Larkworthy, *New Zealand Revisited*, 2nd ed. (London: William Brown, 1882), 24.

WANGANUI BRIDGE, WELLINGTON.

Figure 3.1   The ambitious future prospects ascribed to New Zealand in the 1870s are affirmed by the large new iron bridge that dominates the small town of Wanganui. The bridge is a tangible sign of extensive infrastructure investment, while the empty hills indicate potential for future growth.

the ages during which it has been evolving its grand history, but which, having been transplanted to the Colony, have taken root and flourished as in the most congenial soil."[47] The *Official Handbook*'s detailed survey of the colony, however, seeks out signs of material progress and couples these to a sense of unparalleled future prospects. In the description and accompanying illustration (Figure 3.1) of the town of Wanganui, for example, the progress wrought by investment is put front and center in a description of its "splendid iron bridge, the largest which has yet been built in the North Island, nearly 600 ft. long," which concludes, "The total cost of the bridge was £32,000." At the same time, the vast scale of that infrastructure outlay is markedly out of kilter with the current needs of a settlement that only "contains about 300 houses" and where "the land resources ... are only as yet partially developed."[48] The delicate balance struck

[47] Julius Vogel, ed. *The Official Handbook of New Zealand: A Collection of Papers by Experienced Colonists on the Colony as a Whole, and on the Several Provinces* (London: Wyman, 1875), 25, 43.
[48] Ibid., 194–97.

here between current achievement and future fulfilment points to a more general quality of settler claims on Britishness at this time. The metropolitan-centric Greater Britain movement was actively "leveraged" by colonial politicians and writers, who used the possibilities of speculative utopianism discerned by Butler to appropriate the language and imagery of global Britishness for the purpose of securing metropolitan investment.

The active contestation of Britishness as a category of political identity can be glimpsed in the contrasting uses of the idea of imperial sentiment made in two essays on Greater Britain originating from opposite ends of the settler empire: the metropolitan historian J. A. Froude's "England and Her Colonies" (1870), and the colonial politician Julius Vogel's earliest published pamphlet, *Great Britain and Her Colonies* (1865). Froude envisages the settler empire as a continuation and expansion of English nationalism, in which the fundamental challenge is retaining a sense of patriotic loyalty to the imperial core. Britain's "expatriated swarms" ought to be channeled away from the United States and toward the colonies, where "every acre which they could reclaim from the wilderness [is] so much added to English soil, and themselves and their families fresh additions to our national stability."[49] For Froude, empire is in the first instance a matter of feelings and attachment, rather than financial or strategic calculation: "sentimentalism ... lies at the root of every powerful nationality, and has been the principle of its coherence and growth."[50] In Vogel's hands, however, sentimental attachment to British identity is neither divorced from the political economy of empire nor subordinated to it, but is presented as the ground upon which investment can be conceptualized and legitimated. *Great Britain and Her Colonies* begins by presenting the current state of imperial relations as "vague, shadowy, and undefined," and argues that this is a vulnerability that arises because those bonds are based solely on "sentiment" rather than on "mutual interest."[51] He proposes this state of affairs can only be remedied by Britain's willingness to offer guarantees for capital invested in its settler colonies, and seeks to justify this stance through three related arguments: investments outside the empire diminish Britain's ability to enact an independent foreign policy; by contrast, investing in the colonies will serve to "creat[e] nations to act as her allies in times of danger"; and, moreover, such investments will ensure New Zealand's firm attachment to Britain, because "the colonists [will] owe to the great body of the people at home the capital on which they are

---

[49] Froude, "England and Her Colonies," 151.   [50] Ibid., 159.
[51] Julius Vogel, *Great Britain and Her Colonies* (London: Smith, Elder, 1865), 3.

working their way to wealth."[52] Put another way, what might on the surface seem to be an orthodox assertion of Greater British patriotism – the empire as a global space of Britishness – in fact significantly diverges from that position, by putting imperial "sentiment" to work on behalf of investments to aggrandize the colonies. By the time he was serving in London as New Zealand's agent-general a decade later, Vogel would play on such sentiments ever more explicitly, going so far as to argue that "no greater benefit was ever bestowed upon the money-market of Great Britain than a colony coming forward and asking for money for the purpose of honestly and bravely developing English territory by the countrymen of those who lent the money."[53] Such foregrounding of Britishness amounts to a strategic manipulation of metropolitan rhetoric for the material benefit of the settler colony.

I will argue that speculative utopianism comes into focus in New Zealand in the 1870s as a means of securing two interrelated forms of credit for the settler colony: the reputational credit associated with Britishness – what one of Vogel's successors as agent-general would describe as "the honesty, credit, and standing of industrious, patriotic British communities" – and the financial credit that might as a result be extended from London.[54] In a paper on the subject of national debt from the mid-1870s, R. Dudley Baxter proffered as a thought experiment a global map of credit, organized "round the centre of good credit, London," which would reveal that all credit-worthy nations are found in the northern hemisphere, except for "one great exception": "the English Colonies, – which, whether near the North Pole, or the Equator, or the Antipodes, maintain the credit of their mother country."[55] According to the proponents of Greater Britain, as well as some of its critics, a map surveying reputational credit that was also centered on London would reveal a similar concentration of good character in the settler colonies. In Seeley's eyes, common ethnicity was "fundamental" to the settler empire's "conditions of stability"; for the Fabian, William Clarke, writing in response to *The Expansion of England*, while "it cannot be denied that the idea of a close bond connecting English people acts as a powerful sentiment," it in fact masks an underlying attempt "to divert the broad stream of human progress into the narrow channel of English capitalism."[56] More recently, economic

---

[52] Ibid., 13–14.   [53] Julius Vogel, "New Zealand," *Times*, November 2, 1877.
[54] William Pember Reeves, "New Zealand Finance," *Times*, November 17, 1900.
[55] R. Dudley Baxter, "The Recent Progress of National Debts," *Journal of the Statistical Society of London* 37, no. 1 (1874): 7.
[56] Seeley, *Expansion of England*, 13; Clarke, "English Imperialist Bubble," 71, 72.

historians have similarly stressed the reputational credit secured by claims of Britishness – as individual character, as well as governing structure – in legitimating colonial investments for metropolitan lenders:

> [T]he dominions were regarded as "safe" precisely because the British investor knew what type of behavior to expect from both the borrowers and the state apparatus that ultimately guaranteed their capital's security. For the British therefore, "Britishness" connoted not their parliamentary or legal systems per se, but all the virtues they saw in themselves and that breathed life into their institutions: fairness, justice, reliability, technical competence, accountability, individual freedom and respect for private property.[57]

Gaining credit for the Britishness of New Zealand – and, more specifically, for the presence there of a stable form of British character – was therefore fundamental to securing financial investment in the colony.

To justify the unprecedented scale of New Zealand's borrowing, Vogel and other settler writers sought not only to repeat but also to amplify the rhetoric of Britishness, going so far as to define British identity as a form of potential only capable of ultimate fulfillment in a colonial future. In accordance with this logic, the goal of expanding the settler population becomes so preeminent that it is often pitched as a more important site of colonial investment than the land. In *The Finances of New Zealand by the Premier of the Colonial Government* (1875), written in the midst of the borrowing frenzy, Vogel sounds this note of colonial Britishness at full volume:

> [F]ar above climate, soil, and mineral and other capabilities, the strength of New Zealand depends on its people.... Upon its people depends a country's success; and the colonists of New Zealand have those virtues of frugality, faith, industry, and energy which ensure success and happiness to their possessors.... Generations will live and die in New Zealand, and still the homely virtues of its pilgrim fathers will be reproduced.[58]

The language of settler potential is pegged to the logic of investment, and capital is presented as the means for accelerating its flourishing in the future. The proleptic quality of this rhetoric is usefully demonstrated by one of New Zealand's most prominent London-based financiers, Falconer Larkworthy, whose *New Zealand Revisited* (1881) maintains that Vogel's borrowing policy "originated in the desire, experienced by all young and

---

[57] Magee and Thompson, *Empire and Globalisation*, 212.
[58] Vogel, *Finances of New Zealand*, 20–21.

progressive communities with large resources, to discount the future, and so bring about in a day, and frequently to their own inconvenience, what other communities have taken centuries to accomplish."[59] The conflation of investment with the anticipatory temporality of colonial growth is captured in the term, "discount," a phrase "much used in City circles" that means "to anticipate or expect ... intelligence, and then act as though it had already arrived."[60] Vogel and Larkworthy are effectively asking London investors to also "discount the future," by investing in the seeming certainty of the colony's rosy prospects. Yet those future-focused claims conceal a rhetorical shell game occurring in the present, where the settler business and political elite are borrowing a metropolitan discourse of British identity and presenting it back to metropolitan investors as a form of security for their loans.

Metropolitan Sovereignty and Settler Dystopia: *The Fixed Period*

During the flourishing of the imperial federation movement during the 1870s, the Australasian colonies were held to exemplify the possibility that British institutions could be replicated and patriotic sentiment sustained across the globe. It might therefore seem surprising that, only a few years later, J. A. Froude would record such severe disappointment with New Zealand in his influential travelogue, *Oceana, or, England and Her Colonies* (1886). His impressions were largely shaped by the developing city of Auckland, where he concluded that rapid and unsightly urbanization had displaced the redemptive possibilities of pastoral settlement:

> The English race should not come to New Zealand to renew the town life which they leave behind them.... They will grow into a nation when they are settled in their own houses and freeholds, like their forefathers who drew bow at Agincourt or trailed pike in the wars of the Commonwealth; when they own their own acres, raise their own sheep and cattle, and live out their days with their children and grandchildren around them.[61]

This Carlylean anxiety about the weakening of colonists' moral fiber as a result of their unhealthy physical environs flows over into Froude's critical opinion of the colony's relationship with Britain, which is dominated by his concern for the extent of New Zealand's public borrowing. "The debt was out of all proportion to so small a community," he complains: "The

---

[59] Larkworthy, *New Zealand Revisited*, 4.   [60] *Oxford English Dictionary*, s.v. "Discount."
[61] Froude, *Oceana*, 212.

land, in the North Island at least, was not being developed as it is in Australia. It was falling into the hands of speculators."[62] Rather than providing relief and restoration for Britain's surplus population, this once exemplary colony now appeared more like a parasitic growth, feeding on British capital while inflicting moral damage on British subjects.

Froude's anxieties about New Zealand's likely future, and its implications for the wider empire, were by this point far from unusual. Even during the heyday of speculative utopianism that accompanied Vogel's policy of borrowing, a critical counternarrative had begun to emerge in the metropolitan press, and by the mid-1880s the colony had become a byword for excessive debt. What would become an almost ritual chastisement of the colony by the *Economist* was initiated by a lengthy discussion of Vogel's first budget, which it summed up as "a crude design for encouraging, by methods absolutely opposed to all sound political and economical notions, the speedy advance of the colony in population and production."[63] In 1880, it would describe New Zealand's growth as a "feverish, and partly a fictitious, strength due to the use of stimulants, which impart a present vitality at the expense of the national constitution in the future."[64] By that point such skepticism had by and large achieved the status of received wisdom, following the failure of the City of Glasgow Bank in October 1878: the bank had made significant speculative investments in New Zealand land and, as Larkworthy discreetly put it, "Discredit fell with peculiar force on the financial and mercantile relations of Australia and New Zealand."[65] The bank's association with New Zealand triggered the collapse of the colony's credit, which also coincided with a precipitous decline in export prices, and led to a period of economic stagnation that would last into the 1890s. The second iteration of the *Official Handbook of New Zealand* (1883), written for potential British settlers by the colony's London-based agent-general at the time, Francis Dillon Bell, attests to the scale of this financial and reputational crisis by beginning with a detailed account of the colony's finances. While acknowledging that the colony had amassed a net debt of £22,065,408 since the beginning of the previous decade, Bell valiantly attempts to dispel the considerable suspicion with which it is now viewed:

> Throughout this running survey, as it may be termed, of New Zealand Finance, the endeavour has been to sketch its chief features, to dispel much

---

[62] Ibid., 284–85.   [63] "The Finances of New Zealand," *The Economist* 28, no. 1416 (1870): 1252.
[64] "Our Colonial Possessions," *The Economist* 38, no. 1931 (1880): 1024.
[65] Larkworthy, *New Zealand Revisited*, 5.

misapprehension which exists on the subject of the Public Debt, and to give a true, though faint, idea of the financial condition of the Colony, and of the great future which lies before it in the rapid and continuous development of its industrial resources, infinite in variety and immeasurable in value.[66]

While such statements continued to employ the generic conventions of speculative utopianism, they were now mobilized upon a very different ideological terrain. New Zealand's compromised credit, both financial and reputational, gave rise to a more fraught metropolitan revisioning of Greater Britain, and the potential of the settler colony, that was expressed in markedly dystopian form.

The dystopian counternarrative to speculative utopianism that took shape in metropolitan writing centered on the view that the settler appropriation of Britishness was producing depleted or hollowed-out forms of identity, where "ties to the motherland seemed more instrumental than sentimental."[67] This dystopianism diverged sharply from the more celebratory vision of Greater Britain articulated at the time by Seeley and other imperial federation advocates, and was most fully explored in Trollope's *The Fixed Period* (1882), a "futuristic fantasy" informed by his brief return visit to New Zealand in 1875, during the heyday of Vogel's borrowing policy.[68] Trollope's comments at the time on "Sir Julius Vogel and his loans," made in one of the letters he had contracted to write during his travels for the *Liverpool Mercury*, include commonplace observations about the colony's unparalleled per capita debt, and equally familiar expressions of skepticism toward the populist nature of the borrowing policy. His insights are distinguished, however, by their attention to broader questions of imperial sovereignty:

> [W]ith a country as with an individual, the time will come when debts must be paid or bankruptcy ensue. I do not predict bankruptcy to New Zealand. The mother country would probably save so well-loved a colony from that position. But if she did so, she would demand to have the management of its finances for a time in her own hands. It seems to me to be quite possible that Sir Julius Vogel, if he remain long enough in power, may bring New Zealand to this condition.[69]

---

[66] Francis Dillon Bell, *Official Handbook of New Zealand*, 2nd ed. (London: Edward Stanford, 1883), 37.

[67] Theodore Koditschek, *Liberalism, Imperialism, and the Historical Imagination: Nineteenth-Century Visions of a Greater Britain* (Cambridge: Cambridge University Press, 2011), 195.

[68] Nicholas Birns, "The Empire Turned Upside Down: The Colonial Fictions of Anthony Trollope," *ARIEL: A Review of International English Literature* 27, no. 3 (1996): 15.

[69] Anthony Trollope, *The Tireless Traveler: Twenty Letters to the* Liverpool Mercury, ed. Bradford Allen Booth (Berkeley: University of California Press, 1941), 206.

Trollope envisages a future recalibration of financial and political relations within the Victorian settler empire, as a sovereign penalty imposed by the metropole for preventing the bankrupt colony from further speculation and possible ruin. In the wake of the collapse of New Zealand's credit, Trollope took up and extended these ideas in *The Fixed Period*, the story of a future dispute between Britain and a fictional South Pacific settler colony, which takes aim at the logic of speculative utopianism and settler claims to exemplify the best qualities of Britishness.

The Fixed Period is set a hundred years in the future, in the fictional republic of Britannula, a model colony founded by settlers who first broke away from New Zealand – ironically, over its handling of the colonial debt – and later declared their independence from Britain. The narrator is the colony's charismatic president, Jack Neverbend, who from the outset describes Britannula in the familiar terms of speculative utopianism, stressing the "exuberant fertility" of its agricultural production and presenting the settlers as "the *élite* of the selected population of New Zealand."[70] This sense of elitism has been taken to a bizarre extreme in the Britannulan constitution, specifically the part that gives the novel its name: all citizens who live to the age of 68 are subject to compulsory euthanasia. Helen Lucy Blythe associates the colonial president with "the idealistic discourse of emigration leader Edward Gibbon Wakefield," and argues that the annihilationist constitution he seeks to uphold ironizes the Victorian sense of civilizing mission while also implicitly acknowledging the colonial extinction of indigenous peoples.[71] The settler demagogue who lies more immediately to hand, however, is Julius Vogel. Indeed, President Neverbend justifies the principle of the Fixed Period in developmental terms highly reminiscent of the utopian rhetoric of future fulfilment that pervaded New Zealand's policy discourse in the 1870s:

> [W]e should save on average £50 for each man and woman who had departed. When our population should have become a million, presuming that one only in fifty would have reached the desired age, the sum actually saved to the colony would amount to £1,000,000 a-year. It would keep us out of debt, make for us our railways, render all our rivers navigable, construct our bridges, and leave us shortly the richest people on God's earth. (8)

[70] Anthony Trollope, *The Fixed Period*, ed. David Skilton (Oxford: Oxford University Press, 1993), 16. Hereinafter cited in text.
[71] Blythe, "Euthanasia, Cannibalism, and Colonial Extinction," 168.

By placing *The Fixed Period* in this more immediate context of colonial ambition and financial chicanery, the policy of euthanasia comes into focus as offering an ironic literalizing of the proleptic rhetoric of colonial youth and futurity. After all, this progressive settler colony will never grow old. Neverbend pejoratively associates Britain with an antiquated past – a visiting English cricket team has "no ideas beyond those current in the last century" – while Britannula is "her youngest child" (58, 121). The euthanasia policy perversely exemplifies the colony's unrivalled progressiveness, anticipating Seeley's laudatory descriptions of the settler empire – "the most progressive race put into circumstances most favourable to progress" – in the heavily ironized description of the policy as "an advance in progress and general civilisation never hitherto even thought of among other people" (63). The idea of the Fixed Period therefore performs a double duty in the novel, signifying an extreme form of the social and political innovation associated with the settler colonies, while also disrupting the temporal distinction that values colonial futurity above metropolitan tradition.

The events recounted in *The Fixed Period* are narrated retrospectively, written by the colony's president while he is a prisoner on board the British warship that was to intervene at the first attempt to implement the euthanasia policy, and has restored British rule over the colony. The plot recapitulates the scenario previously envisaged in Trollope's commentary on the stakes of New Zealand's public debt, where Britain "would probably save so well-loved a colony," but only at the cost of restoring a form of metropolitan order, "demand[ing] to have the management of its finances for a time in her own hands." An exchange between Neverbend and a visiting British aristocrat over whether the Britannulans are "foreigners" to the British highlights the novel's probing of the value of the cultural commonalities and national sentiment that were at the center of debates around imperial federation. "What makes a foreigner but a different allegiance?" asks Neverbend, "If we be not foreigners, what are we, my lord?":

> "Englishmen, of course," said he. "What else? Don't you talk English?"
>
> "So do the Americans, my lord," said I, with a smile that was intended to be gracious. "Our language is spreading itself over the world, and is no sign of nationality."
>
> "What laws do you obey?"
>
> "English, – till we choose to repeal them. You are aware that we have already freed ourselves from the stain of capital punishment."
>
> "These coins pass in your market-places?" ... It was one of those pounds which the people will continue to call sovereigns, although the name had

been made actually illegal for the rendering of all accounts. "Whose is this image and superscription?"...

"[A]ccording to my ideas, a nation does not depend on the small external accidents of its coin or its language." (66–67)

The dispute effectively centers on whether the cultural trappings of Britishness have an intrinsic relationship to matters of sovereignty. Neverbend's antagonist asserts that commonalities of race, language, law, and even currency override Britannula's claims to political independence, while the colonial politician argues that cultural forms – "the small external accidents of its coin or its language" – are extraneous to national sentiment. The immediate upshot is a notable failure to establish any clear legal basis for Britain's intervention in what is effectively a local political dispute. Indeed, the novel as a whole is not particularly concerned with offering a coherent account of political relations within the empire. Rather, its most concrete achievement is a realignment of the genre categories used to comprehend colonial Britishness.

The formal critique of speculative utopianism mounted in *The Fixed Period* proceeds by recasting the tropes of colonial youthfulness and futurity in a bounded dystopian temporality. What Seeley calls the "unbounded future" of the settler polity is directly undermined in the novel through the euthanasia policy, which frames colonial progressiveness as a form of cultural and political separation from metropolitan tradition that plays out in demagoguery and national self-annihilation. The instructions given by the Colonial Office to the newly installed British governor accordingly state,

> The country has since undoubtedly prospered, and in a material point of view has given us no grounds for regret. But in their selection of a Constitution the Britannulists have unfortunately allowed themselves but one deliberative assembly, and hence have sprung their present difficulties. It must be, that in such circumstances crude councils should be passed as laws without the safeguard coming from further discussion and thought. (134)

Such concerns might at first seem at several removes from the questions of metropolitan credit and colonial debt, but they in fact constitute an attack on the fundamental claims that settlement might replicate and improve Britishness that were so intrinsic to New Zealand's borrowing policy. Colonial futurity and youthfulness, now redefined as the absence of stabilizing constitutional tradition, becomes a dystopian aberration rather than a source of future value. The reannexation of Britannula therefore amounts to a rejection of speculative utopianism, as Trollope imagines calling in the loan of cultural, political, and racial assets that had founded and sustained this South Pacific settler project.

Speculative Utopianism and Geopolitics: *Anno Domini 2000* and *Decline and Fall of the British Empire*

In the final years of the century the New Zealand economy remained depressed, and it continued to be a byword for debt and imprudence in the pages of the *Economist* and the *Times*, but settler writers and politicians continued to fight a rearguard action to uphold the colony's financial credibility through reaffirming its British qualities. When the financier Falconer Larkworthy took up the subject of the colony's future prospects in his ostensible travel narrative, *New Zealand Revisited* (1881), he began by directly acknowledging the "fashion with the financial papers to rail at the Colony for what was termed its 'spendthrift proclivities.'"[72] Similarly, the colonial press recognized his book as designed to help improve the colony's credit by intervening in that reputational dispute. The reviewer for the *New Zealand Herald* readily discerned that what Larkworthy spuriously called an "independent and trustworthy account" was "calculated to benefit the colony in Great Britain wherever it is read," because of its fervent reaffirmation of the colony's future economic and cultural potential: "So far as it touches upon the affairs of New Zealand, it does so in a clear and trenchant style, and a tone of the fullest confidence as to the future of the colony breathes through every page."[73] Such contestations of the future, aimed at a metropolitan readership, would become central to settler utopian and dystopian novels in the 1880s and 1890s, which now began plotting the subordination of the metropolis to the colony at the same time as continuing to assert the value and importance of a common British identity. Two such works, Julius Vogel's *Anno Domini 2000* and H. C. Marriott Watson's *Decline and Fall of the British Empire*, indicate that debates surrounding transnational British identity were increasingly cast by metropolitan and colonial thinkers alike in a geopolitical light. More specifically, their *fin de siècle* visions of global political upheaval illuminate a shift in the logic of speculative utopianism, whereby the fullest potential value of the settler colonies was increasingly understood in terms of their ability to place a British population in service of metropolitan geopolitical ends.

[72] Larkworthy, *New Zealand Revisited*, 4.
[73] Ibid., 6; "New Zealand Revisited," *New Zealand Herald*, January 14, 1882, 5.

The paradigmatic example of *fin de siècle* speculative utopianism was written, almost inevitably, by Julius Vogel: his *Anno Domini 2000; or, Woman's Destiny* (1889) gives fullest expression to his political commitment to an imperial federation of Britain and its settler colonies. Published after his return to Britain in 1888 – he had previously lived there from 1876 to 1880, while serving as New Zealand's agent-general – the novel was part of a doomed strategy to establish himself in London as a colonial public intellectual, alongside the resumption of the journalistic and public-speaking endeavors he had previously undertaken while agent-general, and corresponding frequently with *The Times* on imperial matters.[74] While Vogel and his publisher disastrously overestimated the level of popular interest in his work, his decision to turn to the utopian novel nevertheless usefully indicates that the relationship between settler futurity and metro-politan financial credit was now framed in overtly geopolitical terms. *Anno Domini 2000* imagines the Victorian settler empire as the end of history, where "not only is it the most powerful empire on the globe, but at present no sign is shown of any tendency to weakness or decay."[75] The limited critical attention that has been paid to the novel has largely focused on the prescience or otherwise of its technological vision, its openness to female political leadership, or the wish-fulfillment of a plot that culminates with the military humbling of the United States. Of greater importance for the current argument is its redeployment of the familiar financial and cultural dimensions of speculative utopianism to assert the future geopolitical preeminence of the settler colonies. From the first chapter of *Anno Domini*, which begins with a general assertion that human history is characterized by "progression, always progression," the novel clearly identifies the settler colony as the catalyst of further imperial development (35). By misrepresenting those frontier spaces as devoid of any indigenous presence, *Anno Domini* retells the enduring settler story of "waste" land capable of ready transformation to bountiful productivity, this time through the kind of large-scale infrastructural investments that also characterized Vogel's public works initiatives. The Malee Scrub Plains in Australia, for example, "were once about as desolate and unromantic a locality as could be found; but a Canadian firm ... had undertaken to turn the wilderness into a garden by irrigation, and they had entirely succeeded" (105). Likewise, the

---

[74] Raewyn Dalziel, *Julius Vogel: Business Politician* (Auckland: Auckland University Press, 1986), 217, 304.
[75] Julius Vogel, *Anno Domini 2000; or, Woman's Destiny* (Honolulu: University of Hawai'i Press, 2002), 37–38. Hereafter cited in text.

novel recounts a privately funded project in New Zealand to recover the gold deposits suspected to lie in a particular river through a vast scheme to "lay bare and clear from water fully fifty miles of the river bed" (120–21). If the conceit of colonial youthfulness is implied when the latter scheme is inaugurated by a child, tasked with pulling the levers that divert the river, the idealized relationship between colonial futurity and metropolitan capital is equally evident when the lowering waters duly reveal vast amounts of gold that will finally reward the watching investors for their persistence with a 50-year project. Such episodes provide the basis for the novel to imagine a form of colonial political agency within Greater Britain, whereby privileging the settler colony as a realm of future wealth generation is integrally related to its status as a global engine of political progress.

Taking up once more Seeley's definition of the settler colony as "the most progressive race put in the circumstances most favourable to progress," *Anno Domini 2000* foregrounds two areas of social and political innovation – imperial federation and gender equality in the public sphere – and attributes the attainment of both to colonial interventions. With the colonies now so "rich, populous, and powerful" that they "far exceeded in importance the original mother-country" (38), they are able to mandate that Britain grant local government to Ireland, which in turn triggers the federation of the empire:

> The Colonies … became every day, as they advanced in wealth and progress, more interested in the nation to which they belonged…. They felt … that the Colonies, which had grown not only materially, but socially, happy under the influence of free institutions, could not regard with indifference the denial of the same freedom to an important territory of the nation. (144)

While the novel does not specifically attribute a colonial origin to its vision of gender equality, its prominence in the novel – its subtitle, after all, is *Woman's Destiny* – reflects the preoccupations of recent settler political debate. Vogel had unsuccessfully sponsored legislation to institute women's suffrage in 1887 in New Zealand, and the suffragist campaign that ultimately succeeded there in 1893 mobilized a rhetoric of civilizational progress that associated women's rights with an emergent sense of nationhood.[76] These questions enter the narrative through a New

---

[76] Dalziel, *Julius Vogel*, 267–69; Raewyn Dalziel, "An Experiment in the Social Laboratory? Suffrage, National Identity, and Mythologies of Race in New Zealand in the 1890s," in *Women's Suffrage in the British Empire: Citizenship, Nation, and Race*, ed. Ian Christopher Fletcher, Philippa Levine, and Laura E. Nym Mayhall (London: Routledge, 2000).

Zealand-born politician, Hilda Fitzherbert, and a creaking love plot that sees her ultimately marry the emperor. The novel concludes with the passage of legislation to allow their daughter to accede to the throne, "an Act considered to be especially memorable, since it removed the last disability under which the female sex laboured" (182). These examples relocate colonial progressivism to the heart of the metropole, and in doing so signal a revaluation of the political balance within the settler empire, where Britain's political leadership is diminished even as the colonies' newfound preeminence remains dependent upon ongoing metropolitan investment.

Alongside such revisionings of speculative utopianism, settler authors at the *fin de siècle* also attempted to reappropriate the dystopian portrayals of colonial debt offered by metropolitan writers such as Froude and Trollope. The most striking, and perhaps unlikely, example is provided by Henry Crocker Marriott Watson, an Anglican minister who emigrated to New Zealand from Australia in 1873, during the heyday of Vogelism, and subsequently published two dystopian narratives set in Britain: *Erchomenon; or, The Republic of Materialism* (1879) and *The Decline and Fall of the British Empire* (1890). The latter work was written during a visit to Britain in the mid-1880s, and a report in the New Zealand press affirms that questions of debt, colonial identity, and narrative production were inextricably linked in his thinking at the time:

> He had also been asked numerous questions respecting New Zealand securities, and had been able to satisfy a good many of those who had been somewhat shaken in their faith in New Zealand through recent Banking uncertainties and commercial failures.... He admitted that he went Home with prejudices in favour of English people and England generally, but, after eighteen months amongst them, his opinions had undergone considerable modification, and, in some instances, were entirely reversed.... His own effort in literature, "The Decline and Fall of the British Empire" ... written during his absence, had now been launched, and had been most favourably reviewed by the leading journals in England.[77]

The novel that emerged from these experiences retraces the broad arc of Marriott Watson's journey to the metropolis, with the fundamental difference that in the future it imagines – it is set in 2990 – its antipodean protagonists are visiting the shattered remnants of an imperial nation now reduced to a state of near barbarism.

---

[77] "The Rev H. C. M. Watson: Home Experiences," *Star*, April 10, 1891, 3.

Marriott Watson's primary concern in *Decline and Fall* is to mount a conservative critique of the degenerative effects of materialism and socialism, and the novel pursues this goal by inverting the dystopian temporal logic previously employed by Froude and Trollope to differentiate the metropolis and colony. Whereas those earlier writers castigated settler progressiveness as the compromised outcome of economic and cultural debt, Marriott Watson now contrasts the "Republic of Australia" favorably with "Ancient Britain."[78] The novel portrays the metropolis as an anachronism, reduced by cultural malaise to a semifeudal state. When the tourists first land at Plymouth, they find it is now just "a small village, built on the site of ancient Plymouth," and the antithesis of modernity and progress:

> The houses in which the natives lived were exceedingly small, the rooms very cramped and confined.... The people lived chiefly by fishing and agriculture; but some cultivated sheep, and were owners of flocks, numbering several thousands each.... Behind and around the village were the cultivated land of the islanders, which seemed to be very fertile.... [T]hat the place had formerly a population of a couple of hundred thousand seemed almost incredible. Equally so was the information that the harbour was then the resort of thousands of large ships every year. (47–49)

Portraying Britain as a society based on small-scale agriculture and pastoralism, and its citizens as "natives," Marriott Watson invokes and inverts some of the most enduring tropes of settler colonialism. Through this reversal, what Froude and Trollope asserted as the virtue of tradition is now reconfigured once more as an archaic state of backwardness.

Despite surveying the ruins of metropolitan British society, *Decline and Fall* does not argue for the dismemberment of the settler empire. Marriott Watson draws on the same logic of colonial progress employed by Seeley and Vogel to portray the settler periphery as now able to repay the cultural and financial investments that have been made in it. The majority of the text is dominated by the narrator's experience of a dream vision, which grants him a privileged insight into the political "theories" that precipitated Britain's decline: "In one word, they were of an artificial character, and tended unduly to the restriction of individual freedom, which is one of the chief factors of progress" (74–75). To mount this critique, Marriott Watson has to ignore the fact that New Zealand's late-century reputation for progressivism was intimately associated with socialistic legislation that

---

[78] Henry Crocker Marriott Watson, *The Decline and Fall of the British Empire, or, the Witch's Cavern* (London: Trischler, 1890), 11. Hereafter cited in text.

reformed working conditions and established the basis of a welfare state. Nevertheless, the novel's vision of the future culminates with the progressive periphery revitalizing the moribund metropolis, in an explicit act of reverse settler colonization: "when Australia is overcrowded," the narrator tells his fiancée at the conclusion, "we will return to the old home and repopulate England. We are English, for England is the home of our fathers" (291). The imaginative investment made by *Decline and Fall* in the cultural commonalities of the settler empire, combined with its determination to view that global terrain from a colonial perspective, defines the novel as a self-conscious engagement with the wider problematic of colonial debt and identity even though it is otherwise never directly addressed in the narrative.

Even into the first decade of the new century, the question of New Zealand's debt continued to generate criticism in Britain, and to be met with colonial defenses couched in the rhetoric of Greater Britain. A letter written to the *Times* on the matter by a disaffected New Zealand settler – "Borrow, borrow, borrow, but never, never, never pay – that is the sum total of Australasian financial statesmanship" – was affirmed in a subsequent editorial, which suggested that British lenders' "faith in the future of the colonies" might be coming to an end, and expressed the hope that "New Zealand is unique in converting a deficiency in the revenue in to a perpetual debt."[79] These statements were met with a rejoinder by the current agent-general, William Pember Reeves, who sought to shift the terms of the debate back onto the terrain of settler character by describing the editorial as "a damning indictment against the honesty, credit, and standing of industrious, patriotic British communities." Even at this point he could maintain that the best "security" that might be afforded to metropolitan lenders was the knowledge of a common British identity:

> I am challenged to say how much of our national debt is reproductive. I unhesitatingly say that nine-tenths of it is so, directly or indirectly. This is the security that the English lenders have – a prosperous, intelligent young nation, the wealth, honesty, and energy of which form, in truth, the safest possible of sinking funds.[80]

In addition to highlighting the longevity of these debates, Reeves's comments confirm that the growing settler population was increasingly seen as the most important outcome of metropolitan investment. Rather than

[79] Wm. Stevenson Aickin, "Australasia's Never, Never Policy," *Times*, November 13, 1900, 5; Unsigned editorial, *The Times*, November 16, 1900, 7.
[80] Reeves, "New Zealand Finance," 14.

being defined in terms of cultural lack or inadequacy, that is, British settler identity was framed more positively as independent yet orientated toward metropolitan interests. As the final chapter will argue, this idealized version of colonial character – and especially those aspects associated with frontier settler masculinity – would become an ever more important imperial resource as the geopolitical confidence reflected in the imperial federation movement was increasingly dissolved by a *fin de siècle* sense of vulnerability.

CHAPTER 4

Manning the Imperial Outpost
The Invasion Novel, Geopolitics, and the Borders of Britishness

> Who can draw the magic circle which is to include the territorial area
> of his duty to die for his country? Home is something more than an
> abstract idea having reference only to locality; its foundations are laid
> in common interests, sympathy, and affection.
>
> J. C. R. Colomb, *The Defence of Great and Greater Britain*

> From the present time forth ... we shall again have to deal with a
> closed political system, and none the less that it will be one of world-
> wide scope.
>
> H. J. Mackinder, "The Geographical Pivot of History"

The invasion novel may be one of the more distinctive variants of the late
Victorian romance revival, but it has only ever occupied the fringes of
critical debate. Its origin is generally asserted with an unusual degree
of specificity – traced to George Chesney's unpropitiously titled *The Battle
of Dorking*, which first appeared in *Blackwood's Magazine* in May 1871 –
yet from this point, as Thomas Richards puts it, the consensus is that the
"new genre ... rarely rose above the generic."[1] Patrick Brantlinger likewise
includes the invasion novel in his broad-brush assessment that the late
Victorian romance "senses its inferiority to realistic narration."[2] What
makes the genre fall under aesthetic suspicion is precisely that which makes
it of interest, namely its willingness to deal directly with late Victorian
geopolitics. It is presumably due to this taint of romance that the invasion
novel is entirely absent from Lauren Goodlad's discussion of what she
terms the Victorian geopolitical aesthetic. Her "framework for studying the
narrative experiments that emerged from a process of capitalist globaliza-
tion" concentrates instead on the cosmopolitan potential of realism to
apprehend the imprint on metropolitan culture of "actually existing"

---

[1] Thomas Richards, *The Imperial Archive: Knowledge and the Fantasy of Empire* (London: Verso,
1993), 113.
[2] Brantlinger, *Rule of Darkness*, 251.

transnationality, seeking "to recognize the globally-inflected spatialities, textures, and experiences that pervade nineteenth-century literature."[3] Set against the intricacies of Collins, Eliot, and Trollope, the invasion novel undoubtedly comes across as a blunt and limited cultural instrument. At the same time, the transnational vision of a project that concentrates on the middle decades of the century with the goal of "deprovincializ[ing] metropolitan forms" is somewhat removed from the hard-edged realities of existing Victorian geopolitics and geostrategy during the period that Eric Hobsbawm terms the "Age of Empire."[4] After all, from the 1870s onward, Britain's global dominance both expanded and was increasingly threatened. While it "increased its territories by some 4 million square miles," most notoriously in Africa following the Berlin Conference of 1884, it also faced intensifying commercial and military competition, from Germany and the United States in particular.[5] In this changing geopolitical environment the settler colonies assumed an increasing prominence in Britain's foreign policy calculations, "in part by reason of their continued growth and prosperity but most of all because of mounting Imperial insecurity and over-extension."[6] It is the geopolitical aesthetic of the invasion novel that most directly registers in formal terms these brute *fin de siècle* facts of territorial domination, capitalist expansion, racism, and imperial competition.

At the same time, although critics associate reflexively the rise of the invasion novel with Britain's changing geopolitical fortunes, little attention has been paid to how this most globally attuned of genres might have developed on the fringes of the empire. The most common stance is that taken by Patrick Brantlinger, who regards the invasion novel – along with cognate popular forms – as "betray[ing] anxieties characteristic of late Victorian and Edwardian imperialism both as an ideology and as a phase of political development."[7] The implication that the invasion novel was solely a product of metropolitan thought and concerns contrasts with the more profound view of global interpenetration offered at the turn of the century in Halford Mackinder's foundational statement of geopolitics and geostrategy, "The Geographical Pivot of History" (1904). Writing in

---

[3] Lauren M. E. Goodlad, *The Victorian Geopolitical Aesthetic: Realism, Sovereignty, and Transnational Experience* (Oxford: Oxford University Press, 2015), 38, 33.
[4] Ibid., 38.   [5] E. J. Hobsbawm, *The Age of Empire, 1875–1914* (New York: Vintage, 1989), 59.
[6] Andrew Porter, "Introduction: Britain and Empire in the Nineteenth Century," in *The Nineteenth Century*, ed. Andrew Porter, The Oxford History of the British Empire (Oxford: Oxford University Press, 1999), 26.
[7] Brantlinger, *Rule of Darkness*, 236.

the aftermath of the Second Anglo-Boer War, Mackinder saw the end of the nineteenth century as marking the conclusion of a *longue durée* of international politics, which he labeled the "Columbian epoch," characterized by European expansion. Echoing Conrad's recent description in *Heart of Darkness* (1899) of a world map where the blank spaces have been filled in, he argued that the globe's "virtually complete political appropriation" meant that every action on the periphery was now potentially fraught with ramifications for metropolitan powers:

> From the present time forth … we shall again have to deal with a closed political system, and none the less that it will be one of world-wide scope. Every explosion of social forces, instead of being dissipated in a surrounding circuit of unknown space and barbaric chaos, will be sharply re-echoed from the far side of the globe, and weak elements in the political and economic organism of the world will be shattered in consequence.[8]

This "closed political system" became increasingly visible from the 1870s onward, and the emergence of the invasion novel provided a powerful means for Victorian writers around the globe to map that changing strategic terrain. The settler empire gained new prominence in this environment, as the relationships between metropole and colony that had primarily been understood in commercial terms were increasingly seen as being of military importance. The settler colonies, by the turn of the century, "began to take up the part of Britain's most reliable allies, bound to her 'system' by deep ties of self-interest and self-identification."[9] Indeed, the rapid spread of *The Battle Dorking* testifies to that growing interconnection, as it was extensively reviewed and reprinted around the settler empire within months of its publication in Britain.[10] Within this increasingly militarized and embattled understanding of imperial belonging and allegiance, the invasion novel provided a powerful means for settler writers to imagine locally distinct forms of what Richards has termed a "war interiority."[11] Not only was the form of novel that emerged in Australia and New Zealand markedly different from its metropolitan progenitor, but I shall argue that the new kind of protagonist that settler writers sought to

[8] H. J. Mackinder, "The Geographical Pivot of History," *The Geographical Journal* 23, no. 4 (1904): 421, 422.

[9] Darwin, *Empire Project*, 145. Hobsbawm makes the important point, however, that "speaking globally, India was the core of British strategy." Hobsbawm, *Age of Empire*, 68.

[10] I. F. Clarke identifies "editions immediately printed in Australia, Canada, New Zealand and the United States." I. F. Clarke, *Voices Prophesying War, 1763–3749*, 2nd ed. (Oxford: Oxford University Press, 1992), 35.

[11] Richards, *Imperial Archive*, 114.

mobilize in response to the threat of invasion would contribute to reshaping the genre in Britain.

The distinctive qualities of the settler colonial invasion novel can be better grasped by first revisiting the metropolitan template offered by Chesney's *Battle of Dorking*. Despite being informed by a broad geopolitical perspective, the British invasion novel offers a narrowly focalized national tale, with the empire little more than a vague background presence. *The Battle of Dorking* presents the empire as a cause of Britain's military weakness – widespread unrest has left "our ships all over the world, and our little bit of an army cut up into detachments" – but also as the source of Britain's wealth, albeit an "artificial ... prosperity" that "rested on foreign trade and financial credit."[12] Chesney instead brings to the fore a more localized series of problems and solutions. As he put it in his original proposal to John Blackwood, the narrative was intended as "a useful way of bringing home to the country the necessity for a thorough reorganization" of the army.[13] *The Battle of Dorking* presents the retrospective narrative of an unnamed volunteer in the British army, whose regiment is hurriedly mobilized upon news of a successful German landing. Stressing the ensuing logistical chaos, the novel clearly signals the likelihood of disaster even before battle is joined: "We could not but depict to ourselves the enemy as carrying out all the while firmly his well-considered scheme of attack, and contrasting it with our own uncertainty of purpose."[14] The volunteer soon becomes a participant-observer in an unfolding catastrophe as the defenders' ramshackle arrangements prove no match for the superior organization and advanced technologies of the invading forces. Out of a tale of disorganization and unpreparedness, I. F. Clarke argues, the nation emerges as the tragic hero of the tale.[15] In A. Michael Matin's analysis, Chesney's plot established several themes of strategy and geopolitics among an array of features that came to be "virtually constitutive" of the invasion novel:

> [D]emonstrations of the vulnerability of the territories of the British Empire in addition to that of England or Great Britain; ... [F]ailures to

---

[12] George Tomkyns Chesney, *The Battle of Dorking: Reminiscences of a Volunteer*, in *The Next Great War*, ed. I. F. Clarke, British Future Fiction (London: Pickering & Chatto, 2001), 9, 39.

[13] Clarke, *Voices Prophesying War*, 40–41. A. Michael Matin points out that a number of subsequent invasion novels were written by "career army or navy officers and government officials whose duties included responsibilities for war planning." A. Michael Matin, "The Creativity of War Planners: Armed Forces Professionals and the Pre-1914 British Invasion-Scare Genre," *ELH* 78, no. 4 (2011): 803.

[14] Chesney, *Battle of Dorking*, 18.   [15] Clarke, *Voices Prophesying War*, 30.

support strategic and tactical innovations, including those associated with technological advancements; ... [G]eographical specificity and depictions of familiar local detail, such as English national landmarks (monuments of power and national pride that are usually damaged or destroyed).[16]

Motivated by the political goal of spurring military reform, Chesney and other metropolitan proponents of the genre stressed issues of policy, centralized planning, and technological advancement. As advocates for the professionalization of Britain's armed forces, they also manifested a "scorn for the civilian public ... copiously illustrated in the literature of the several decades before World War One."[17] Translated to the settler colonies, however, the invasion novel was not only imitated but also extensively reorganized in response to local conditions and concerns.

The sudden prominence of *The Battle of Dorking* coincided in Australia and New Zealand with growing public debates among the settler populations about perceived threats to their emerging economies and positions of racial dominance that were also couched in the language of invasion. Writing about Australia just a few years before Chesney's novel arrived on its shores, C. W. Dilke had commented at length on the growing support for tariff protection of the colonial economy against foreign imports, and the equally strong feeling against immigration from non-English-speaking nations. Despite being a strong advocate of free trade, Dilke credited the arguments of colonial protectionists with a surprising degree of force and persuasiveness. As he relayed to his British readers, unfettered movements of trade and labor were viewed as grave threats to the attempt to establish new outposts of racially homogeneous British culture and capitalism:

> Unrestricted immigration may destroy the literature, the traditions, the nationality itself of the invaded country, and it is a question whether these ideas are not worth preserving at a cost of a few figures in the returns of imports, exports, and population. A country in which Free Trade principles have been carried to their utmost logical development must be cosmopolitan and nationless, and for such a state of things to exist universally without danger to civilization the world is not yet prepared.[18]

Economic threats to the colonies were perceived from several quarters, including other colonies, but perhaps surprisingly concern focused especially on the low wages and efficient production of Britain. By contrast, while anxieties about immigration potentially encompassed a range of

---

[16] Matin, "Creativity of War Planners," 804.   [17] Ibid., 806.   [18] Dilke, *Greater Britain*, 2.69.

nationalities – Dilke refers dismissively to "a mixed multitude of negroes, Chinamen, Hill-coolies, Irish, and Germans" – they were most consistently and firmly centered upon neighboring Asian nations.[19] Those racial antipathies are further intensified in Dilke's account by the ability of new technologies to annihilate distance, which casts the project of settler colonization in a distinctively antimodern light. "Protection in the colonies is to a great degree a revolt against steam," he concludes: "When steam brings all races into competition with each other, the cheaper races will extinguish the dearer, till at last some one people will inhabit the whole earth."[20] Thus, while the model of invasion offered by Chesney dwelt on the potential for metropolitan decline from a position of dominance, equivalent narratives on the settler periphery would instead more often proceed from a position of isolation from the metropole and opposition to the technologies of modernity.

In this chapter I argue that the invasion novel provides a powerful example of the mobility of Victorian forms, and highlights the role of colonial conditions in generating significant changes to familiar metropolitan genres. Not only did a distinctive form of the invasion novel emerge in Australia and New Zealand between the 1870s and 1890s, centered on a model of British character increasingly – yet without irony – colored by qualities drawn from indigenous populations, but as a result of the settler empire's participation in the Second Anglo-Boer War these genre innovations were in turn able to infuse later metropolitan narratives of invasion. The extent of the shift away from the British model of the invasion novel is evident in two Australian texts – George Ranken's *The Invasion* (1877) and Kenneth Mackay's *The Yellow Wave: A Romance of the Asiatic Invasion of Australia* (1895) – that jointly demonstrate the fostering of a form of British masculinity that made a virtue of the failings of organization and technology that were anathematized in Chesney's foundational work. Yet what was initially posed in these novels as a defensive formulation was soon reframed in more aggressive terms, and ultimately translated into a metropolitan context, through the enthusiastic participation of settler polities in the Second Anglo-Boer War, and the associated mythologizing of a frontier sensibility as particularly suited to the demands of guerrilla warfare. This act of global translation can be seen most clearly in the work of a veteran of the South African conflict, Erskine Childers, whose account of the war's guerrilla phase for the multivolume *Times History of the War in South Africa* (1907) overlapped with his authorship of the "one masterpiece of the invasion

[19] Ibid., 2.70.   [20] Ibid., 2.61.

genre," *The Riddle of the Sands: A Record of Secret Service* (1903).[21] In Childers's hands, the improvisatory frontier skills ascribed to British settlers are adopted by metropolitan protagonists, and applied no longer to the defense of British territory but to the preemptive surveillance of a hostile Europe. The chapter concludes by considering the afterlife of this militarized conception of settler masculinity as a strategic resource for the empire in World War I, specifically in works such as John Masefield's *Gallipoli* (1916) that eulogized the Australian and New Zealand soldiers (the so-called Anzacs) who fought in the doomed invasion of the Dardanelles.

The Invasion Novel in the Settler Colony: From *The Battle of Dorking* to *The Invasion*

I. F. Clarke's standard history of narratives of conflict set in the future, *Voices Prophesying War* (1992), has taught us that the formula for the invasion novel laid out in *The Battle of Dorking* was simply translated wholesale into Europe and the United States. "The nationality of the writers does not in any way affect the medium of communication," he maintains, so that Chesney's novel "gave rise to an international practice in the composition of these imaginary wars."[22] Although Clarke's extensive bibliography of "imaginary wars" narratives omits colonial texts entirely, it might seem at first glance that such claims are affirmed in the earliest Australian invasion novel, George Ranken's *The Invasion* (1877), published some three years before the first known example in the United States. Ranken's tale of a Russian invasion of Sydney draws heavily on the plot and structure of *The Battle of Dorking*, and further follows Chesney's lead in seeking to mobilize public opinion through the scenario of an underprepared and ill-equipped defending force facing off against a vast and seemingly overwhelming display of imperial might. Russia had for some time been seen as a potential threat to the Victorian settler empire in the antipodes, especially in light of the Crimean War and visits by Russian naval ships to Australian harbors in the early 1860s:

> The Australian Colonies, fed by speculation in the *Times* and other British newspapers, reprinted in the Australian newspapers, had lively visions, in the event of war breaking out between Britain and Russia, of "hit and run" naval raids in the Pacific by Russian cruisers, and swoops on major Australian cities and seaports by raiders.[23]

---

[21] Richards, *Imperial Archive*, 115.   [22] Clarke, *Voices Prophesying War*, 42, 45.
[23] Clem Llewellyn Lack, "Russian Ambitions in the Pacific: Australian War Scares of the Nineteenth Century," *Journal of the Royal Historical Society of Queensland* 8, no. 3 (1968): 441.

More immediately, the publication of Ranken's *Invasion* also coincided with two developments that granted the settler colonies a new geopolitical importance. The outbreak of war in 1877 between Russia and Turkey further heightened the status of Russia as an expansionist imperial power, while in the same year the colonial-commissioned Jervois-Scratchley reports offered "the first detailed analysis of Australia's strategic environment," concluding that the most immediate risk to colonial security was posed by naval raids from imperial powers with Pacific bases.[24] Yet if Ranken also draws on Chesney in foregrounding the nation's isolation at the point of invasion, the Australian novel presents a much deeper sense of imperial abandonment: Britain deprives the colony of naval protection just at the point when steam has brought it within reach of rival powers. "We Australians naturally acquired a complete distrust of the Imperial military system," the narrator comments acerbically, "but equally there rose among us a very resolute determination to defend our homes against the enemy."[25] Such sentiments usefully highlight the point where *The Invasion* takes its leave from *The Battle of Dorking*. In attempting to imagine what kind of defense might be grounded in patriotic sentiment in the absence of any of the trappings of imperial power, Ranken begins to articulate a new understanding of settler masculinity as a key strategic resource.

The formal changes to the invasion novel produced by its relocation to the settler colonies start to come into focus through the divergence between metropolitan and colonial treatments of civilian populations and their capacities for military discipline. In *The Defence of Great and Greater Britain* (1880), the imperial defense strategist J. C. R. Colomb identified population as a primary "war resource" to be taken into account in any geopolitical calculations. Proceeding from the basis that the empire's British population ought to be viewed collectively as a unified strategic resource, he nevertheless acknowledges that frontier conditions might produce a more "hardy Englishman" than the "fœtid atmosphere of an overcrowded manufacturing town at home."[26] Yet above the fighting potential afforded by environmental determination, Colomb argues that

---

[24] Anthony Burke, *Fear of Security: Australia's Invasion Anxiety* (Cambridge: Cambridge University Press, 2008), 24–25; Luke Trainor, *British Imperialism and Australian Nationalism: Manipulation, Conflict and Compromise in the Late Nineteenth Century* (Cambridge: Cambridge University Press, 1994), 21–22.

[25] W. H. Walker [George Ranken], *The Invasion* (Sydney: Turner & Henderson, 1877), 21. Hereafter cited in text.

[26] J. C. R. Colomb, *The Defence of Great and Greater Britain: Sketches of Its Naval, Military, and Political Aspects* (London: Stanford, 1880), 165.

discipline and training remain the most important determinants of a population's military value: "Men ... are 'raw materials,' but the trained seaman and disciplined soldier are 'developed resources,'" just as the raw materials of coal and iron reach "the perfect product of their development" in the ironclad warship.[27] Similar sentiments are expressed in J. T. Barrington's nonfictional *England on the Defensive* (1881), which argues that volunteer troops should never be placed in the front lines, for fear "they would fail, through want of training and solidity, and communicate their unsteadiness to the rest."[28] The metropolitan invasion novel likewise presents the unformed and undisciplined volunteer soldier – however patriotic – as symptomatic of the nation's strategic weaknesses. Hence Chesney's narrator and his ill-equipped regiment, for all their martial intentions, are shown to buckle under pressure almost as soon as battle commences:

> [S]omebody on horseback called out from behind – I think it must have been the brigadier – "Now, then, Volunteers! give a British cheer, and go at them – charge!" and, with a shout we rushed at the enemy.... [W]e were now all out of order; there was no one to say what to do.... [I]n a few moments the whole slope of the hill became a scene of confusion that I cannot describe, regiments and detachments mixed up in hopeless disorder. (29–30)

In light of this consensus, the portrait of war offered in Ranken's account is all the more striking. *The Invasion* presents the familiar scenario of a ruthless European "military mechanism," whose "tactics and discipline were perfect," facing off against disorganized and amateurish British defenders: "it could hardly be said that tactics or discipline were their chief moving principles, or that they constituted a united organism.... They formed rather a band of highly galvanized atoms" (126). Yet rather than succumbing to those superior tactics and discipline, it is the volunteer soldier who proves most capable of protecting the colony. His apparent disorganization becomes a source of strength, and this capacity is derived directly from the formative experience of inhabiting colonial territory.

Faced with the Russians' overwhelming technological and organizational superiority, the "war interiority" that Ranken imagines to be capable of mounting a successful defense rests upon three principles: the fighting

---

[27] Ibid., 161.
[28] J. T. Barrington, *England on the Defensive, or, the Problem of Invasion Critically Examined under the Aspect of a Series of Military Operations with Special Reference to the Character of the Country and of the National Forces* (London: Paul, Trench, 1881), 47.

qualities and patriotic sentiments seemingly inherent in British blood; the shaping environment of the colonial frontier; and precedents of successful guerrilla warfare and resistance in recent imperial history. In *The Invasion*, that is, settler violence becomes a strategic resource. Stripped of all traces of injustice and culpability, that history of conflict is now repurposed as the legitimate basis for imagining a national defense. Describing the formation of rifle clubs and a widespread arming of the colonial population prior to the invasion, the narrator reflects,

> Naturally, this irregular movement was from the side of authority, con-demned as wholly irrational and useless, but it came quite naturally to many of the colonists. Not a few had spent years of their lives in districts where a loaded rifle hung above the bed was a necessary part of the furniture of the hut. Most of the colonists came of races from which they inherited far more valuable qualities than drill or barrack-yard routine. They had warlike blood in their veins, and warlike traditions in their memories. (24)

Despite his standing as a professional soldier, the commander of the colonial forces, Major Livingstone, is willing to credit his troops' propen-sities for instinctive and unstructured violence, for he has also experienced "rough and irregular frontier service on the scattered outposts of the Empire" (115). What therefore comes into focus is the very different historical and military context shaping the colonial invasion novel, as compared to the concerns with rising European powers and rapidly evolving military technology typically cited in critical accounts of the genre's emergence and defining features. Rather than foregrounding the need to compete on equal terms with other Great Powers, *The Invasion* is instead animated by the lessons of "irregular" colonial policing and resist-ance, and the belief that "bank clerks in New Zealand and boatmen in Ontario make uncommonly good shooting against tatooed [*sic*] warriors and heroes in green uniforms" (115). Focusing on a mythologized frontier experience, rather than on military structure, Ranken signals the beginning of a turn in the colonial novel toward locating strategic value in a particular kind of British character.

The Invasion thus offers a first glimpse of the extent to which the revaluation of British character in light of the colonies' emerging geopolit-ical sensibilities would draw on and repurpose their violent origins in invasion. David Walker points out that, in contrast to contemporaneous examples from Britain and the United States, the anxiety that propels the Australian invasion novel "is not loss of cultural identity so much as a fear that Australia's historically shallow and remote colonies might not be given long enough to establish coherent identities at all."[29] Yet in addition to registering anxieties, the colonial invasion novel becomes the vector for a more productive cultural work. This arises as the structural asymmetry baked into the genre – whereby underresourced and scattered defenders are faced with advanced and numerous invaders – becomes the means of imagining settler resilience in localized, nontechnological, and increasingly racialized terms. Hence Ranken's narrator can reflect, in relation to a skirmish that helped slow the Russian advance,

> We were beaten – a panic had begun – we were broken and dispersed. Still the cohesion was not dissolved. The atoms came together again and joined spontaneously.
>
> Was this from drill or from the want of it? Or was it from another cause altogether? Was it in the blood? (142)

The question of blood remains central to the novel's vision of settlement. In the kind of memorializing that Benedict Anderson identifies as emblematic of modern nationalist sentiment, the dead colonial defenders are interred in "one common sepulchre" and marked with a "massive column," the place "hallowed by the blood and tears of a nation" (155–56). That nationalist sentiment remains underpinned by a wider sense of imperial affiliation, however, for the qualities of militarism and patriotism that it celebrates are directly attributed to British "blood." The redefinition of British identity in a context of colonial geopolitics would be extended further in subsequent years, as settler writers sharpened the invasion novel's vision of patriotic defense by the audacious act of aligning it not with colonial policing but with indigenous anticolonial resistance.

Māori Resistance and Settler Masculinity: *New Zealand in the Next Great War*

In making his case for a "correlation between the larger geographical and the larger historical generalizations," Halford Mackinder argued that accounts of world history as a civilizing process attributed too great an agency to the spread of abstract ideas and principles. Turning attention from this "literary conception of history" to the material facts of geography required that the Victorian understanding of the locus of historical agency

[29] David Walker, *Anxious Nation: Australia and the Rise of Asia, 1850–1939* (St. Lucia: University of Queensland Press, 1999), 101.

be broadened out beyond Europe and the Mediterranean, and Asia's
military aggression placed at its center instead:

> [I]t was under the pressure of external barbarism that Europe achieved her
> civilization. I ask you, therefore, for a moment to look upon Europe and
> European history as subordinate to Asia and Asiatic history, for European
> civilization is, in a very real sense, the outcome of the secular struggle
> against Asiatic invasion.[30]

What might have seemed a novel approach to Mackinder's metropolitan
audience had acquired the status of received wisdom among British settlers
in Australia and New Zealand over the previous few decades. Indeed, as far
back as 1868, Dilke had commented on the increasingly virulent anti-
Chinese attitude in Australia, and hazarded a guess that such sentiments
might offer a glimpse into Britain's future: "They fear that ... they will live
to see the English element swamped in the Asiatic throughout Australia. It
is not certain that we may not some day have to encounter a similar danger
in Old England."[31] Indeed, the emergence around this time of powerful
organized labor movements in the colonies exacerbated these racist tendencies, as "working class identities were constituted in a discourse of racial
difference that defined the white worker as the bearer of civilisation and its
responsibilities."[32] Shaped by this charged environment, the invasion
novel served during the 1880s and 1890s to help redefine British identity
in the settler colonies through direct opposition to Asia. While their plots
directly attest to the intensification of geopolitical anxieties regarding
China in particular, the evolving portrayal of colonial defense – and
especially the military potential of the central "Volunteer" protagonist –
demonstrates that this intensely racialized sense of strategic isolation was
paralleled by the appropriation of an indigenizing rhetoric of territorial
knowledge and belonging.

　　Much settler antipathy toward Asia centered on the idea that the
colonies were insufficiently populated by white people given their vast
land areas and quantities of natural resources, which were perceived as twin
temptations to the burgeoning and modernizing populations of the East.
Coupled with a climatic determinism that viewed Australia's tropical
regions as potentially inhospitable to European populations, and the
adoption of the language of Darwinian struggle, many saw the settler
population not merely struggling to compete with Asian immigrants but

---

[30] Mackinder, "Geographical Pivot of History," 422, 423.   [31] Dilke, *Greater Britain*, 2.73.
[32] Marilyn Lake and Henry Reynolds, *Drawing the Global Colour Line: White Men's Countries and the
International Challenge of Racial Equality* (Cambridge: Cambridge University Press, 2008), 32.

at threat of racial extinction.[33] The academic and one-time minister in the Victorian parliament, C. H. Pearson, put the case with bracing directness in *National Life and Character* (1893): "We know that coloured and white labour cannot exist side by side; we are well aware that China can swamp us with a single year's population.... We are guarding the last part of the world, in which the higher races can live and increase freely, for the higher civilization."[34] Such anxieties took the concrete political form of financial and numerical restrictions on Chinese immigration and institutionalized discrimination against Chinese residents, culminating in the infamous "White Australia" policy of 1901, and these measures were frequently framed as preemptive responses to the threat of invasion. This ethos is readily evident in the writing of the Fabianist New Zealand historian and politician, William Pember Reeves, whose charting of the emergence of a nascent colonial welfare state in *State Experiments in Australia and New Zealand* (1902) concludes with a final chapter, "The Exclusion of Aliens and Undesirables." Maintaining that the overarching predominance of the settler population meant that Australia and New Zealand were unique within the empire in not being divided by "race fissures," Reeves argues that the racial threat posed by Chinese immigration is inseparable from the advent of steam technology:

> They come of their own accord only too readily; the difficulty is to keep them out. For steam has brought Australia within a few weeks' voyage from the swarming hives of Southern and Eastern Asia, within easy reach of races which, though without the ability to discover the Far South for themselves, or build a civilisation there, are prepared in multitudes to use the discoveries of the white man and build on the foundations laid by his pioneers.[35]

Reeves's analysis turns inside out one of the most familiar tropes invoked by the advocates of Greater Britain to articulate the idea of a transnational British identity. The ability of communication and transportation technologies to overcome distance was "considered essential" by many proponents of a global British polity, promising to bring about a sufficient sense of proximity as to sustain an empire-wide imagined community.[36] The anxieties surrounding Chinese immigration produced a sharply contrasting vision of technology's spatial influence on British identity. Even as a common racial affiliation is affirmed across the empire, steam brings

[33] See, for example, Walker, *Anxious Nation*, 4–6.   [34] Pearson, *National Life and Character*, 16.
[35] William Pember Reeves, *State Experiments in Australia and New Zealand*, 2 vols. (London: Allen & Unwin, 1902), 2.328.
[36] Bell, *Idea of Greater Britain*, 88.

potential invaders closer while Britain seems further away. Out of this geopolitical environment, a strident sense of British racial identity came more and more into alignment both with a rejection of technology and finance capitalism, and with the assertion of a localized sense of settler belonging.

This new rhetoric of settler belonging and vulnerability is reflected in the invasion novel's plotting of national defense as a matter of instinctive, improvisational guerrilla warfare that originates in frontier experience. In these narratives it was "bushmen from the rough interior who inevitably formed the core of a guerrilla resistance to Asiatic armies," because they exemplified the vigor necessary to subdue an empty continent and defend it from hostile outsiders.[37] This logic animates one of the most notorious and influential of Australian invasion novels, the radical journalist and trades unionist William Lane's *White or Yellow? A Story of the Race War of A.D. 1908* (1887), which hinges on the contrast between the passionate identification with the soil felt by the settler working classes and the "heartless calculation" of a pro-British ruling class unwilling to prevent Chinese immigration or investment.[38] The colonial resistance to the ensuing Chinese invasion is led by John Saxby, owner of the region's only unmortgaged farm, and the distinctive fighting qualities of the force he rapidly gathers around him – "dash" and "wild enthusiasm" – are born out of their attachment to the land and their status as civilian soldiers: "sailors and farmers and volunteers and diggers and shopkeepers, all with some training and everyone burning for a fight."[39] In later novels, this belief in the British settler's guerrilla qualities is increasingly colored by an indigenizing logic whereby a detailed knowledge of, and identification with, the landscape is explicitly aligned with histories of anticolonial resistance. It was the colonial history of New Zealand rather than Australia, however, which proved the most fertile ground for this act of appropriation.

The sustained and wide-ranging armed resistance by Māori to the colonization of New Zealand was typically likened at the time by British commentators to a guerrilla insurgency, and after peaking in the 1860s was rapidly recuperated by the victorious settler population as motivated by patriotic sentiment.[40] This is in striking contrast to the more caustic or

---

[37] Walker, *Anxious Nation*, 5.

[38] Sketcher [William Lane], "White or Yellow? A Story of the Race-War of A.D. 1908," *The Boomerang*, March 31, 1888, 9.

[39] Ibid.

[40] The definitive account of this reinterpretation of the so-called New Zealand Wars is offered by Belich, *New Zealand Wars*, 311–35. Belich points out that an "emphasis on Maori courage and

dismissive portrayals of indigenous armed resistance in Australia, despite it also taking the form of guerrilla campaigns throughout the course of the end of the nineteenth century.[41] Dilke gives a rough-and-ready indication of these divergent colonial orthodoxies in his late-century assessment of the settler empire's military capabilities, *Problems of Greater Britain* (1890): whereas he deems Australia to be "virtually without a native race" because its indigenous population has failed to cultivate the soil, Māori are "warlike and intelligent" and their fighting prowess has "won the respect of the white colonists – a most unusual thing in the case of any dark-skinned race."[42] The possibility of directly appropriating the history of Māori anticolonial resistance for the purpose of rethinking British settler identity in response to invasion first appears in *New Zealand in the Next Great War: A Note of Warning* (1894), published anonymously by the colonial journalist and short story writer A. A. Grace. Although ostensibly a nonfiction pamphlet, Grace – writing as "Artemidorus," a classical Greek diviner of dreams – imagines the scenario of a war between the empire and a Franco-Russian alliance, where the settler colonies are left vulnerable to the depredations of Russia. In keeping with the tradition of settler invasion writing stretching back to Ranken, Grace portrays New Zealand as a beleaguered outpost failed by imperial military orthodoxy, populated by a harmonious, peaceful settler population that is simply too small to defend the territory it claims to possess. The invading Russian force is depicted as a savage horde ("'Scratch the Russian and you find the Tartar' is a common saying – and the Tartar is cruel") descending upon the defenseless pastoral landscape:

> I fear that no force that we possess would be able to prevent them from extending their conquests southwards. In other words, we could not call the property, which we have acquired with so much labour, the land, which we have changed from a wilderness to fertile fields, our own, but would have the chagrin of seeing men of a foreign nation possessed of what we so value.[43]

While there is an indigenizing logic implicit in this identification with the settled landscape, this impulse becomes more more explicit in Grace's proposal that such an invasion should be met with a form of guerrilla resistance.

---

chivalry began during the wars, but it increased greatly soon after them, growing almost to the point where it subsumed all else…. [I]t perpetuated the notion of the wars as a limited fight with gloves on, a breeding-ground of mutual respect." Ibid., 319.

[41] Carey and Edmonds, "Australian Settler Colonialism," 372–76.

[42] C. W. Dilke, *Problems of Greater Britain* (London: MacMillan, 1890), 248, 257.

[43] Artemidorus [A. A. Grace], *New Zealand in the Next Great War: A Note of Warning* (Nelson: Betts, 1894), 18, 21-22.

Faced with the overwhelming force and technology of a hostile imperial power, Grace proposes that the settlers' intimate knowledge of the colony's complex terrain might constitute a strategic resource of sorts. Richards argues that the invasion novel as first envisaged by Chesney "performed a simple operation: it linked the control of territory with a hermeneutics of information."[44] Whereas Richards finds the invasion novel assigning to the metropolitan state the task of acquiring geographic knowledge, however, in the colonial context this demand is coupled with recognition of a more practical form of expertise. Specifically, Grace derives a settler "hermeneutics of information" from the Māori resistance in New Zealand's own recently completed colonial wars: "New Zealand is an easy land to defend on account of the numberless natural defences it possesses," he observes, "We have the recollection of our struggles with the Maoris to remind us of the fact" (22–23). This fleeting observation provides the springboard for a proposal to militarize the civilian male population, with its combination of British fighting instincts and intimate local frontier knowledge, deeming it capable of recapitulating and rewriting the history of colonial warfare in New Zealand. The strength of Grace's imagined "force of armed guerillas [*sic*]" lies precisely in its rejection of forms of modernity, notably technology and military discipline, characteristic of the empire that has abandoned the colony as much as the one now invading it:

> [W]ith such a force of armed men in this country it would be impossible for any armed force … to subjugate any part of it.… I believe that with such a force of armed men, roughly drilled and trained though they might be, our lives and those of our wives and children, together with the bulk of our property, would be safe so long as we chose to fight.…
> I take it for granted that each colonist worth calling a man … would like to have the means of defence in his hands in case of invasion. (23)

Confronted with geopolitical threat, in other words, settler writers respond by reconfiguring the relationship between the male British subject and the territory he inhabits. If Grace's settlers do not become Māori, they certainly become like them.

Indigenized British Character in Australia: *The Yellow Wave*

Having traced the transformation of the invasion novel in the course of its transit from Dorking to New Zealand, what follows will take up the

---

[44] Richards, *Imperial Archive*, 113.

genre's return journey to the point where its reformation of Britishness was able to intervene once more in metropolitan culture. The first stage of that journey can be glimpsed, in an example of what Lydia Wevers calls the "cross-colonial transference of narratives of legitimacy," through the adoption and expansion of Grace's indigenizing narrative in the most developed Australian example of the invasion novel, Kenneth Mackay's *The Yellow Wave: A Romance of the Asiatic Invasion of Australia* (1895).[45] Mackay was seen as an "archetypal representative" of Australian frontier character, "a bushman and balladeer, a celebrator of the values of the outback," and his proto-nationalist writings were complemented by political and military interests. Elected to the parliament of New South Wales in the year of the novel's publication, he would spearhead the formation of a cavalry regiment recruited from rural parts of the colony in 1897.[46] *The Yellow Wave* offers a version of the familiar invasion-scare scenario of British distraction from colonial concerns: this time, a Russian-Chinese alliance against the British Empire, where Britain's total focus is on the Russian invasion of India, gives the Chinese free reign to descend upon the colony of Queensland. This horde of "Mongol" soldiers is represented in virulently racist terms, and is graphically shown engaging in wanton violence, rape, and pillage. Also familiar is Mackay's emphasis on the relative paucity of the isolated settler population, rendering Australia acutely vulnerable to the invasion: the leader of the invasion fleet, General Leroy, reflects that "in its [Australia's] colossal limits lay its impotency."[47] This territorial vulnerability is further exacerbated by steam transportation and telegraph communications, which have already brought a flood of foreign capital and labor into Australia and are now employed to speed the progress of the invasion. The importance of territorial knowledge is signaled from the outset by the inclusion of a map of the colony (Figure 4.1), but in representing the railways – the technological vector of the invasion – it in fact signals the need for another mode of understanding and encountering the local terrain. In contrast to the invaders' dependence on technologies associated with the annihilation of distance

[45] Lydia Wevers, "Becoming Native: Australian Novelists and the New Zealand Wars," *Australian Literary Studies* 22, no. 3 (2006): 327.

[46] Neville Meaney, "'The Yellow Peril,' Invasion Scare Novels and Australian Political Culture," in *The 1890s: Australian Literature and Literary Culture*, ed. Ken Stewart (St. Lucia: University of Queensland Press, 1996), 243.

[47] Kenneth Mackay, *The Yellow Wave: A Romance of the Asiatic Invasion of Australia*, ed. Andrew Enstice and Janeen Webb (Middletown: Wesleyan University Press, 2003), 165. Hereafter cited in text.

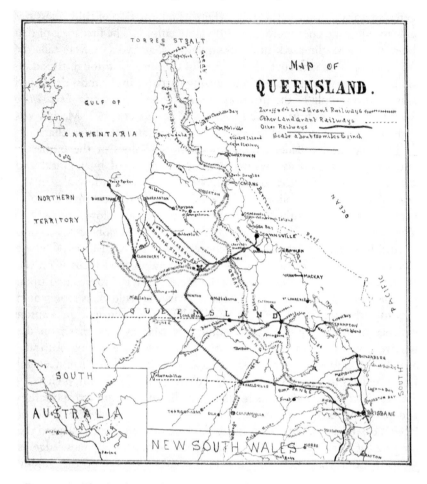

Figure 4.1   The sketch map that accompanied Alexander Mackay's *The Yellow Wave*,
where the railways signify the extent of the colony's vulnerability to the superior
technology of the imperial invaders. The spiritual home of the settler resistance,
Fort Mallaraway, is located far from urban centers, at a point near where the railway
from Townsville branches.

and the homogenization of imperial territory, *The Yellow Wave* also follows
Grace in presenting a need for the isolated colony to rely on less modern
and more autochthonous means of defense.

Following the collapse of the unprepared and underresourced Queensland
defense forces, resistance to the invaders begins to coalesce around a rugged
colonial bushman, Dick Hatten. Renowned as the "Admirable Crichton

of the North," especially for his horse-riding expertise, he is an archetype of colonial masculinity, yet is already something of an anachronism in a modernizing nation where "the wonderful horsemen of Australia were growing fewer and fewer" (37, 150). Before the invasion, Hatten had been commissioned by a sympathetic member of the Queensland government to take charge of a mounted infantry unit that had fallen on hard times. Faced with a shortage of weapons, which must be ordered from England, he strikes on a method for improvising lances out of obsolete shearing shears:

> Now that the machines have taken their place, the store-keepers will, I dare say, let us have them for the asking. Let each man get a pair, break off one blade, and level down the shoulder so that it will offer no resistance when being withdrawn, then sharpen the back and rivet the handle on to a strong, light shaft of wood, and he will have an Australian lance, not as well finished, certainly, as an English one, but quite as reliable as most of them. (186–87)

At first glance, the enthusiasm of Hatten's troops is remarkable – "Struck by the originality of the idea, the men took it up on the spot" – considering that they are being told to fight the Mongols' machine guns with little more than scissors bolted onto broom handles. Yet the positive reception given to this absurd strategy derives from its avowedly archaic qualities. The shears are remnants of an outmoded, preindustrial form of agriculture, and this helps guarantee their value as a specifically "Australian" weapon attuned to the requirements of local conditions.

The cultural logic behind the valorization of the local and the premodern in *The Yellow Wave* is brought to the fore through two analogies drawn from recent imperial campaigns against indigenous populations. One invokes the first use of the Maxim gun on an imperial battlefield, during the recent Matabele War (1893–94), as a means of conveying the vulnerability of the settler population:

> At present they were no more fit to face Leroy's machine-guns and automatic weapons than were the gallant Matabeles who fell fighting for their country before the Maxims of the English invaders, who differed only from the Mongols in that they cloaked their designs and justified their actions under the twin catch words of English hypocrisy, "God and free trade." (213)

Here the reference to indigenous struggle allows Mackay to cast Australia's settlers as innocent victims of a rapacious imperialism, while the offshore reference also evades the need to acknowledge the ongoing campaign of Aboriginal dispossession much closer to home. The second imperial analogy seeks to articulate a stronger sense of settler agency by drawing on the same historical example as A. A. Grace: the success of Māori opposition to colonial invasion in New Zealand, particularly in its postwar framing as patriotic resistance. The spiritual center of Hatten's resistance is an isolated enclave for white settlers, Fort Mallarraway, which is distinguished by its innovative defensive structure:

> Before him rose a line of iron-bark and box logs, set after the fashion of a Maori pah [*sic*], and as he rode up under them, he noticed that the outer line stood between two trenches, and that the stakes, while loose at the bottom, were securely bound together by chains along the top.... "It's ingenious," [he] mused ... admiringly. "This palisade, while letting [rifle] balls through without injury to self, should stop any rush if well defended." (144)

Critics have noted the anachronism of this structure in light of the novel's mid-twentieth-century setting. "It is not that Mackay failed to anticipate that a box log fortification was unlikely to be state of the art defence in 1954," David Walker argues, "but rather that his purpose was to depict a stout guerrilla action mounted by a troop of race patriots true to their bush inheritance."[48] Yet as the passage makes clear, the logic of "stout guerrilla action" is not derived from Australian soil. In likening Fort Mallarraway to a Māori *pa*, or defensive fortification, *The Yellow Wave* draws instead on a more distant yet still readily available history of recent anticolonial resistance. As Belich puts it:

> In military terms, the most remarkable thing about the New Zealand Wars was not the eventual Maori defeat, but the degree of their success along the way.... The key to Maori success was the modern *pa* system; an innovative military method designed as an antidote to the British system, a form of counter-European warfare.[49]

Belich further argues that, despite these innovative Māori tactics, "there is no evidence of any transference of knowledge – on the contrary, the British rapidly forgot what they had learned."[50] This is not strictly true, however, for a form of trans-Tasman knowledge transfer clearly occurs in the settler invasion novel. Settlers' repeated characterization as guerrilla fighters taps into that history to imagine their resistance as both patriotic and autochthonous.

Mackay's bastion of settler resistance, Fort Mallarraway, further indigenizes its British patriots by conforming them to a premodern form of social organization. Established in opposition to the capitalist economy, which is seen as dangerously transnational, the novel's "bush patriots" have

---

[48] Walker, *Anxious Nation*, 107.   [49] Belich, *New Zealand Wars*, 298.   [50] Ibid., 297.

instead adopted a cooperative model. Most immediately – and ironically – this scheme is based on an essay by George Ranken, author of the earlier *The Invasion*, which argues that Australia could only be brought into agricultural production and fully populated if British settlers followed the example of Chinese immigrants. Despite viewing them as "mere sojourners," Ranken found the Chinese to be "the only people in Australia who make the land yield certain crops by systematic cultivation."[51] Arguing that the challenges posed by the Australian landscape and climate are too great for any individual to overcome, he pointed admiringly to the Chinese "habit or instinct of co-operation native in his race," and went on to propose a model of large-scale, self-supporting, cooperative rural settlements.[52] Just a few years earlier again, Dilke had also proposed cooperative labor arrangements as a democratic solution to colonial labor disputes, and he too traced their origin to other cultures: "a return to the earliest and noblest form of labor; the Arabs, the Don Cossacks, the Maori tribes are all cooperative farmers; it is the mission of the English race to apply the ancient principle to manufactures."[53] In Mackay's hands, such a scheme – shorn of its inconvenient associations with cultural difference – becomes an expression of settler autochthony, as the economic ground upon which patriotic resistance might be built.

While *The Yellow Wave* is motivated by geopolitical anxiety, its response centers on turning away from the modern trappings of empire to produce a form of indigenized British character. The ability of Fort Mallaraway's leader to see in Dick Hatten "the beau-ideal of a guerilla [*sic*] leader" indicates the prominence of tropes of self-reliance and unconventionality as the joint bases of a newly militarized sense of settler masculinity (147). That is, the novel's investment in the idea of guerrilla warfare goes beyond expertise in firearms and the ability to know and master the intricacies of local terrain, to propose that it characterizes a distinct colonial mentality born out of frontier conditions and the "self-reliant" and "dare-devil" qualities that find an "ideal prototype" in the rural settler (266). As the novel proceeds and Hatten's band of mounted fighters repeatedly proves its mettle, however, they are more than matched by the overwhelming force of the invaders, who continue their relentless onslaught. By the novel's conclusion, it is unclear whether any resistance will ever have a chance of success, but whatever hope there is for the settlers is emphatically

---

[51] Capricornus [George Ranken], "Co-operative Settlement," in *Bush Essays* (Edinburgh: Black, 1872), 39–40.
[52] Ibid., 40.   [53] Dilke, *Greater Britain*, 2.74–75.

located by Mackay in their ability to exploit the resources that lie immediately to hand: "Not only armies, but also arms and ammunition, must now be evolved from local resources, if the enemy were to be seriously resisted" (290). Such intensely local ideas would seem to have minimal mobility within a wider imperial context. Within a few years, however, they would become reconfigured and set in motion following the outbreak of large-scale imperial war in South Africa.

The Settler Soldier in South Africa

In April 1900, three years after the publication of *The Yellow Wave*, Kenneth Mackay boarded a steamship for South Africa, as commander of the New South Wales Imperial Bushmen's Contingent. In doing so, he joined more than 16,000 Australians and almost 6,500 New Zealanders who enlisted to fight for the empire in the Second Anglo-Boer War (1899–1902), the "first major war against a white settler population."[54] The majority of Australasian enlistments to fight in South Africa took place during the fever of proimperial sentiment that swept the Victorian settler empire following "Black Week," in December 1899, when hopes of a quick victory were dashed by a series of British defeats that cost more than 2,700 soldiers killed, wounded, or captured. The shocking prospect of Boer victory presented an opportunity for a rousing affirmation of a global "Britannic" sentiment. As Arthur Conan Doyle wrote in *The Great Boer War: A Two Years' Record, 1899–1901* (1901), a work he began while serving as a volunteer doctor in Bloemfontein, "the whole existence of the empire" appeared to depend on the outcome of the war, because of what it would reveal of the colonies' relationship to Britain: "Had we really founded a series of disconnected nations, with no common sentiment or interest, or was the empire an organic whole, as ready to thrill with one emotion or to harden into one resolve as are the several States of the Union?"[55] Those early defeats also spurred a stinging critique of the British Army's rigid structures and inflexible tactics, and the perceived shortcomings of metropolitan masculinity. As a result, the vast colonial frontier on which the South African war was taking place also encouraged commentators to privilege the militarized sense of settler masculinity that had

---

[54] Paula M. Krebs, *Gender, Race, and the Writing of Empire: Public Discourse and the Boer War* (Cambridge: Cambridge University Press, 1999), 145.

[55] Arthur Conan Doyle, *The Great Boer War: A Two Years' Record, 1899–1901*, enl. ed. (London: Smith, Elder, 1901), 72.

Morant, in early 1902.[63] Critical voices could also be heard in the settler colonies, as in the final chapter of *Tommy Cornstalk* (1902), by the war veteran J. H. M. Abbott, arguably the first work of Australian war literature:

> It is a land drenched with the best blood of its people, and with the best of ours; a land ravaged, and wasted, and made empty; a land afflicted with the curse of the soldier from end to end.... There is nothing there. Its industries are man killing and maiming; its exports are human lives.[64]

Vigorous debate also centered on whether the guerrilla phase of the war offered any broader lessons for the security of the empire. In response to the enthusiastic pronouncements of Arthur Conan Doyle, for example, the military writer William Elliott Cairnes would complain that "the lessons of the Boer war may be so misread as to induce people to believe in the invincibility of an untrained citizen army."[65] One of the most prominent commentators on the question was the Anglo-Irish writer Erskine Childers, who had parlayed his service in South Africa as an artillery driver into a successful memoir, *In the Ranks of the C.I.V.* (1900), before being commissioned to write the volume of the *Times History of the War in South Africa* devoted to the guerrilla campaign. Convinced that his subject offered insights of more general applicability, Childers's analysis hinged on extending the kind of indigenized logic of British masculinity previously formulated in the invasion novel in Australia and New Zealand.

For Childers, the empire's struggle to achieve victory in South Africa went beyond mere historical interest to lay bare fundamental insights into the nature of modern warfare. Fired by this vision, he commenced his history of the guerrilla campaign with a series of claims for its wider theoretical significance:

> [I]t is the peculiar interest of guerilla [*sic*] war that it illuminates much that is obscure and difficult in regular war. Just as the Röntgen rays obliterate fleshy tissues and reveal the bony structure, so in the incidents of guerilla warfare there may be seen, stripped of a mass of secondary detail,

---

[63] According to a sympathetic contemporary biographer, it was Kenneth Mackay – author of *The Yellow Wave* – who recommended Morant to a unit that understood itself to be outside the rules of warfare: "It was on the whole a 'no-quarter' war which was being waged in the outer Pietersburg district.... The Bushveldt Carbineers played the part of remorseless guerillas [*sic*]." Frank Renar [Frank Fox], *Bushman and Buccaneer: Harry Morant: His 'Ventures and Verses* (Sydney: Dunn, 1902), 20.

[64] J. H. M. Abbott, *Tommy Cornstalk: Being Some Account of the Less Notable Feature of the South African War from the Point of View of the Australian Ranks* (London: Longmans, Green, 1902), 252.

[65] William Elliot Cairnes, *The Army from Within* (London: Sands, 1901), 42.

the few dominant factors which sway the issue of great battles and great campaigns....

It will be found that the qualities which made for success in it are qualities which make for success in operations of the grandest scope.[66]

Childers deploys this history in the hope of effecting change in a metropolitan mindset that he associates with monolithic attitudes and tactics. Arguing that successful prosecution of the campaign demanded "vigorous originality," he instead finds that British tactics were marked by a "mechanical and statistical character" and directed by "centralised intelligence, depending rather on symmetry and punctuality than on dash and cunning" (69, 263, 269). (Returning to the subject in a later work on military tactics, *War and the Arme Blanche* [1910], Childers goes further to assert that it was Australian and New Zealand cavalry who showed greatest aptitude in mastering the skills of guerrilla combat, "seem[ing] always to have shown the most tactical vigour," and surpassing all other imperial forces in "sheer fighting efficiency").[67] The central insight that Childers derives from the history of the war is the need for mobility, which he understands and applies across the broadest possible range of domains, "physical and mental, strategical, tactical and individual" (xii). As a spatial metaphor, the demand for mobility is derived from the settler's individual encounter with the volatile environment of the frontier. For this reason, the call for a new national mindset is grounded in a vision of individual character: "Analysing the matter to its roots, we come finally to the individual efficiency of the private soldier in marksmanship, cleverness and dash, and we find that this individual efficiency governed in varying degrees all other questions, even to the highest" (91). What animates Childers's history, in other words, is the romanticized image of the indigenized British patriot, who originated in the settler invasion novel and is now writ large across the empire.

Metropolitan Territory and Colonial Subjectivity:
The Riddle of the Sands

Just as South Africa was pivotal in the webs of material exchange that sustained the settler empire, its ports "vital strategic links in the empire's

---

[66] Erskine Childers, *The Times History of the War in South Africa, 1899–1902*, ed. L. S. Amery, vol. 5 (London: Low, Marston, 1907), xi–xii. Hereafter cited in text. For the origin of the *Times History*, and its relationship to other early accounts of the South African conflict, see Ian F. W. Beckett, "The Historiography of Small Wars: Early Historians and the South African War," *Small Wars and Insurgencies* 2, no. 2 (1991).

[67] Erskine Childers, *War and the Arme Blanche* (London: Arnold, 1910), 196, 217.

far-flung network of steamer lanes, coaling stations and naval bases," so I am arguing that it was a crucial waypoint in the transnational literary exchanges and adaptations that allowed the reverse migration of the invasion novel from Australasia to Britain at the very end of the Victorian era.[68] Blind to those distant processes, scholars have struggled to account for what is generally seen as a fundamental transformation of the genre, from invasion novel to spy novel, commonly attributed to Childers's most famous work, *The Riddle of the Sands: A Record of Secret Service* (1903). For Thomas Richards, the novel is simply *sui generis*, "the one masterpiece of the invasion genre": "In *The Riddle of the Sands* the invasion novel both reaches maturity and undergoes mitosis: for it is not only the first spy novel (with its archetypal synthesis of the military and the police) but the first sustained narrative of ... 'pure logistics.'"[69] In David Stafford's more nuanced telling, the military concerns of Chesney's *Battle of Dorking* were leavened during the 1890s by an increasing concern with espionage, prompted especially by the rise of anti-German sentiment, so that *Riddle of the Sands* "merely fell within an existing tradition, although its huge impact and its durability as a piece of writing endowed it with particular significance."[70] Reading the novel within a purely metropolitan context is perhaps understandable, given the novel's setting on the European coast of the North Sea, in and around the German Frisian Islands, and its intense focus on the stakes of European geopolitics. Yet Childers's willingness within such a setting to imagine "a different kind of hero," as David Trotter observes, one who is "regenerated by adventure ... [to] save the nation," offers an initial indication that these ostensibly metropolitan horizons are to a large extent reconceived of in the novel in profoundly colonial terms.[71] Put simply, *The Riddle of the Sands* offers a rethinking of the relationship between British character and territoriality that is as much a product of the Boer War as of Europe's shifting power balance, and as a result it expresses its concerns in a form more closely resembling the colonial invasion novel than its metropolitan counterpart.

On first glance, it would be hard to imagine how any narrative commonalities might arise between the expansive landscapes of South Africa – a "theatre of war so vast as to stagger imagination," Childers put it in his

---

[68] Thomas Pakenham, *The Boer War* (London: Weidenfield & Nicolson, 1993), 60.
[69] Richards, *Imperial Archive*, 115, 123–24.
[70] David A. T. Stafford, "Spies and Gentlemen: The Birth of the British Spy Novel, 1893–1914," *Victorian Studies* 24, no. 4 (1981): 498.
[71] David Trotter, "The Politics of Adventure in the Early British Spy Novel," *Intelligence and National Security* 5, no. 4 (1990): 40.

history (270) – and the maritime environs and intricate shorelines at the center of *The Riddle of the Sands*. The novel is narrated by Carruthers, a minor functionary in the Foreign Office, who agrees to a mysterious request from an eccentric acquaintance, Davies, to join him on his yacht, the *Dulcibella*, for a duck shooting expedition around the German Frisian Islands at the end of the yachting season, a daunting proposition given the likelihood of treacherous weather. The challenge is further heightened by the hazardous and poorly charted sandbanks that define the region's geography: even the little information that does appear on those charts, "a confusion of winding and intersecting lines and bald spaces," is rendered virtually useless by the action of the tide, for "at half flood all those banks are covered; the islands and coasts are scarcely visible, they are so low, and everything looks the same."[72] Davies has become fixated upon this unpicturesque locale through an encounter with a German yachtsman, Dollmann, who once attempted to drown him by piloting him onto a sandbank in a storm, and who he has since come to believe is some kind of spy. Davies is convinced that the Germans are secretly fortifying the islands, but cannot comprehend precisely how or why, and has enlisted Carruthers's physical help and language expertise in undertaking the accurate charting of the treacherous waterways that surround them. The protracted investigations of what the novel describes as "two young gentlemen in a seven-ton pleasure boat, with a taste for amateur hydrography and police duty combined" lead to the realization that they have fundamentally misunderstood the evidence of German activity they have witnessed, and what they have uncovered is not defensive preparation but an elaborate scheme to enable the invasion of Britain (121).

The likelihood of an impending military confrontation between Britain and Germany is consistently framed by Childers not in national or even European terms, but as a clash between empires. Colonial analogies sustain the narrative from the very first page, when Carruthers likens his reluctant presence in London in September to an isolated imperial administrator, sustaining social norms to "prevent a relapse into barbarism" (27). A sharper geopolitical edge is revealed as Carruthers departs from London for the continent: the steamship "slid through the calm channels of the Thames estuary, passed the cordon of scintillating light-ships that watch over the sea-roads to the imperial city like pickets round a sleeping army, and slipped out into the dark spaces of the North Sea" (37). Obsessed as it

---

[72] Erskine Childers, *The Riddle of the Sands: A Record of Secret Service* (London: Penguin, 1978), 60, 61. Hereafter cited in text.

is with the everyday realities of the sea and sailing, the novel is also permeated with an awareness of the maritime basis of Britain's imperial strength and national survival. Davies constantly refers to Alfred Thayer Mahan's canonical work of naval strategy, *Influence of Sea Power upon History* (1890), and echoes the programmatic goals of metropolitan invasion novelists in frequently inveighing against widespread British apathy regarding its own naval forces. Alongside that instinctive patriotism, the diplomatist Carruthers is able to articulate a wider understanding of Britain's geopolitical vulnerability, describing "our delicate network of empire, sensitive as gossamer to external shocks, and radiating from an island whose commerce is its life, and which depends even for its daily ration of bread on the free passage of the seas" (120). These anxieties are raised in a context of heightened awareness of Germany's growing power – "a thundering great nation," as the schoolboyish Davies puts it (68) – which is directly construed as imperial ambition. At the very beginning of their voyage, Carruthers and Davies come across a monument to recent German aggression, "a slender Gothic memorial in grey stone," dating from the Second Schleswig War of 1864 and "inscribed with bas-reliefs of battle scenes, showing Prussians forcing a landing in boats and Danes resisting with savage tenacity" (68). Later, it is the German-speaking Carruthers who is once more able to place this episode in a wider geopolitical perspective:

> I described her marvelous awakening in the last generation, under the strength and wisdom of her rulers; her intense patriotic ardor; her seething industrial activity, and, most potent of all, the forces that are moulding modern Europe, her dream of a colonial empire, entailing her transformation from a land-power to a sea-power. (120)

Perhaps the most direct consequence for the novel of adopting this imperial perspective is to maximize the stakes of the sailors' exploration of this otherwise obscure coastline. More subtly, yet significantly, it also presents the Frisian Islands as if they were another colonial frontier, such that the "riddle" they pose cannot be resolved by the protagonists through metropolitan patterns of thought.

The Riddle of the Sands responds to this environment of imperial competition by a restructuring of the invasion novel away from actual conflict and toward defining a form of British masculinity capable of acquiring deep territorial knowledge. The line of filiation between Childers's novel and earlier colonial invasion novels, such as *The Yellow Wave*, is evident in the foregrounding of local territorial detail both in the narrative and in the maps that preface it (Figure 4.2). Richards describes it as a work

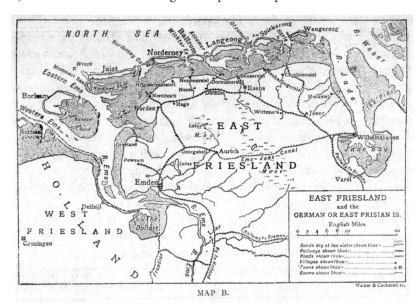

Figure 4.2   One of three maps included in Erskine Childers's *The Riddle of the Sands*, depicting the wider region where Davies and Carruthers conduct their investigations. The complexity of landscape features, combined with railway and canal infrastructure, conveys the importance of territorial knowledge and the need for its correct military interpretation.

of "thick geography," with much of the narrative consisting of "a detailed actuarial anatomy of sea, sand, wind, rain, and mud," which proceeds by gradually zooming in on an ever more precise and particular sense of location: "This graduated reading ... does not lead to a major military action; no invasion or occupation takes place; no high-tech instruments take center stage."[73] Although he argues that the novel delineates an "imperial archive," Richards places this achievement within a narrowly metropolitan intellectual history that elides Childers's firsthand insights into frontier conflict.[74] The two British sailors are first ascribed a frontier masculinity when they begin their illicit surveying mission – in a chapter entitled "The Pathfinders" – and Davies is soon after credited with having the "intuition" characteristic of the "perfect guide or scout" (143). Davies

---

[73] Richards, *Imperial Archive*, 123, 125.
[74] Richards's sole reference to Childers's experience in South Africa is to point out that, as an artillery driver, he "had experienced war exclusively as a series of logistical details" due to the challenge of moving artillery across country "and caring for his horses." Ibid., 124.

embodies a "nautical version of Cooper's Natty Bumppo," Trotter argues, so that metropolitan spycraft is figured as "an extension of scouting by other means."[75] The effete Carruthers is initially horrified to be so fully and unglamorously immersed in the physical environment. He soon comes to view his experiences more positively, however, as a kind of frontier education, and also likens this to the practical experience of military service:

> I hardened to the life, grew salt, tough, and tolerably alert. As a soldier learns more in a week of war than in years of parades and pipeclay, so ... moving from bivouac to precarious bivouac, and depending, to some extent, for my life on my muscles and wit, I rapidly learnt my work and gained a certain dexterity. (144)

Such comparisons do not simply draw on a generalized understanding of the colonial frontier, I wish to suggest, but emerge directly out of the history of the war in South Africa. The focal point of this act of imperial translation is the male British subject, reimagined along the lines of a guerrilla fighter.

This is to say that the geopolitical vision of *The Riddle of the Sands* is inseparable from its desire to reimagine metropolitan subjectivity along colonial lines, a project made visible as much through the protagonists' amateurism as through their adoption of a rugged, frontier lifestyle and mindset. Even though their activities are likened throughout to military actions, great weight is placed upon Davies and Carruthers's nonprofessional status and lack of affiliation with any branch of the armed services. This dimension of their characters reflects the conclusions of commentaries on the war in South Africa, such as W. E. Cairnes's *An Absent-Minded War* (1900), which stressed the inadequacy of routinized soldier training in comparison to the skills possessed by their Boer opponents simply through their everyday immersion in the frontier: "Ignorant farmers as they were, I tell you that they knew more of war in its grim reality than all our regulars put together.... These ignorant farmers had been at war with nature and the wilderness all their lives. They could read the skies and the sounds and signs of the veldt, a sealed book to our town-bred Tommies."[76] This critique is mirrored exactly in Davies's expertise as a sailor and navigator, an instinctive and practical mastery that is presented as the outcome of a deep and sustained familiarity with the natural

---

[75] Trotter, "Politics of Adventure," 46.

[76] British Staff Officer [W. E. Cairnes], *An Absent-Minded War: Being Some Reflections on Our Reverses and the Causes Which Have Led to Them*, 12th ed. (London: Milne, 1900), 95.

environment rather than routine training or theory. "Even in the dim gaslight he clashed on my notions of a yachtsman," Carruthers recalls, "no cool white ducks or neat blue serge.... The hand he gave me was horny, and appeared to be stained with paint" (38). His later observation that Davies "looked the amateur through and through" – a complimentary rather than critical assessment – silently follows the example of the colonial invasion novel, which finds military virtue rather than vulnerability in the citizen's everyday expertise (66). The refined Davies is gradually acclimated to this amateur ethos as he comes to embrace the physical privations and sense of mission that are equally characteristic of life on the *Dulcibella* – its "world of physical endeavour" (48). This process of personal restoration is cast as a recovery of a rugged masculinity through a concomitant rejection of metropolitan habits. On first leaving London for his mysterious European assignation, Carruthers pictures himself as a "nerve-sick townsman" experiencing a "delicious physical awakening" as he sheds his office routine; following his first nighttime surveying adventure with Davies, he is "finally cured of funk" (37, 140). Childers would reiterate these sentiments in more prosaic terms a few years later, in the context of British efforts in South Africa, finding that "[l]ong years of peace and civil prosperity had softened the national fibre."[77] Yet the lessons that he derived from the guerrilla conflict went beyond concerns with metropolitan physical degeneracy. While spycraft, subterfuge, and physical exertion are the hallmarks of Childers's adventure, it is crucial for the political vision of the novel that their motivation is derived from a fiercely patriotic sentiment.

The romanticized idea of the guerrilla fighter that emerged from the conflict in South Africa was underpinned by the idea of an autochthonous patriotism, and in *The Riddle of the Sands* that principle is actively extended to imagine such a local attachment might be able to function beyond the borders of the nation. Conan Doyle had described the Boers as fired by an "an ardent and consuming patriotism," and Childers would also argue that "local patriotism" was the force that enabled them to fight "with so much local success and for so long."[78] In the novel, such values are again translated most directly into the portrayal of Davies, who is motivated by "a fire of pent-up patriotism struggling incessantly for an outlet in strenuous physical expression" (118). Because of the strength of

[77] Childers, *War and the Arme Blanche*, 175.
[78] Doyle, *Great Boer War*, 1–2; Childers, *Times History of the War*, 23.

this conviction, Carruthers accords his compatriot's homespun and halting opinions an almost mystical value:

> [H]e seemed to have caught his innermost conviction from the very soul of the sea itself. An armchair critic is one thing, but a sunburnt, brine-burnt zealot ... athirst for a means, however tortuous, of contributing his effort to the great cause, the maritime supremacy of Britain, that was quite another thing. He drew inspiration from the very wind and spray. (121)

The value of such prophetic zeal is heightened by its contrast to two flawed models of national affiliation also on display in the novel. On the one hand, there is Dollmann, the instigator of the German invasion scheme, who is revealed to be a traitorous British subject who formerly served in the Royal Navy. On the other, there is Carruthers, whose nationalism is initially shallow and reflexive, limited to espousing "sonorous generalities" without ever doing anything "so vulgar as to translate them into practice" (121). "Just as the peevish dandy had been transformed into an outdoorsman," Trotter notes, "so the civil servant joins the civilian agitators."[79] Given the lack of any overt violence in the novel, the earnest Davies may seem an unlikely candidate for a guerrilla fighter, yet his embodiment of precisely those qualities central to so much commentary on the Boer War provides the means for *The Riddle of the Sands* to begin reimagining acts of metropolitan aggression as if they were an extension of a patriotic defensiveness.

Conan Doyle described it as "somewhat of the nature of an anti-climax" to have to publish a new edition of *Great Boer War*, after the conflict inconsiderately refused to come to an end, one that would also encompass the "scattered operations" of the guerrilla conflict that broke out. The war's prolongation posed a formal challenge to his romance-inflected narrative of imperial conquest: "daily bulletins of sniping, skirmishes, and endless marchings" produce a "dull chronicle," he complains, while the irregular and localized nature of such episodes means they "must be enumerated without any attempt at connecting them."[80] In Childers's hands, however, the "irregular and localized" is made central to the concerns of the metropolitan invasion novel. Although the geopolitical stakes of the genre may appear to have been misplaced in the narrow confines of the *Dulcibella* and the mind games undertaken by its inhabitants, *The Riddle of the Sands* in fact reimagines the location and spatial logic of imperial warfare as part and parcel of its colonial rethinking of British identity. In marked contrast

---

[79] Trotter, "Politics of Adventure," 41.   [80] Doyle, *Great Boer War*, 515, 557.

to prior invasion novels, after all, it is hard to discern what or where is being invaded. While Davies and Carruthers ultimately stumble upon the true, aggressive meaning of the German activity along the coastline – a scheme for "flinging themselves on a correspondingly obscure and therefore unexpected portion of the enemy's coast" – no invasion ever takes place (305). Instead it is the protagonists who have encroached nefariously upon foreign territory: when they entered the German canal system at the beginning of their quest, Carruthers recalls, "the sleepy officials ... little knew what an insidious little viper they were admitting into the imperial bosom" (116). *The Riddle of the Sands* therefore undertakes a twofold realignment of the genre, blurring the distinction between defense and attack at the same time as establishing Europe – rather than Britain, or the wider empire – as a potential theater for war. For Richards, Davies's defensive strategy marks a crucial turning point in the evolution of imperial power, revealing that the nation's security depends upon the extent to which the civilian population is integrated into a state apparatus geared toward war. Yet more significant than this is the manner in which, writing in the shadow of World War I, Childers marshals the invasion novel's investments in sentiment and strategy so that an aggressive, offshore incursion can be justified and even romanticized under the guise of local patriotism.

Gallipoli and the Surplus Value of the Settler Colony

The cataclysmic war that began in Europe in 1914 was wholly unlike the mobile and small-scale encounters envisaged by Childers, or the defiantly low-technology strategies and heroic actions proposed by his settler precursors, its sheer scale seemingly antithetical to any lingering traces of romanticized frontier thinking about territorial knowledge and individual character. Winston Churchill's history of World War I maintains that, within a year, "the opportunity was lost of confining the conflagration within limits which though enormous were not uncontrolled": "Governments and individuals conformed to the rhythm of the tragedy, and swayed and staggered forward in helpless violence, slaughtering and squandering on ever-increasing scales, till injuries were wrought to the structure of human society which a century will not efface, and which may conceivably prove fatal to the present civilisation."[81] Churchill played a direct role

---

[81] Winston Churchill, *The World Crisis, Part Two, 1915*, The Collected Works of Sir Winston Churchill (London: Library of Imperial History, 1974), 17.

in this expansion of "slaughtering and squandering" by initiating the Dardanelles campaign, a calamitous attempt to open a new front in the conflict by invading Turkey's Gallipoli peninsula. This of all the battles and campaigns in the war would became most strongly associated with the exploits of settler soldiers from Australia and New Zealand, through the Australian and New Zealand Army Corps (Anzac), which constituted approximately half of the 489,000 soldiers that made up the Mediterranean Expeditionary Force. In the course of the campaign, between January 1915 and February 1916, almost 11,500 Anzac troops were killed and more than 24,600 wounded. Alongside them, some 21,200 British and Irish soldiers were killed and 52,200 wounded, while the Turkish and Arab soldiers fighting for the Ottoman Empire are estimated to have suffered more than 250,000 casualties, of which more than 86,600 were killed.[82] Rapidly memorialized by British and colonial reporters, veterans, and historians, Gallipoli constitutes a grim apotheosis of the Victorian settler project, one final recombination of the elements of British masculinity, frontier territory, and romance, familiar from the colonial invasion novel and now relocated directly onto European terrain.

Amid all the blood shed by settler soldiers during World War I, the Gallipoli campaign was portrayed as uniquely revelatory both of imperial spirit and colonial distinctiveness, and these apparently contradictory impulses were held in suspension by way of a logic established through the invasion novel. *The Riddle of the Sands* articulates the kind of double movement that enabled this conflict to be redeemed through narrative as a triumph of the settler empire: the romanticized image of the settler guerrilla fighter is translated onto European territory, along with his autochthonous connection to place, at the same time as the strategic distinction is blurred between aggression and defense, so that the act of invasion might be figured as a sign of local patriotism. The application of this logic to the Gallipoli campaign was further catalyzed by the rugged nature of the landscape, and the act of invasion, so that commentators were able to cast it in terms that were more or less inconceivable in other theaters of the war:

> Gallipoli's physical separation from France and Flanders, its decisively different topology and climate are potent factors. Also of significance is the way in which it was fought: the extraordinary achievement of the

[82] NZHistory, "Gallipoli Casualties by Country," Ministry for Culture and Heritage.

initial amphibious attack, and the subsequent contrast with the anonymous, industrial killing of the Western Front made Gallipoli seem to some extent to be war as it should be: noble, daring, imaginative, chivalrous and tragic.[83]

Even a campaign history by C. E. Callwell, one of its planners and author of an influential manual on asymmetric warfare, while ostensibly focused on the "broad strategical aspect of the operations," would describe Gallipoli as "the great adventure."[84] The geopolitical stakes involved in romancing the invasion are most clearly on display in John Masefield's vivid and propagandistic *Gallipoli* (1916). Masefield, who would later succeed Robert Bridges as poet laureate, had served for a brief time as a hospital orderly during the campaign, and he turned to history after a lecture tour of America where he was frequently confronted by criticism of the Dardanelles campaign.[85] "No army in history made a more heroic attack," he writes of the initial landings on April 25, 1915, "no army in history has been set such a task."[86] Masefield's *Gallipoli* exemplifies what Jenny Macleod terms the British "heroic-romantic myth" of the campaign, which foregrounds the valor of its participants as part of a strategy to displace criticism by a "simplified and benign shared understanding of the campaign."[87] That project centered on asserting a romanticized vision of British identity that was found to be most powerfully embodied in soldiers from the settler colonies.

Masefield approached his task of exculpation in the first instance not by directly invoking the invasion novel but by seeking to elevate its subject matter to the status of epic romance. Sustained intertextual references to the medieval epic *The Song of Roland* – memorializing a clash between the armies of Charlemagne and those of Marsile, the Muslim king of Spain – serve to ascribe a chivalric quality to the individual soldier and establish a sense of the campaign, in its broadest terms, as a clash between

[83] Jenny Macleod, "The British Heroic-Romantic Myth of Gallipoli," in *Gallipoli: Making History*, ed. Jenny Macleod (London: Cass, 2004), 82–83. Commenting on C. E. W. Bean's monumental, state-sanctioned *Official History of Australia in the War of 1914–1918* (1921–42), Alistair Thomson similarly observes: "Assaults like the Gallipoli landing could be experienced and depicted in active, exhilarating terms. By contrast, the artillery barrage which became a dominant feature of the Great War, especially on the Western Front, imposed a vulnerable and passive role upon participants, and demanded a different style of writing about soldiers." Alistair Thomson, "'Steadfast Until Death'? C. E. W. Bean and the Representation of Australian Military Manhood," *Australian Historical Studies* 23, no. 93 (1989): 467.

[84] C. E. Callwell, *The Dardanelles* (London: Constable, 1919), vii.

[85] Constance Babington-Smith, *John Masefield: A Life* (Oxford: Oxford University Press, 1978), 158.

[86] John Masefield, *Gallipoli* (London: Heinemann, 1916), 25. Hereafter cited in text.

[87] Macleod, "British Heroic-Romantic Myth," 75.

civilizations. Beginning each part of his history with an epigraph from the poem, Masefield likens the present-day invasion to past conflict between Christian Franks and Muslim Saracens, and draws especially on the parallels with its tale of noble but hopelessly outnumbered warriors:

> The Franks answered: "We will not fail. If it be God's will, we will not murmur. We will fight against our enemies; we are few men, but well hardened."
> They spurred forward to fight the pagans. The Franks and Saracens are mingled. (57)

The recurrent imagery of knightly combat is further layered over classical epic. Masefield makes much of the Gallipoli peninsula's proximity to the ruins of Troy – he consistently refers to the Hellespont, "the most important channel of water in the world," rather than the Dardanelles (9) – to heighten the heroic qualities ascribed to the British forces and broaden the geopolitical context in which the fighting might be understood. The parallel between these ancient and contemporary conflicts, and the resultant attempt to dignify the latter, is made explicit in the account of the fighting to establish a British foothold on the peninsula, some two weeks after the initial landing:

> Samothrace and Eubœa were stretched out in the sunset like giants watching the chess, waiting, it seemed, almost like human things, as they had waited for the fall of Troy and the bale-fires of Agamemnon.... They saw ... more men, and yet more men, from the fields of sacred France, from the darkness of Senegal, from sheep-runs at the ends of the earth, from blue-gum forests, and sunny islands ... from Irish pastures and glens, and from many a Scotch and English city and village and quiet farm; they went on and they went on, up ridges blazing with explosion into the darkness of death. (82)

If such intertexts seem far removed from the more recent concerns of the colonial invasion novel, they nevertheless contribute to the genre's expansion that was previously initiated by Childers. "Despite its quixotic elements," Macleod observes, the overall effect of Masefield's mythmaking is "melancholy in tone."[88] Where settler novelists had first imagined a form of British identity defined equally by innate military prowess, patriotic attachment, and isolation – and further colored, in texts such as *The Yellow Wave*, with a sense of nobility in defeat – Masefield's *Gallipoli* employs its

---

[88] Ibid.

melancholy precursors to translate that formal logic of invasion into a context of metropolitan aggression.

Perhaps the most obvious yet important sign of the indebtedness of *Gallipoli* to the settler invasion novel, however, is the simple fact of Masefield's decision to place the Anzac soldier at the center of his narrative, where he is valorized as much for his territorial instincts as for his fighting qualities. Military historian Chris Pugsley stresses the difficulty of the terrain that confronted the invaders, which ensured that "from the beginning the fight was as much with the landscape as it was with the Turk."[89] Masefield prioritizes the difficulty of this landscape, and makes sense of it by describing it as if it were an unmapped colonial space. It is a "cracked and fissured jungle" (47); "a savage rough country" (49); and "trackless, waterless, and confused, densely covered with scrub (sometimes with forest), littered with rocks, an untamed savage country" (104). Indeed, the distance between Gallipoli and the Boer War is compressed in the summer months to the point of disappearance, when the peninsula acquires a "savage and African look of desolation" (96). Faced with a colonial landscape, Masefield responds by praising the physical excellence of settler masculinity for what the final page remarkably terms a display of "sheer naked manhood" (183). It is therefore the settler soldier who is most closely aligned with the romance values of the *Song of Roland* because frontier experience produces the fullest flourishing of British character and subjectivity. "For physical beauty and nobility of bearing they surpassed any men I have ever seen; they walked and looked like the kings in old poems," he observes, coupling that exemplary physicality with the familiar assertion of the settler's resistance to stultifying discipline: "As their officers put it, 'they were in the pink of condition and didn't care a damn for anybody'" (19–20). Figuring the terrain in such terms constitutes an attempt to naturalize the British presence, and that of settler soldiers in particular, yet it does so at the cost of bringing into focus the commonalities between invasion and colonization.

In the midst of the carnage of the Dardanelles campaign, commentators thus found a settler colony taking shape. War correspondent Ellis Ashmead-Bartlett would refer to a "southern colony, so strangely and suddenly planted on the bleak inhospitable Gallipoli coast."[90] More allusively,

---

[89] Christopher Pugsley, *Gallipoli: The New Zealand Story* (North Shore: Penguin, 2008), 15. For a broader discussion of the cultural logic informing the parallels drawn between the landscapes of Australian colonization and World War I, see Peter H. Hoffenberg, "Landscape, Memory and the Australian War Experience, 1915–18," *Journal of Contemporary History* 36, no. 1 (2001).

[90] Ellis Ashmead-Bartlett, *The Uncensored Dardanelles* (London: Hutchinson, 1928), 57.

Churchill wrote that "the power did not exist in the Turkish Empire to shake from its soil the grip of the Antipodes."[91] Again it is Masefield who takes up the idea at greatest length. At points, he finds the Anzac presence akin to the most primitive and elemental form of belonging, with soldiers eking out their existence in trenches and caves as if "put back to Cro-Magnon or Tampa, into some swarming tribe of cave-dwellers" (167). As his narrative comes to a close and he reflects on the deserted encampments of the retreating invaders, he finds the scene recapitulating some of the best-known scenes of Victorian settler colonialism:

> Those lines at Cape Helles, Anzac, and Suvla, were once busy towns, thronged by thousands of citizens, whose going and coming and daily labour were cheerful with singing, as though those places were mining camps during a gold rush, instead of a perilous front where the fire never ceased and the risk of death was constant....
>
> I have said that those positions were like mining camps during a gold rush. Ballarat, the Sacramento, and the camps of the Transvaal, must have looked strangely like those camps at Suvla and Cape Helles. (162)

The invading forces have also accomplished the colonial task of renaming the landscape. Bloodshed has transformed parts of the Gallipoli peninsula, "unnamed till then, probably, save by some rough Turkish place-name," so that names such as Anzac Cove are now likely to be "printed on all English maps" (55). The Gallipoli campaign would soon become mythologized in both Australia and New Zealand as the sacrificial origin of a new national identity, yet nationalism does not explain why it might also be celebrated in such similar terms by a British advocate of empire such as Masefield.[92]

Masefield's hyperbolic mythologizing of settler soldiers is nevertheless able to offer genuine insight into the role of British political identity within the Victorian settler empire because his valorization of the campaign as a colonial invasion is accompanied throughout by his assertion of what might be called an imperial necropolitics. His portrait of Gallipoli is pervaded by a melancholy recognition of the human toll that has been paid by the invaders to sustain their presence. There is a "tragical feeling"

---

[91] Churchill, *World Crisis*, 324.

[92] Adrian Caesar surveys the outpouring of writing about the war in Australia throughout the 1920s, and its role in the creation of an "Anzac myth" that "the Australian 'character' was tried, tested, and not found wanting in the crucible of war, so that Australian nationhood was confirmed in the heights of Gallipoli in 1915." Adrian Caesar, "National Myths of Manhood: Anzacs and Others," in *The Oxford Literary History of Australia*, ed. Bruce Bennett and Jennifer Strauss (Melbourne: Oxford University Press, 1998), 147.

overlaying this European settler colony, "the sense that Death was at work there, that Death lived there, that Death wandered up and down there and fed on Life" (168). Such imagery is no doubt intended to help romanticize the settler, elevating him to the level of an epic hero, so that the eventual withdrawal of the troops is not seen in the light of a failure or a defeat. "They had lost no honour," he maintains, "They were not to blame, that they were creeping off in the dark, like thieves in the night" (176). One unintended consequence of portraying the Anzac trenches as colonies of the dead is the retrospective illumination it casts upon the settler project as it took shape in Australia and New Zealand across the nineteenth century. Patrick Wolfe has influentially argued that settler colonialism is defined by a "logic of elimination," stressing that the destruction of indigenous society is perpetrated to establish a new society in its place.[93] The logic of elimination is manifested both through the decimation of indigenous populations during the process of invasion, and through ongoing efforts to supplant that population and its rights to territory: in this latter regard, "the logic of elimination marks a return whereby the native repressed continues to structure settler-colonial society."[94] Yet if there is an uncanny element to the intimacy between settlement and death revealed on the rugged terrain of Gallipoli, it does not arise from a "native repressed" external to the idea of colonial British identity. Instead, what becomes manifest in the slaughter – when the "souls of a race, all the company of a nation's dead" are imagined in the presence of "this death and mangling and dying misery and exultation" (146) – is somehow intrinsic to the idea of settler identity, and to its perceived value within the empire.

I am therefore arguing that while the mythologizing of colonial invasion in the Dardanelles campaign marks the apotheosis of a global circulation of bodies and ideas that spanned the Victorian settler empire, Masefield's narrative also brings into new focus that the political identity of British settler masculinity can be conceived of as a form of surplus value. In using this term, I wish to invoke both meanings of "surplus" – profitability, and unvalued excess. On the one hand, the contribution of the Anzac troops appears the ultimate fulfilment of the settler colony's promise to produce superlative or exemplary British social and physical qualities, offering "a new reservoir of British virility, preserving British virtues somewhat better than the old."[95] On the other hand, the project of settlement was also inextricably associated from the outset with the kind of excess or extraneous population that Marx described as "a disposable industrial

---

[93] Wolfe, "Settler Colonialism," 388.   [94] Ibid., 390.   [95] Belich, *Replenishing the Earth*, 467.

reserve army," "a mass of human material always ready for exploitation by capital in the interests of capital's own changing valorization require-ments."[96] That doubled sense of surplus value can be traced at least as far back as Wakefield's *Letter from Sydney*, which both celebrated colonial masculinity – "I cannot help feeling envious and jealous of their personal beauty," his settler reflects – and proffered emigration as a biopolitical solution to British social and economic malaise:

> If an Englishman who ardently desires the greatest good of his country ... were offered the gratification of one wish, however extravagant, for what would he ask? ... His sole object would be to put an end to that portion of crime and misery which in Britain is produced by an excess of people in proportion to territory....
>
> The object is, to reduce, as much as the system would allow, the population of the emigrating country, and to increase, as much as possible, that of the immigrating countries.[97]

These ideas are taken up fully in the vision of a settler colony established on the Gallipoli peninsula, revealing by way of the invasion novel that British masculinity is ultimately figured as little more than the most valuable of the colony's abundant natural resources. It was as a surplus that British subjects were first set in motion at the beginning of the Victorian era, to wreak havoc upon the indigenous populations and landscapes of Australia and New Zealand; it was as a surplus that they returned to the battlefields of Europe, to be decimated in turn. The fatal collision in Gallipoli of surplus value with romance – of political economy with literary form – therefore stands as one final grim skirmish at the borders of Britishness that constituted the Victorian settler empire.

[96] Marx, *Capital*, 784.   [97] Wakefield, *Letter from Sydney*, 146, 163, 164.

Conclusion

There is a great difference, in short, between looking *to* a place and looking *from* it.

Edward Gibbon Wakefield, *A Letter from Sydney:*
The Principal Town of Australasia

In one way, this book is an attempt at a sustained reckoning with Edward Gibbon Wakefield, and the remarkably persuasive Victorian story he told about the settler colonies. His words implicate me as a Pākehā New Zealander, the product of settlement, and they shadow my argument in uncomfortable ways. He sat in a British jail and fabricated his letter from Sydney, but about one thing he wasn't entirely wrong: "There is a great difference, in short, between looking *to* a place and looking *from* it."[1] In retrospect, such insights as I have to offer about the influence of place have themselves been the product of located thinking. One moment: arriving at graduate school in the United States, a long way from home and knowing little else apart from New Zealand literature, and sensing those powers of distance but also realizing that being in the metropole didn't mean you could see everything. A second moment: Kathy Psomiades allowing a harebrained assignment on Trollope's *Australia and New Zealand*, driven by a naïve sense of wonder that someone who had made it into the Penguin Classics had also made that long, long journey south, and wondering what difference it might have made, and how or why we should talk about it when everyone already knew but no one seemed to care. A third moment: sitting in a library carrel working on loaner laptop on a chapter that seemed to have something to do with colonial debt, at the time when the banks started to collapse, and the entire economy of Greece imploded, and sensing amidst the fear old echoes in the language of "credit crisis" and the limited but surprising power that a small place on the

---

[1] Wakefield, *Letter from Sydney*, 141.

periphery might derive from claims of a shared identity and from the simple fact of financial interconnection. This doesn't quite add up to Edward Said's idea of traveling theory – and to be honest, I never was very good at theory – but I want to agree with his general observation:

> Like people and schools of criticism, ideas and theories travel – from person to person, from situation to situation, from one period to another.... Such movement into a new environment is never unimpeded. It necessarily involves processes of representation and institutionalization different from those at the point of origin. This complicates any account of the transplant-ation, transference, circulation, and commerce of theories and ideas.[2]

Thinking about this in relation to the Victorian past, I just couldn't buy the idea that British identity didn't change through its imperial career. It didn't make sense that colonial experience and insight didn't occasionally make its way back to Britain again. Thinking about this in relation to the Victorianist present, it seemed like it should make some kind of a difference to approach this field from a place where so much of everyday life – the street names, the landscape, the economy, the political dilemmas – follows routes laid down in the nineteenth century.

Then again, this book is also an attempt at a sustained reckoning with Edward Gibbon Wakefield, who reminds us that to understand the culture of settler colonialism we must follow the money. If he teaches us one thing that we can still bear to hear, it is perhaps that it is impossible to talk meaningfully about the literature of the Victorian settler empire – to grasp its formal qualities, to recognize its stakes – without also talking about the financial and economic dimensions of those imperial connections. Yet in looking for a theory of the Victorian settler empire – as a system, rather than its discrete parts – it seemed necessary to stray into the territory of the historians. Literary criticism offered stories of national literatures in Australia and New Zealand that were often rich and complex but neverthe-less bounded, or work about British writing that focused narrowly on "myths" of settlement or the experience of emigration.[3] By contrast, a rush of historical works, each bigger than the last – Bell, Magee and Thompson,

[2] Edward W. Said, "Traveling Theory," in *The World, the Text and the Critic* (London: Faber, 1984), 226.

[3] Myth is invoked by Brantlinger, *Rule of Darkness*, 132; Lansbury, *Arcady in Australia*, 3. Emigration is of recurring interest to Kranidis, *Victorian Spinster and Colonial Emigration*; Piesse, *British Settler Emigration*; Janet C. Myers, *Antipodal England: Emigration and Portable Domesticity in the Victorian Imagination* (Albany: State University of New York Press, 2009); and Tamara S. Wagner, *Victorian Narratives of Failed Emigration: Settlers, Returnees, and Nineteenth-Century Literature in English* (Abingdon: Routledge, 2016).

Darwin, Belich – placed the settler colonies at the center of transnational stories about imperial politics, capital, and commerce. There was a sense of purpose in these male tomes, of mission even, in revealing not only that the settler colonies really mattered to Victorian Britain but that they also occupied center stage of a new global history. For Darwin, "their contribution to British world power [cannot] be treated as less important than India's"; for Belich, "It was settlement, not empire, that had the spread and staying power in the history of European expansion, and it is time that historians of that expansion turned their attention to it."[4] Such claims and perspectives cannot be ignored – indeed, there is something seductive about their scope and scale, the sense of importance they bestow on the colonies. I now see this is a seduction I have only partly resisted. In pursuing the idea that the novel and political economy played distinctive roles in those transnational networks, and in seeking out more material connections between colonial and metropolitan texts than simple homologies or resemblances, the book tells a different story than the imperial historians yet inevitably remains wedded to their themes. There are too many men in these pages, and all of them are British in some form or other, and while I remain convinced of the importance of recovering this dimension of the Victorian settler empire, it is emphatically the case that this is not the only story that literary criticism can or should tell about it.

In another way this book is also an attempt at a sustained reckoning with Edward Gibbon Wakefield, whose words helped radically upend all forms of life on the opposite side of the world. Around the time I was completing this project, my family and I visited the graveyard in Kaponga, a tiny settlement at the foot of Mount Taranaki, where my grandparents, Len and Doreen Prestidge, lie buried. I never knew my grandfather, and I can barely remember my mother, but my grandmother was so kind, and gentle, and quiet. The Prestidge family first arrived in New Zealand in 1856 – Henry and Mary Prestidge, and their four young children – when they disembarked in Nelson, along with more than 160 other passengers, after the hundred-day journey from London. I think of this, and of my own four children, and also of Wakefield's nephew, Edward Jerningham, who wrote of one of the transactions with a *rangatira* (chief) that enabled the systematic colonization of New Zealand – of Nelson, among other places – that it was "in order to receive a population beyond his imagination of numbers, and to be made available with a rapidity beyond what he

---

[4] Darwin, *Empire Project*, 16; Belich, *Replenishing the Earth*, 23.

could conceive."[5] It was one of Henry's sons, Joel, who purchased a rural section on the Waimate Plain, near what would become the settlement of Kaponga. That section was part of more than 800,000 acres that had been confiscated from Taranaki Māori during the 1860s, the spoils of three wars that had crushed their sovereignty, and that had been surveyed in the late 1870s. "I never saw such earth-hunger as prevails in New Zealand amongst all its classes of people," Julius Vogel wrote in a pamphlet published in London in the year the survey began.[6] Joel and his family arrived in the Taranaki region in November 1881. It was also in November 1881 that colonial forces invaded the Māori settlement of Parihaka, center of the passive resistance movement led by Te Whiti o Rongomai and Tohu Kākahi in opposition to those land surveys and sales. My ancestors took up their land, felled the trees, went about their daily routines. "Prestidge took almost no part in public life," according to the historian of Kaponga, Rollo Arnold.[7] I think of this, and of a poem I now teach, by Apirana Taylor, that begins,

> roads in Taranaki
> zigzag and snake their way
> over the bitter earth
> they seldom run straight[8]

This history is so close, and yet I cannot grasp it, cannot reconcile its parts, cannot quite place where it leaves us all now. Such concerns are ultimately not for Victorian studies, they are for those of us who have to live this out as best we can, but perhaps they have infused a book that has sought to see some parts of that past a little more clearly, to understand a little better the narratives that brought us to this point.

---

[5] Edward Jerningham Wakefield, *Adventure in New Zealand, from 1839 to 1844: With Some Account of the Beginning of the British Colonization of the Islands*, 2 vols. (London: Murray, 1845), 1.87.

[6] Vogel, *New Zealand and the South Sea*, 29.

[7] Rollo Arnold, *Settler Kaponga, 1881–1914: A Frontier Fragment of the Western World* (Wellington: Victoria University Press, 1997), 18.

[8] Apirana Taylor, "zigzag roads," in *Mauri Ola: Contemporary Polynesian Poems in English*, ed. Robert Sullivan, Albert Wendt, and Reina Whaitiri (Auckland: Auckland University Press, 2010), 222.

Bibliography

Abbott, J. H. M. *Tommy Cornstalk: Being Some Account of the Less Notable Feature of the South African War from the Point of View of the Australian Ranks.* London: Longmans, Green, 1902.

Aickin, Wm. Stevenson. "Australasia's Never, Never Policy." *Times*, November 13, 1900, 12.

Amery, L. S. "General Editor's Preface." In *The Times History of the War in South Africa, 1899–1902*, edited by L. S. Amery. Vol. 5, v–x. London: Low, Marston, 1907.

Anderson, Amanda. *The Powers of Distance: Cosmopolitanism and the Cultivation of Detachment.* Princeton: Princeton University Press, 2001.

Anderson, Benedict R. O'Gorman. *Imagined Communities: Reflections on the Origin and Spread of Nationalism.* Rev. ed. London: Verso, 2006.

"Another 'El Dorado.'" *The Illustrated London News* 19, no. 514 (September 6, 1851): 273–74.

Argyle, Barry. *An Introduction to the Australian Novel, 1830–1930.* Oxford: Clarendon Press, 1972.

Arnold, Rollo. *Settler Kaponga, 1881–1914: A Frontier Fragment of the Western World.* Wellington: Victoria University Press, 1997.

Artemidorus [A. A. Grace]. *New Zealand in the Next Great War: A Note of Warning.* Nelson: Betts, 1894.

Ashmead-Bartlett, Ellis. *The Uncensored Dardanelles.* London: Hutchinson, 1928.

Australian Bureau of Statistics. "Australian Historical Population Statistics, 2008." Commonwealth of Australia, www.abs.gov.au/AUSSTATS/abs@.nsf/Details Page/3105.0.65.0012008?OpenDocument.

Babington-Smith, Constance. *John Masefield: A Life.* Oxford: Oxford University Press, 1978.

Bagehot, Walter. "The Danger of Lending to Semi-civilised Countries." In *The Collected Works of Walter Bagehot*, edited by Norman St John-Stevas, 419–23. London: Economist, 1978.

Ballantyne, Tony. "The Changing Shape of the Modern British Empire and Its Historiography." *The Historical Journal* 53, no. 2 (2010): 429–52.

——— "Race and the Webs of Empire." In *Webs of Empire: Locating New Zealand's Colonial Past*, 24–47. Wellington: Bridget Williams Books, 2012.

"Remaking the Empire from Newgate: Wakefield's *A Letter from Sydney*." In *Ten Books That Shaped the British Empire: Creating an Imperial Commons*, edited by Antoinette M. Burton and Isabel Hofmeyr, 29–49. Durham: Duke University Press, 2014.

Barrell, John. "Geographies of Hardy's Wessex." In *The Regional Novel in Britain and Ireland, 1800–1990*, edited by K. D. M. Snell, 99–118. Cambridge: Cambridge University Press, 1998.

Barrington, J. T. *England on the Defensive, or, the Problem of Invasion Critically Examined under the Aspect of a Series of Military Operations with Special Reference to the Character of the Country and of the National Forces*. London: Paul, Trench, 1881.

Baucom, Ian. *Out of Place: Englishness, Empire, and the Locations of Identity*. Princeton: Princeton University Press, 1999.

Baxter, R. Dudley. "The Recent Progress of National Debts." *Journal of the Statistical Society of London* 37, no. 1 (1874 1874): 1–20.

Beckett, Ian F. W. "The Historiography of Small Wars: Early Historians and the South African War." *Small Wars and Insurgencies* 2, no. 2 (1991): 276–98.

Belich, James. *Making Peoples: A History of the New Zealanders, from Polynesian Settlement to the End of the Nineteenth Century*. Auckland: Penguin, 1996.
　The New Zealand Wars and the Victorian Interpretation of Racial Conflict. Auckland: Penguin, 1998.
　Replenishing the Earth: The Settler Revolution and the Rise of the Anglo-World, 1783–1939. Oxford: Oxford University Press, 2009.

Bell, Duncan. *The Idea of Greater Britain: Empire and the Future of World Order, 1860–1900*. Princeton: Princeton University Press, 2007.
　"John Stuart Mill on Colonies." *Political Theory* 38, no. 1 (2010): 34–64.
　Reordering the World: Essays on Liberalism and Empire. Princeton: Princeton University Press, 2016.

Bell, Francis Dillon, ed. *Official Handbook of New Zealand*. 2nd ed. London: Stanford, 1883.

Bentham, Jeremy. "Panopticon *versus* New South Wales: Or, the Panopticon Penitentiary System, and the Penal Colonization System, Compared." In *The Works of Jeremy Bentham*, edited by John Bowring, 173–211. Edinburgh: Tait, 1843.

Bigelow, Gordon. *Fiction, Famine, and the Rise of Economics in Victorian Britain and Ireland*. Cambridge: Cambridge University Press, 2003.

Bird, Delys. "The 'Settling' of English." In *The Oxford Literary History of Australia*, edited by Bruce Bennett and Jennifer Strauss, 21–43. Melbourne: Oxford University Press, 1998.

Birns, Nicholas. "The Empire Turned Upside Down: The Colonial Fictions of Anthony Trollope." *ARIEL: A Review of International English Literature* 27, no. 3 (1996): 7–23.

Black, R. D. Collison. *Economic Thought and the Irish Question, 1817–1870*. Cambridge: Cambridge University Press, 1960.

Blainey, Geoffrey. *The Rush That Never Ended: A History of Australian Mining*. 2nd ed. Melbourne: Melbourne University Press, 1969.

A History of Victoria. 3rd. ed. Melbourne: Cambridge University Press, 2006.

Blythe, Helen Lucy. "*The Fixed Period* (1882): Euthanasia, Cannibalism, and Colonial Extinction in Trollope's Antipodes." *Nineteenth-Century Contexts* 25, no. 2 (2003): 161–80.

Bodenheimer, Rosemarie. *Knowing Dickens*. Ithaca: Cornell University Press, 2007.

Boucher, Leigh. "Victorian Liberalism and the Effect of Sovereignty: A View from the Settler Periphery." *History Australia* 13, no. 1 (2016): 35–51.

Boylan, Thomas A., and Timothy P. Foley. "'Tempering the Rawness': W. E. Hearn, Irish Political Economist, and Intellectual Life in Australia." In *The Irish-Australian Connection*, edited by Seamus Grimes and Gearóid Ó Tuathaigh, 91–19. Galway: University College Galway, 1989.

Braddon, Mary Elizabeth. *Lady Audley's Secret*, edited by David Skilton. Oxford: Oxford University Press, 1987.

Brantlinger, Patrick. *Rule of Darkness: British Literature and Imperialism, 1830–1914*. Ithaca: Cornell University Press, 1988.

Brantlinger, Patrick, and Donald Ulin. "Policing Nomads: Discourse and Social Control in Early Victorian England." *Cultural Critique* 25 (1993): 33–63.

Bridge, Carl, and Kent Fedorowich. "Mapping the British World." In *The British World: Diaspora, Culture and Identity*, edited by Carl Bridge and Kent Fedorowich, 1–15. London: Frank Cass, 2003.

Bright, Rachel K., and Andrew R. Dilley. "After the British World." *The Historical Journal* 60, no. 2 (2017): 547–68.

British Staff Officer [W. E. Cairnes]. *An Absent-Minded War: Being Some Reflections on Our Reverses and the Causes Which Have Led to Them*. 12th ed. London: Milne, 1900.

Bulwer-Lytton, Edward. *The Caxtons: A Family Picture*. 3 vols. Edinburgh: Blackwood, 1849.

Burke, Anthony. *Fear of Security: Australia's Invasion Anxiety*. Cambridge: Cambridge University Press, 2008.

Burroughs, Peter. *Britain and Australia, 1831–1855: A Study in Imperial Relations and Crown Lands Administration*. Oxford: Clarendon Press, 1967.

"Defence and Imperial Disunity." In *The Nineteenth Century*, edited by Andrew Porter. The Oxford History of the British Empire, 320–45. Oxford: Oxford University Press, 1999.

Butler, Samuel. *A First Year in Canterbury Settlement*, edited by A. C. Brassington and Peter Bromley Maling. Auckland: Blackwood & Paul, 1964.

Erewhon, or, Over the Range, edited by Peter Mudford. London: Penguin, 1970.

Buzard, James. *Disorienting Fiction: The Autoethnographic Work of Nineteenth-Century British Novels*. Princeton: Princeton University Press, 2005.

"Portable Boundaries: Trollope, Race, and Travel." *Nineteenth-Century Contexts* 32, no. 1 (2010): 5–18.

Caesar, Adrian. "National Myths of Manhood: Anzacs and Others." In *The Oxford Literary History of Australia*, edited by Bruce Bennett and Jennifer Strauss, 147–65. Melbourne: Oxford University Press, 1998.

Cain, P. J. "Economics and Empire: The Metropolitan Context." In *The Nineteenth Century*, edited by Andrew Porter. The Oxford History of the British Empire, 31–52. Oxford: Oxford University Press, 1999.

——— "Empire and the Languages of Character in Later Victorian and Edwardian Britain." *Modern Intellectual History* 4, no. 2 (2007): 249–73.

——— "The Economics and Ideologies of Anglo-American Settlerism, 1780–1939." *Victorian Studies* 53, no. 1 (2010): 100–7.

Cain, P. J., and A. G. Hopkins. *British Imperialism, 1688–2000*. 2nd ed. Harlow: Longman, 2002.

Cairnes, William Elliot. *The Army from Within*. London: Sands, 1901.

Calder, Alex. "Introduction." In *Old New Zealand and Other Writings*, 1–14. London: Leicester University Press, 2001.

Callwell, C. E. *The Dardanelles*. London: Constable, 1919.

Calvert, John. *The Gold Rocks of Great Britain and Ireland: And a General Outline of the Gold Regions of the World, with a Treatise on the Geology of Gold*. London: Chapman and Hall, 1853.

Capricornus [George Ranken]. "Co-operative Settlement." In *Bush Essays*, 36–45. Edinburgh: Black, 1872.

Carey, Jane, and Penelope Edmonds. "Australian Settler Colonialism over the Long Nineteenth Century." In *The Routledge Handbook of the History of Settler Colonialism*, edited by Edward Cavanagh and Lorenzo Veracini, 371–89. London: Routledge, 2016.

Carlyle, Thomas. *Past and Present*. London: Ward, Lock and Bowden, 1897.

Carter, Paul. *The Road to Botany Bay: An Exploration of Landscape and History*. Minneapolis: University of Minnesota Press, 2010.

Casanova, Pascale. *The World Republic of Letters*. Translated by M. B. DeBevoise. Cambridge: Harvard University Press, 2007.

Chandler, James. *England in 1819: The Politics of Literary Culture and the Case of Romantic Historicism*. Chicago: University of Chicago Press, 1998.

Chesney, George Tomkyns. *The Battle of Dorking: Reminiscences of a Volunteer*. In *The Next Great War*, edited by I. F. Clarke, British Future Fiction, 1–40. London: Pickering & Chatto, 2001.

Childers, Erskine. *In the Ranks of the C.I.V.: A Narrative and Diary of Personal Experiences with the C.I.V. Battery (Honourable Artillery Company) in South Africa*. London: Smith, Elder, 1900.

——— *The Times History of the War in South Africa, 1899-1902*, edited by L. S. Amery. Vol. 5. London: Low, Marston, 1907.

——— *War and the Arme Blanche*. London: Arnold, 1910.

——— *The Riddle of the Sands: A Record of Secret Service*. London: Penguin, 1978.

Churchill, Winston. *The World Crisis, Part Two, 1915*. The Collected Works of Sir Winston Churchill. Vol. 9. London: Library of Imperial History, 1974.

Clarke, I. F. *Voices Prophesying War, 1763–1749.* 2nd ed. Oxford: Oxford University Press, 1992.

Clarke, William. "An English Imperialist Bubble." *The North American Review* 141, no. 344 (1885): 60–72.

Colley, Linda. *Britons: Forging the Nation, 1707–1837.* New Haven: Yale University Press, 1992.

Collini, Stefan. *Public Moralists: Political Thought and Intellectual Life in Britain, 1850–1930.* Oxford: Clarendon Press, 1991.

Collins, Philip. *Dickens and Crime.* London: Macmillan, 1962.

Colomb, J. C. R. *The Defence of Great and Greater Britain: Sketches of Its Naval, Military, and Political Aspects.* London: Stanford, 1880.

Dalley, Hamish. "The Meaning of Settler Realism: (De)Mystifying Frontiers in the Postcolonial Historical Novel." *Novel* 51, no. 3 (2018): 461–81.

Dalziel, Raewyn. *Julius Vogel: Business Politician.* Auckland: Auckland University Press, 1986.

——— "An Experiment in the Social Laboratory? Suffrage, National Identity, and Mythologies of Race in New Zealand in the 1890s." In *Women's Suffrage in the British Empire: Citizenship, Nation, and Race,* edited by Ian Christopher Fletcher, Philippa Levine, and Laura E. Nym Mayhall, 87–102. London: Routledge, 2000.

Darwin, John. *The Empire Project: The Rise and Fall of the British World-System, 1830–1970.* Cambridge: Cambridge University Press, 2009.

Delany, Paul. "Land, Money, and the Jews in the Later Trollope." *Studies in English Literature* 32, no. 4 (1992): 765–87.

Denoon, Donald. "Re-Membering Australasia: A Repressed Memory." *Australian Historical Studies* 34, no. 122 (2003): 290–304.

Dickens, Charles. *Great Expectations,* edited by Charlotte Mitchell. London: Penguin, 1996.

——— "Home for Homeless Women." *Household Words* 7, no. 161 (April 23, 1853): 169–75.

——— *The Letters of Charles Dickens,* edited by Margaret Brown, Nina Burgis, Angus Easson, K. J. Fielding, Madeline House, Graham Storey, and Kathleen Tillotson. 12 vols. Oxford: Clarendon Press, 1965–2002.

——— *David Copperfield,* edited by Jeremy Tambling. London: Penguin, 1996.

Dilke, C. W. *Greater Britain: A Record of Travel in English-Speaking Countries during 1866 and 1867.* London: MacMillan, 1868.

——— *Problems of Greater Britain.* London: MacMillan, 1890.

Dolin, Tim. "First Steps toward a History of the Mid-Victorian Novel in Colonial Australia." *Australian Literary Studies* 22, no. 3 (2006): 273–93.

Dooley, Elizabeth Eileen. "Sir Walter Crofton and the Irish or Intermediate System of Prison Discipline." *Modern Penal Practice* 7, no. 1 (1981): 72–96.

Doyle, Arthur Conan. *The Great Boer War: A Two Years' Record, 1899–1901.* Enl. ed. London: Smith, Elder, 1901.

Duncan, Ian. "Primitive Inventions: *Rob Roy*, Nation, and World System." *Eighteenth-Century Fiction* 15, no. 1 (2002): 81–102.

During, Simon. "Out of England: Literary Subjectivity in the Australian Colonies, 1788–1867." In *Imagining Australia: Literature and Culture in the New New World*, edited by Judith Ryan and Chris Wallace-Crabbe, 3–21. Cambridge: Harvard University Press, 2004.

"Samuel Butler's Influence." In *A History of New Zealand Literature*, edited by Mark Williams, 44–55. Cambridge: Cambridge University Press, 2016.

Editorial, *The Morning Chronicle*, October 8, 1829.

Editorial, *The Times*, November 16, 1900.

Edwards, P. D. *Anthony Trollope, His Art and Scope*. New York: St. Martin's Press, 1978.

Ermarth, Elizabeth Deeds. *Realism and Consensus in the English Novel: Time, Space and Narrative*. Edinburgh: Edinburgh University Press, 1998.

Esty, Jed. *Unseasonable Youth: Modernism, Colonialism, and the Fiction of Development*. Oxford: Oxford University Press, 2013.

Field, L. M. *The Forgotten War: Australia and the Boer War*. Carlton: Melbourne University Press, 1995.

"The Finances of New Zealand." *The Economist* 28, no. 1416 (October 15, 1870): 1252–53.

Fowler, Frank. *Southern Lights and Shadows: Being Brief Notes of Three Years' Experience of Social, Literary, and Political Life in Australia*. London: Sampson Low, 1859.

Frederickson, Kathleen. "Liberalism and the Time of Instinct." *Victorian Studies* 49, no. 2 (2007): 302–12.

Freedgood, Elaine. "Realism, Fetishism, and Genocide: 'Negro Head' Tobacco in and around *Great Expectations*." *Novel* 36, no. 1 (2002): 26–41.

Froude, James Anthony. "The Colonies Once More." In *Short Studies on Great Subjects*, 280–312. New York: Scribner, Armstrong, 1874.

"England and Her Colonies." In *Short Studies on Great Subjects*, 149–77. New York: Scribner, Armstrong, 1874.

Oceana, or, England and Her Colonies London: Longmans Green, 1898.

Gagnier, Regenia. *The Insatiability of Human Wants: Economics and Aesthetics in Market Society*. Chicago: University of Chicago Press, 2000.

Galbraith, John Kenneth. *A History of Economics: The Past as the Present*. London: Hamilton, 1987.

Gallagher, Catherine. *The Body Economic: Life, Death, and Sensation in Political Economy and the Victorian Novel*. Princeton: Princeton University Press, 2005.

NZHistory. "Gallipoli Casualties by Country." Ministry for Culture and Heritage, https://nzhistory.govt.nz/media/interactive/gallipoli-casualties-country.

Gardner, W. J. "A Colonial Economy." In *The Oxford History of New Zealand*, edited by Geoffrey Rice, 57–86. 2nd ed. Auckland: Oxford University Press, 1992.

Gelder, Ken, and Rachael Weaver. "Beginnings and Endings: The Precarious Life of a Colonial Journal." In *The Colonial Journals: And the Emergence of Australian Literary Culture*, edited by Ken Gelder and Rachael Weaver, 6–18. Crawley: UWA Publishing, 2014.

Ghosh, Durba. "Another Set of Imperial Turns?" *American Historical Review* 117, no. 3 (2012): 772–93.

"Gold-Seeking at Home." *Chambers's Edinburgh Journal,* July 24, 1852, 60–63.

Goodlad, Lauren M. E. *Victorian Literature and the Victorian State: Character and Governance in a Liberal Society.* Baltimore: Johns Hopkins University Press, 2003.

——— *The Victorian Geopolitical Aesthetic: Realism, Sovereignty, and Transnational Experience.* Oxford: Oxford University Press, 2015.

Goodman, David. *Gold Seeking: Victoria and California in the 1850s.* St. Leonards: Allen & Unwin, 1994.

Goodwin, Craufurd D. *Economic Enquiry in Australia.* Durham: Duke University Press, 1966.

——— "British Economists and Australian Gold." *The Journal of Economic History* 30, no. 2 (1970): 405–26.

Grant, Robert. "Edward Gibbon Wakefield, England and 'ignorant, dirty, unsocial, . . . restless, more than half-savage' America." *Comparative American Studies* 1, no. 4 (2003): 471–87.

Grossman, Jonathan H. "Living the Global Transport Network in *Great Expectations.*" *Victorian Studies* 57, no. 2 (2015): 225–50.

Hadley, Elaine. *Living Liberalism: Practical Citizenship in Mid-Victorian Britain.* Chicago: University of Chicago Press, 2010.

Hall, N. John. *Trollope: A Biography.* Oxford: Clarendon Press, 1991.

Hartley, Jenny. "Undertexts and Intertexts: The Women of Urania Cottage, Secrets and *Little Dorrit.*" *Critical Survey* 17, no. 2 (2005): 63–76.

——— *Charles Dickens and the House of Fallen Women.* London: Methuen, 2009.

Hearn, William Edward. *Plutology: or, the Theory of the Efforts to Satisfy Human Wants.* London: Macmillan, 1864.

Hensley, Nathan K. *Forms of Empire: The Poetics of Victorian Sovereignty.* Oxford: Oxford University Press, 2016.

Herbert, Christopher. *Culture and Anomie: Ethnographic Imagination in the Nineteenth Century.* Chicago: University of Chicago Press, 1991.

Hickford, Mark. *Lords of the Land: Indigenous Property Rights and the Jurisprudence of Empire.* Oxford: Oxford University Press, 2011.

Higgins, David. "Writing to Colonial Australia: Barron Field and Charles Lamb." *Nineteenth-Century Contexts* 32, no. 3 (2010): 219–33.

Hobsbawm, E. J. *The Age of Empire, 1875–1914.* New York: Vintage, 1989.

Hochstetter, Ferdinand von. *New Zealand: Its Physical Geography, Geology and Natural History, with Special Reference to the Results of Government Expeditions in the Provinces of Auckland and Nelson.* Translated by Edward Sauter. Stuttgart: Cotta, 1867.

Hoffenberg, Peter H. "Landscape, Memory and the Australian War Experience, 1915–18." *Journal of Contemporary History* 36, no. 1 (2001): 111–31.

Hofmeyr, Elizabeth. *The Portable Bunyan: A Transnational History of* The Pilgrim's Progress. Princeton: Princeton University Press, 2004.

Horne, R. H. *Australian Facts and Prospects: To Which Is Prefixed the Author's Australian Autobiography*. London: Smith, Elder, 1859.

Howe, Stephen. "British Worlds, Settler Worlds, World Systems, and Killing Fields." *Journal of Imperial and Commonwealth History* 40, no. 4 (2012): 691–725.

Howitt, William. *The Rural Life of England*. 2 vols. London: Longman, Orme, Brown, Green, and Longmans, 1838.

———. *Land, Labour, and Gold; or, Two Years in Victoria: With Visits to Sydney and Van Diemen's Land*. 2 vols. London: Longman, Brown, Green, and Longmans, 1855.

Hughes, Robert. *The Fatal Shore*. New York: Knopf, 1987.

Indyk, Ivor. "Pastoral and Priority: The Aboriginal in Australian Pastoral." *New Literary History* 24, no. 4 (1993): 837–55.

Jaffe, Audrey. "Trollope in the Stock Market: Irrational Exuberance and *The Prime Minister*." In *Victorian Investments: New Perspectives on Finance and Culture*, edited by Cannon Schmitt and Nancy Henry, 143–60. Bloomington: Indiana University Press, 2009.

Jameson, Fredric. *The Political Unconscious: Narrative as a Socially Symbolic Act*. Ithaca: Cornell University Press, 1981.

Jevons, William Stanley. *Money and the Mechanism of Exchange*. 13th ed. London: Kegan Paul, Trench, Trubner, 1902.

———. *The Principles of Science: A Treatise on Logic and Scientific Method*. 2nd ed. London: Macmillan, 1913.

———. Review of *Plutology; or, the Theory of the Efforts to Satisfy Human Wants*, by W. E. Hearn. *The Spectator* 37, no. 1862 (March 5, 1864): 276.

———. *The Theory of Political Economy*, edited by R. D. Collison Black. Harmondsworth: Penguin, 1970.

———. *Papers and Correspondence of William Stanley Jevons*, edited by R. D. Collison Black and Rosamond Könekamp. 7 vols. London: Macmillan, 1972–1981.

Johnston, Anna. "'Greater Britain': Late Imperial Travel Writing and the Settler Colonies." In *Oceania and the Victorian Imagination: Where All Things Are Possible*, edited by Richard D. Fulton and Peter H. Hoffenberg, 31–44. Farnham: Ashgate, 2013.

Johnston, Judith. "William Howitt, Australia and the 'Green Language.'" *Australian Literary Studies* 29, no. 4 (2014): 36–47.

Jones, Joseph. *The Cradle of Erewhon: Samuel Butler in New Zealand*. Austin: University of Texas Press, 1959.

Keene, J., and W. H. Wills. "A Golden Newspaper." *Household Words* 4, no. 87 (November 22, 1851): 207–8.

Kendrick, Walter M. *The Novel-Machine: The Theory and Fiction of Anthony Trollope*. Baltimore: Johns Hopkins University Press, 1980.

Kennedy, Dane. *The Imperial History Wars: Debating the British Empire*. London: Bloomsbury Academic, 2018.

Kingsley, Henry. *The Recollections of Geoffry Hamlyn*, edited by Paul Eggert, J. S. D. Mellick, and Patrick Morgan. St. Lucia: University of Queensland Press, 1996.

Koditschek, Theodore. *Liberalism, Imperialism, and the Historical Imagination: Nineteenth-Century Visions of a Greater Britain.* Cambridge: Cambridge University Press, 2011.

Kranidis, Rita S. *The Victorian Spinster and Colonial Emigration: Contested Subjects.* Basingstoke: Macmillan, 1999.

Krebs, Paula M. *Gender, Race, and the Writing of Empire: Public Discourse and the Boer War.* Cambridge: Cambridge University Press, 1999.

Lack, Clem Llewellyn. "Russian Ambitions in the Pacific: Australian War Scares of the Nineteenth Century." *Journal of the Royal Historical Society of Queensland* 8, no. 3 (1968): 432–59.

Lake, Marilyn. "The White Man under Siege: New Histories of Race in the Nineteenth Century and the Advent of White Australia." *History Workshop Journal* 58, no. 1 (2004): 41–62.

———. "'The Day Will Come': Charles H. Pearson's *National Life and Character: A Forecast.*" In *Ten Books That Shaped the British Empire: Creating an Imperial Commons*, edited by Antoinette M. Burton and Isabel Hofmeyr, 90–111. Durham: Duke University Press, 2014.

Lake, Marilyn, and Henry Reynolds. *Drawing the Global Colour Line: White Men's Countries and the International Challenge of Racial Equality.* Cambridge: Cambridge University Press, 2008.

Lamb, Jonathan. "The Idea of Utopia in the European Settlement of New Zealand." In *Quicksands: Foundational Histories in Australia and Aotearoa New Zealand*, edited by Hilary Ericksen, Klaus Neumann, and Nicholas Thomas, 79–97. Sydney: University of New South Wales Press, 1999.

La Nauze, John Andrew. *Political Economy in Australia: Historical Studies.* Melbourne: Melbourne University Press, 1949.

Lansbury, Coral. *Arcady in Australia: The Evocation of Australia in Nineteenth-Century English Literature.* Carlton: Melbourne University Press, 1970.

Larkworthy, Falconer. *New Zealand Revisited.* 2nd ed. London: William Brown, 1882.

Lazarus, Mary Ellen. *A Tale of Two Brothers: Charles Dickens's Sons in Australia.* Sydney: Angus and Robertson, 1973.

Le Rossignol, James Edward, and William Downie Stewart. "The Public Debt of New Zealand." *The Journal of Political Economy* 17, no. 8 (1909): 509–27.

Lesjak, Caroline. *Working Fictions: A Genealogy of the Victorian Novel.* Durham: Duke University Press, 2006.

Levine, Caroline. "From Nation to Network." *Victorian Studies* 55, no. 4 (2013): 647–66.

———. *Forms: Whole, Rhythm, Hierarchy, Network.* Princeton: Princeton University Press, 2015.

Levinson, Marjorie. "What Is New Formalism?" *PMLA* 122, no. 2 (2007): 558–69.

Locke, John. *Second Treatise of Government*, edited by C. B. Macpherson. Indianapolis: Hackett, 1980.

Lyall, A. C. Review of *National Life and Character: A Forecast*, by Charles H. Pearson. *The Nineteenth Century* 33, no. 195 (1893): 892–96.

Mackay, Kenneth. *The Yellow Wave: A Romance of the Asiatic Invasion of Australia*, edited by Andrew Enstice and Janeen Webb. Middletown: Wesleyan University Press, 2003.

Mackinder, H. J. "The Geographical Pivot of History." *The Geographical Journal* 23, no. 4 (1904): 421–44.

Macleod, Jenny. "The British Heroic-Romantic Myth of Gallipoli." In *Gallipoli: Making History*, edited by Jenny Macleod, 73–85. London: Cass, 2004.

Maconochie, Alexander. *Australiana: Thoughts on Convict Management, and Other Subjects Connected with the Australian Penal Colonies*. London: Parker, 1839.

——— *Crime and Punishment: The Mark System, Framed to Mix Persuasion with Punishment, and Make Their Effect Improving, Yet Their Operation Severe*. London: Hatchard, 1846.

——— *Comparison between Mr. Bentham's Views on Punishment, and Those Advocated in Connexion with the Mark System*. London: Compton, 1847.

——— *The Principles of Punishment on Which the Mark System of Prison Discipline Is Advocated*. London: Ollivier, 1850.

Maddox, Alan. "On the Machinery of Moral Improvement: Music and Prison Reform in the Penal Colony on Norfolk Island." *Musicology Australia* 34, no. 2 (2012): 185–205.

Magarey, Susan. *Unbridling the Tongues of Women: A Biography of Catherine Helen Spence*. Sydney: Hale & Iremonger, 1985.

Magee, Gary B., and Andrew S. Thompson. *Empire and Globalisation: Networks of People, Goods and Capital in the British World, c. 1850–1914*. Cambridge: Cambridge University Press, 2010.

Mahood, Linda. *The Magdalenes: Prostitution in the Nineteenth Century*. London: Routledge, 1990.

Makdisi, Saree. "Riding the Whirlwind of Settler Colonialism." *Victorian Studies* 53, no. 1 (2010): 108–15.

Maning, F. E. *Old New Zealand: A Tale of the Good Old Times*. Auckland: Creighton and Scales, 1863.

Marx, Karl. *Capital: A Critique of Political Economy: Volume One*. Translated by Ben Fowkes, edited by Ernest Mandel. London: Penguin, 1976.

Masefield, John. *Gallipoli*. London: Heinemann, 1916.

Matin, A. Michael. "The Creativity of War Planners: Armed Forces Professionals and the Pre-1914 British Invasion-Scare Genre." *ELH* 78, no. 4 (2011): 801–31.

McCombie, Thomas. *Arabin; or, the Adventures of a Settler in New South Wales*. London: Simmonds and Ward, 1845.

——— *Essays on Colonization*. London: Smith, Elder, 1850.

McCormick, E. H. *Letters and Art in New Zealand*. Wellington: Department of Internal Affairs, 1940.

McCulloch, J. R. *The Principles of Political Economy; With a Sketch of the Rise and Progress of the Science*. 2nd ed. London: Tait, 1830.

McMichael, Philip. *Settlers and the Agrarian Question: Foundations of Capitalism in Colonial Australia*. Cambridge: Cambridge University Press, 1984.

Meaney, Neville. "'The Yellow Peril,' Invasion Scare Novels and Australian Political Culture." In *The 1890s: Australian Literature and Literary Culture*, edited by Ken Stewart, 228–63. St. Lucia: University of Queensland Press, 1996.

Meckier, Jerome. "Dating the Action in *Great Expectations*: A New Chronology." *Dickens Studies Annual* 21 (1992): 157–94.

Meek, Ronald L. *Social Science and the Ignoble Savage*. Cambridge: Cambridge University Press, 1976.

Mein Smith, Philippa, Peter Hempenstall, and Shaun Goldfinch. *Remaking the Tasman World*. Christchurch: Canterbury University Press, 2008.

Meisel, Martin. "Miss Havisham Brought to Book." *PMLA* 81, no. 3 (1966): 278–85.

Merivale, Herman. *Lectures on Colonization and Colonies*. 2 vols. London: Longman, Orme, Brown, Green, and Longmans, 1841.

Mill, John Stuart. "Civilization." In *Essays on Politics and Society*, edited by J. M. Robson. Collected Works of John Stuart Mill, 117–47. Toronto: University of Toronto Press, 1977.

——— *On Liberty*. In On Liberty *and Other Writings*, edited by Stefan Collini, 1–115. Cambridge: Cambridge University Press, 1989.

Mitchell, W. J. T. "The Commitment to Form; or, Still Crazy after All These Years." *PMLA* 118, no. 2 (2003): 321–25.

Moore, Grace. *Dickens and Empire: Discourses of Class, Race and Colonialism in the Works of Charles Dickens*. Aldershot: Ashgate, 2004.

Moore, Gregory C. G. "The Anglo-Irish Context for William Edward Hearn's Economic Beliefs and the Ultimate Failure of His *Plutology*." *The European Journal of the History of Economic Thought* 18, no. 1 (2011): 19–54.

Moore, J. M. "Reformative Rhetoric and the Exercise of Corporal Power: Alexander Maconochie's Regime at Birmingham Prison, 1849–51." *Historical Research* 89, no. 245 (2016): 510–30.

Moretti, Franco. *Atlas of the European Novel, 1800–1900*. London: Verso, 1998.

——— *The Way of the World: The Bildungsroman in European Culture*. Translated by Albert Sbragia. New ed. London: Verso, 2000.

Myers, Janet C. "'Verily the Antipodes of Home': The Domestic Novel in the Australian Bush." *Novel: A Forum on Fiction* 35, no. 1 (2001): 46–68.

——— *Antipodal England: Emigration and Portable Domesticity in the Victorian Imagination*. Albany: State University of New York Press, 2009.

"New Zealand Revisited." *New Zealand Herald*, January 14, 1882.

"Our Colonial Possessions." *The Economist* 38, no. 1931 (September 4, 1880): 1023–25.

Pakenham, Thomas. *The Boer War*. London: Weidenfeld & Nicolson, 1993.

Pappe, H. O. "Wakefield and Marx." *Economic History Review* 4, no. 1 (1951): 88–97.

Parsonson, Ann. "The Challenge to Mana Māori." In *The Oxford History of New Zealand*, edited by Geoffrey Rice, 167–98. 2nd ed. Auckland: Oxford University Press, 1992.

Patterson, R. H. *The Economy of Capital, or, Gold and Trade.* Amended ed. Edinburgh: Blackwood, 1865.

Pearson, Charles H. *National Life and Character: A Forecast.* London: Macmillan, 1893.

Piesse, Jude. *British Settler Emigration in Print, 1832–1877.* Oxford: Oxford University Press, 2016.

Pike, Douglas. *Paradise of Dissent: South Australia 1829–1857.* 2nd ed. Melbourne: Melbourne University Press, 1967.

Piterberg, Gabriel, and Lorenzo Veracini. "Wakefield, Marx, and the World Turned Inside Out." *Journal of Global History* 10, no. 3 (2015): 457–78.

Plotz, John. *Portable Property: Victorian Culture on the Move.* Princeton: Princeton University Press, 2008.

Pocock, J. G. A. "The Neo-Britains and the Three Empires." In *The Discovery of Islands: Essays in British History*, 181–98. Cambridge: Cambridge University Press, 2005.

"*Tangata Whenua* and Enlightenment Anthropology." In *The Discovery of Islands: Essays in British History*, 199–225. Cambridge: Cambridge University Press, 2005.

Poovey, Mary. *Making a Social Body: British Cultural Formation, 1830–1864.* Chicago: University of Chicago Press, 1995.

A History of the Modern Fact: Problems of Knowledge in the Sciences of Wealth and Society. Chicago: University of Chicago Press, 1998.

Genres of the Credit Economy: Mediating Value in Eighteenth- and Nineteenth-Century Britain. Chicago: University of Chicago Press, 2008.

Porter, Andrew. "Introduction: Britain and Empire in the Nineteenth Century." In *The Nineteenth Century*, edited by Andrew Porter. The Oxford History of the British Empire, 1–28. Oxford: Oxford University Press, 1999.

Pugsley, Christopher. *Gallipoli: The New Zealand Story.* North Shore: Penguin, 2008.

Raby, Peter. *Samuel Butler: A Biography.* London: Hogarth, 1991.

Reade, Charles. *"It Is Never Too Late to Mend": A Matter-of-Fact Romance.* 2nd ed. 3 vols. London: Bentley, 1856.

Rees, W. L. *The Coming Crisis: A Sketch of the Financial and Political Condition of New Zealand, with the Causes and Probable Results of That Condition.* Auckland: Reed and Brett, 1874.

Reeves, William Pember. "New Zealand Finance." *Times*, November 17, 1900.

State Experiments in Australia and New Zealand. 2 vols. London: Allen & Unwin, 1902.

Renar, Frank [Frank Fox]. *Bushman and Buccaneer: Harry Morant: His 'Ventures and Verses.* Sydney: Dunn, 1902.

"The Rev H. C. M. Watson: Home Experiences." *Star*, April 10, 1891.

Review of *National Life and Character: A Forecast* by Charles H. Pearson. *The Edinburgh Review* 178, no. 366 (1893): 277–304.

Review of *National Life and Character: A Forecast* by Charles H. Pearson. *The Athenaeum*, no. 3410 (1893): 273–74.

Review of *Old New Zealand, a Tale of the Good Old Times. The Athenaeum*, no. 2560 (1876): 653–54.

Reynolds, Henry. *The Law of the Land.* 3rd ed. Camberwell: Penguin, 2003.

Richards, Thomas. *The Imperial Archive: Knowledge and the Fantasy of Empire.* London: Verso, 1993.

Rowcroft, Charles. *Tales of the Colonies, or, the Adventures of an Emigrant.* London: Saunders & Otley, 1843.

Rudy, Jason R. *Imagined Homelands: British Poetry in the Colonies.* Baltimore: Johns Hopkins University Press, 2017.

"On Literary Melbourne: Poetry in the Colony, ca. 1854." *BRANCH: Britain, Representation and Nineteenth-Century History*, edited by Dino Franco Felluga, www.branchcollective.org/?ps_articles=jason-r-rudy-on-literary-melbourne-poetry-in-the-colony-ca-1854.

Said, Edward W. "Traveling Theory." In *The World, the Text and the Critic*, 226–47. London: Faber, 1984.

Culture and Imperialism. New York: Knopf, 1993.

Sala, George Augustus. "Cheerily, Cheerily!" *Household Words* 6, no. 131 (September 25, 1852): 25–31.

Sargent, Lyman Tower. "Colonial and Postcolonial Utopias." In *The Cambridge Companion to Utopian Literature*, edited by Gregory Claeys, 200–22. Cambridge: Cambridge University Press, 2010.

Sartori, Andrew. *Liberalism in Empire: An Alternative History.* Oakland: University of California Press, 2014.

Schabas, Margaret. *A World Ruled by Number: William Stanley Jevons and the Rise of Mathematical Economics.* Princeton: Princeton University Press, 1990.

Schwarz, Bill. "An Unsentimental Education: John Darwin's Empire." *Journal of Imperial and Commonwealth History* 43, no. 1 (2015): 125–44.

Scott, Walter. "An Essay on Romance." In *Essays on Chivalry, Romance, and the Drama.* The Miscellaneous Prose Works of Walter Scott, 129–216. Edinburgh: Cadell, 1834.

Seeley, John Robert. *The Expansion of England: Two Courses of Lectures.* 2nd ed. London: Macmillan, 1921.

Serle, Geoffrey. *Golden Age: A History of the Colony of Victoria, 1851–1861.* Carlton: Melbourne University Press, 1977.

From Deserts the Prophets Come: The Creative Spirit in Australia 1788–1972. New ed. Clayton: Monash University Publishing, 2014.

"Seven Tons of Australian Gold." *The Times*, November 24, 1852.

Sinnett, Frederick. "The Fiction Fields of Australia." In *The Writer in Australia: A Collection of Literary Documents, 1856 to 1964*, edited by John Barnes, 8–32. Melbourne: Oxford University Press, 1969.

Sketcher [William Lane]. "White or Yellow? A Story of the Race-War of A.D. 1908." *The Boomerang*, March 31, 1888, 9.

Smalley, Donald Arthur, ed. *Trollope: The Critical Heritage.* London: Routledge, 1969.

Smith, Adam. *Lectures on Jurisprudence*, edited by Ronald L. Meek, D. D. Raphael, and Peter Stein. The Glasgow Edition of the Works and Correspondence of Adam Smith. Oxford: Clarendon Press, 1978.

Smith, Rosalind. "*Clara Morison*: The Politics of Feminine Heterotopia." *Southerly* 61, no. 3 (2001): 40–51.

Smithies, James. "Return Migration and the Mechanical Age: Samuel Butler in New Zealand 1860–1864." *Journal of Victorian Culture* 12, no. 2 (2007): 203–24.

Smits, Katherine. "John Stuart Mill on the Antipodes: Settler Violence against Indigenous Peoples and the Legitimacy of Colonial Rule." *Australian Journal of Politics and History* 54, no. 1 (2008): 1–15.

Spence, Catherine Helen. *Clara Morison: A Tale of South Australia during the Gold Fever.* 2 vols. London: Parker, 1986.

Stafford, David A. T. "Spies and Gentlemen: The Birth of the British Spy Novel, 1893–1914." *Victorian Studies* 24, no. 4 (1981): 489–509.

Stafford, Jane. "Alfred Domett, Robert Browning and a Dream of Two Lives." *Journal of New Zealand Literature* 21 (2003): 32–53.

———. "'Remote Must Be the Shores': Mary Taylor, Charlotte Brontë, and the Colonial Experience." *Journal of New Zealand Literature* 10 (1992): 8–15.

Stafford, Robert A. "Preventing the 'Curse of California': Advice for English Emigrants to the Australian Goldfields." *Historical Records of Australian Science* 7, no. 3 (1988): 215–30.

Statistics New Zealand. "Historical Population Estimates Tables." Statistics New Zealand, http://archive.stats.govt.nz/browse_for_stats/population/estimates_and_projections/historical-population-tables.aspx.

Steer, Philip. "On Systematic Colonization and the Culture of Settler Colonialism: Edward Gibbon Wakefield's *A Letter from Sydney* (1829)." *BRANCH: Britain, Representation and Nineteenth-Century History*, edited by Dino Franco Felluga, http://www.branchcollective.org/?ps_articles=philip-steer-on-systematic-colonization-and-the-culture-of-settler-colonialism-edward-gibbon-wakefields-a-letter-from-sydney-1829.

Stewart, Garrett. "The Foreign Offices of British Fiction." *Modern Language Quarterly* 61, no. 1 (2000): 181–206.

Stocking, George W. *Victorian Anthropology.* New York: Free Press, 1987.

Taylor, Apirana. "Zigzag Roads." In *Mauri Ola: Contemporary Polynesian Poems in English*, edited by Robert Sullivan, Albert Wendt, and Reina Whaitiri, 222. Auckland: Auckland University Press, 2010.

Thomas, David Wayne. *Cultivating Victorians: Liberal Culture and the Aesthetic.* Philadelphia: University of Pennsylvania Press, 2004.

Thomson, Alistair. "'Steadfast Until Death'? C. E. W. Bean and the Representation of Australian Military Manhood." *Australian Historical Studies* 23, no. 93 (1989): 462–78.

Timpe, Kevin. "Moral Character." *The Internet Encyclopedia of Philosophy*, edited by Bradley Dowden and James Fieser, www.iep.utm.edu/moral-ch/.

Trainor, Luke. *British Imperialism and Australian Nationalism: Manipulation, Conflict and Compromise in the Late Nineteenth Century.* Cambridge: Cambridge University Press, 1994.

Trollope, Anthony. *Australia and New Zealand.* 2nd ed. 2 vols. London: Chapman and Hall, 1873.

The Tireless Traveler: Twenty Letters to the Liverpool Mercury, edited by Bradford Allen Booth. Berkeley: University of California Press, 1941.

Can You Forgive Her? London: Oxford University Press, 1973.

Phineas Finn. London: Oxford University Press, 1973.

An Autobiography, edited by Frederick Page and Michael Sadleir. Oxford: Oxford University Press, 1980.

The Fixed Period, edited by David Skilton. Oxford: Oxford University Press, 1993.

John Caldigate, edited by N. John Hall. Oxford: Oxford University Press, 1993.

Trotter, David. "The Politics of Adventure in the Early British Spy Novel." *Intelligence and National Security* 5, no. 4 (1990): 30–54.

Trumpener, Katie. *Bardic Nationalism: The Romantic Novel and the British Empire.* Princeton: Princeton University Press, 1997.

Tucker, Irene. "International Whiggery." *Victorian Studies* 45, no. 4 (2003): 687–97.

Turner, Stephen. "Settlement as Forgetting." In *Quicksands: Foundational Histories in Australia and Aotearoa New Zealand*, edited by Klaus Neumann, Nicholas Thomas and Hilary Ericksen, 20–38. Sydney: University of New South Wales Press, 1999.

Tyrrell, Alex. "'No Common Corrobery': The Robert Burns Festivals and Identity Politics in Melbourne, 1845–59." *Journal of the Royal Australian Historical Society* 97, no. 2 (2005): 161–80.

Vogel, Julius. *Great Britain and Her Colonies.* London: Smith, Elder, 1865.

The Finances of New Zealand by the Premier of the Colonial Government. London: Longmans, Green, 1875.

"New Zealand." *Times*, November 2, 1877.

New Zealand and the South Sea Islands, and Their Relation to the Empire. London: Stanford, 1878.

New Zealand: Its Past, Present and Future. London: Waterlow and Sons, 1893.

Anno Domini 2000; or, Woman's Destiny. Honolulu: University of Hawai'i Press, 2002.

ed. *The Official Handbook of New Zealand: A Collection of Papers by Experienced Colonists on the Colony as a Whole, and on the Several Provinces.* London: Wyman, 1875.

Wagner, Tamara S. *Victorian Narratives of Failed Emigration: Settlers, Returnees, and Nineteenth-Century Literature in English.* Abingdon: Routledge, 2016.

Wahrman, Dror. "The Meaning of the Nineteenth Century: Reflections on James Belich's *Replenishing the Earth.*" *Victorian Studies* 53, no. 1 (2010): 91–99.

Waite, Robert G. "From Penitentiary to Reformatory: Alexander Maconochie, Walter Crofton, Zebulon Brockway, and the Road to Prison Reform – New South Wales, Ireland, and Elmira, New York, 1840–70." *Criminal Justice History* 11 (1991): 85–105.

Wakefield, Edward Gibbon. "Australia." *The Morning Chronicle*, August 21, 1829.
———. "Australia." *The Morning Chronicle*, October 6, 1829.
———. *England and America: A Comparison of the Socia and Political State of Both Nations*. In *The Collected Works of Edward Gibbon Wakefield*, edited by M. F. Lloyd Prichard, 311–636. Glasgow: Collins, 1968.
———. *A Letter from Sydney: The Principal Town of Australasia*. In *The Collected Works of Edward Gibbon Wakefield*, edited by M. F. Lloyd Prichard, 93–185. Glasgow: Collins, 1968.
Wakefield, Edward Jerningham. *Adventure in New Zealand, from 1839 to 1844: With Some Account of the Beginning of the British Colonization of the Islands*. 2 vols. London: Murray, 1845.
Walker, David. *Anxious Nation: Australia and the Rise of Asia, 1850–1939*. St. Lucia: University of Queensland Press, 1999.
Walker, W. H. [George Ranken]. *The Invasion*. Sydney: Turner & Henderson, 1877.
Wallace, Edgar. *Unofficial Dispatches*. London: Hutchinson, 1901.
Walsh, Susan. "Bodies of Capital: *Great Expectations* and the Climacteric Economy." *Victorian Studies* 37, no. 1 (1993): 73–98.
Watson, Henry Crocker Marriott. *The Decline and Fall of the British Empire, or, the Witch's Cavern*. London: Trischler, 1890.
Wells, H. G. *The War of the Worlds*, edited by Andy Sawyer. London: Penguin, 2005.
Wevers, Lydia. *Country of Writing: Travel Writing and New Zealand, 1809–1900*. Auckland: Auckland University Press, 2002.
———. "Becoming Native: Australian Novelists and the New Zealand Wars." *Australian Literary Studies* 22, no. 3 (2006): 319–28.
———. *Reading on the Farm: Victorian Fiction and the Colonial World*. Wellington: Victoria University Press, 2010.
White, Michael V. "Jevons in Australia: A Reassessment." *Economic Record* 58, no. 1 (1982): 32–45.
Whitelock, Derek. *Adelaide: A Sense of Difference*. Kew: Arcadia, 2000.
Wiener, Martin J. *Reconstructing the Criminal: Culture, Law, and Policy in England, 1830–1914*. Cambridge: Cambridge University Press, 1990.
Wilcox, Craig. *Australia's Boer War: The War in South Africa, 1899–1902*. South Melbourne: Oxford University Press, 2002.
Williams, Raymond. *Marxism and Literature*. Oxford: Oxford University Press, 1977.
Winch, Donald N. "Classical Economics and the Case for Colonization." *Economica* 30, no. 120 (1963): 387–99.
Withers, Charles W. J. *Placing the Enlightenment: Thinking Geographically about the Age of Reason*. Chicago: University of Chicago Press, 2007.
Wolfe, Patrick. *Settler Colonialism and the Transformation of Anthropology: The Politics and Poetics of an Ethnographic Event*. London: Cassell, 1999.
———. "Settler Colonialism and the Elimination of the Native." *Journal of Genocide Research* 8, no. 4 (2006): 387–409.
Zemka, Sue. "*Erewhon* and the End of Utopian Humanism." *ELH* 69, no. 2 (2002): 439–72.

Index

CAMBRIDGE STUDIES IN NINETEENTH-CENTURY
LITERATURE AND CULTURE

General editor
Gillian Beer, *University of Cambridge*